BATMAN • JESUS CHRIST SUPERSTAR • EVELYN • **HARRY POTTER & THE PRISONER OF AZKABAN**
SHINE • THELMA & LOUISE • **ALIEN** • MUSEUM PIECE • PYGMALION • THIS M   ELLO
VER TWIST • THE BEACH • THE IMPORTANCE OF BEING EARNEST • MICKEY BLU   UALLY
ETH • LOST IN SPACE • RESTORATION • TIGER IN THE SMOKE • THE COLDITZ S   E AND
ES • **BLADE RUNNER** • A NIGHT TO REMEMBER • THE THIRTY NINE STEPS • FER   TO HONG KONG • THE
ND DOWNSTAIRS • SINK THE BISMARCK • GULLIVER'S TRAVELS • THE BOUNTY • CONSPIRACY OF HEARTS
ENTLEMEN • HEAR MY SONG • **GANDHI** • SONS AND LOVERS • DOCTOR IN LOVE • NEVER ENDING STORY
NG • **GOLDFINGER** • HIGH WIND IN JAMAICA • CARRY ON CLEO • CITY UNDER THE SEA • KHARTOUM •
BANG BANG • 1492:CONQUEST OF PARADISE • CARRY ON UP THE KHYBER • **SLIDING DOORS** • CARRY
BLE • JANE EYRE • THE PROFESSIONALS • CARRY ON REGARDLESS • **ROLLERBALL** • CARRY ON HENRY •
• LIVE AND LET DIE • VICTOR/VICTORIA • NEAREST AND DEAREST • KILLING ME SOFTLY • **FIDDLER ON**
T GATSBY • JUGGERNAUT • THE MAN WITH THE GOLDEN GUN • CRIMINAL LAW • MOONRAKER • **BUGSY**
ME • THE PEOPLE THAT TIME FORGOT • THE MEDUSA TOUCH • BREAD & ROSES • **SUPERMAN** • CLASH
E OF THE PINK PANTHER • SUPERMAN 3 • OCTOPUSSY • SUPERGIRL • A VIEW TO A KILL • MY HOUSE IN
JACKET • HELLBOUND: HELLRAISER II • **MEMPHIS BELLE** • ALIEN 3 • THE RUSSIA HOUSE • WILDE • 5
S • **INTERVIEW WITH THE VAMPIRE** • HARRY POTTER & THE CHAMBER OF SECRETS • HACKERS • FIRST
ITH LOVE • DOCTOR AT SEA • HELLRAISER • LUTHER • **EYES WIDE SHUT** • THE DRESSER • TOMORROW
ENT • THE WORLD IS NOT ENOUGH • EXISTENZ • **TOMB RAIDER** • THE MUMMY RETURNS • BLAME IT ON
TICAL LIMIT • INKHEART • THE HOURS • **IRIS** • POSSESSION • PLANET OF THE APES • THE RED SHOES •
THE LAST TEN DAYS • DESIGNING WOMEN • LEST WE FORGET • BIRDS OF A FEATHER • RADIO PIRATES •
E HOUSE • CURTAIN UP • THE DECEIVERS • THE WOODEN HORSE • THE CRYING GAME • **THE AFRICAN**
LIFE • BANG,YOU'RE DEAD • **PHANTOM OF THE OPERA** • THE BELLES OF ST. TRINIANS • LAST ORDERS
OVED REDHEADS • CROUPIER • THE ADMIRABLE CRICHTON • JACK THE RIPPER • ROOM AT THE TOP • A
ED • BILLY LIAR • **MIX ME A PERSON** • BIRTHDAY GIRL • CATACOMBS • THE BABYSITTER • WHITE SQUALL
ARIS • LAND GIRLS • ROTTEN TO THE CORE • THE SICILIANS • DOCTOR WHO AND THE DALEKS • **SYLVIA**
AT THE TOP • HALF A SIXPENCE • A MAN FOR ALL SEASONS • TILL DEATH US DO PART • THE COUNT OF
D • THE MAN WHO FELL TO EARTH • VERONICA GUERIN • **THE PINK PANTHER STRIKES AGAIN** • THE
BLE • THE-BOYS FROM BRAZIL • KILLING DAD • THE MAN WHO KNEW TOO LITTLE • DOMINIQUE • FORCE
THE AFFAIR • BLACKBALL • FLASH GORDON • **OLIVER!** • THE ELEPHANT MAN • LITTLE LORD FAUNTLEROY
NGER • THE HOUND OF THE BASKERVILLES • BOOMERANG • STILL CRAZY • OUT OF AFRICA • ABSOLUTE
ES • **GORILLAS IN THE MIST** • CHILDREN OF MEN • HOW TO GET AHEAD IN ADVERTISING • MOUNTAINS
MEN AND A LITTLE LADY • THE OTHER WOMAN • SPLITTING HEIRS • **FOUR WEDDINGS AND A FUNERAL**
MLET • 101 DALMATIANS • SENSE & SENSIBILITY • THE ADVENTURES OF BARON MUNCHAUSEN • THE
THE PARENT TRAP • GLADIATOR • LOVE'S LABOUR'S LOST • **BILLY ELLIOT** • SLEEPY HOLLOW • MAYBE
END IT LIKE BECKHAM • **GOSFORD PARK** • DIRTY PRETTY THINGS • THE GATHERING STORM • EXTREME
HERS • TROY • DRACULA • THE LIFE & DEATH OF PETER SELLERS • COMPLEAT FEMALE STAGE BEAUTY •
T JONES 2 • ALEXANDER • THUNDERBIRDS • BATMAN BEGINS • CHILDREN OF MEN • CHARLIE AND THE

... to be continued

PINEWOOD
STUDIOS

PINEWOOD
STUDIOS

70 YEARS OF FABULOUS FILM-MAKING

FOREWORD BY DAME JUDI DENCH

INTRODUCTION BY TIM BURTON

MORRIS BRIGHT

CARROLL & BROWN PUBLISHERS LIMITED

First published in 2007 in the United Kingdom by

Carroll & Brown Publishers Limited
20 Lonsdale Road
London NW6 6RD

Text © Morris Bright, 2007
Compilation © Carroll & Brown Limited, 2007

A CIP catalogue record for this book is available from the British Library.

ISBN 978-1-904760-63-4

10987654321

Reproduced by RALI, Spain
Printed and bound in Italy by MS Printing, Milan

CONTENTS

14 — 41

From Mansion to Movies 1

42 — 61

Less Light but Still
Cameras 2 and Action

162 — 201

Carrying 6 On

202 — 237

Heroes 7 and Heroines

238 — 275

Nobody Does 8 It Better

FOREWORD

Although I had a made a few films in the 1960s, at that time in my career I was concentrating on stage and television work, and so I did not find myself filming at Pinewood until relatively late in its long history. My husband, Michael Williams, was a much earlier visitor to the Studios, first working on a film there – *The Marat Sade*, with Glenda Jackson, Patrick Magee and Ian Richardson – back in 1966.

I came to Pinewood to film *Jack and Sarah* with Richard E. Grant, Eileen Atkins and Ian McKellen in 1994 – a time of change for the Studios. The previous year, Pinewood had had no films on its stages at all. It was a bad time for the industry in general and a low point for Pinewood in particular. Yet just months later, things had begun to turn – thanks I am sure, in no small part, to the efforts of a management team determined to pull the Studios around.

Like most big studios, there are various activities going on at any one time. While I was involved with *Jack and Sarah* on one sound stage, Richard Gere and Sean Connery were on the back lot making *First Knight*, Tom Cruise and Brad Pitt were on another stage shooting *Interview With the Vampire*, Julia Roberts was filming *Mary Reilly* and, I recall, Ted Danson and Ian Holm were picking up interior shots for *Loch Ness*. Quite a mix of pictures, with very different stories, very different budgets and very different talents, but that is exactly what film studios are like most days of the week – great melting pots of talent creating such varied and interesting bodies of work.

This book, published to celebrate 70 years of filmmaking at Pinewood, pays tribute to that work. However, it does more than just pay lip-service to the history of a favourite institution. It brings together, in the way only a book can, not just the thoughts and memories of those who have worked both in front of and behind the cameras over the years, but also hundreds of carefully chosen images from seven decades of production at this special site.

Which fan of film could not fail to be impressed by the sight of Alec Guinness in costume as Fagin, taking a cigarette break during the filming of *Oliver Twist* in 1947? Who cannot raise a wry smile witnessing a young Prince of Wales coming to Pinewood to visit – of all films being made at the Studios in 1962 – the sets of *Doctor in Distress* and *Carry On Cabby*? And which lover of the cinema would not be excited at seeing Alfred Hitchcock overseeing a music recording session at Pinewood during production of his penultimate film, *Frenzy*, back in 1972? Such images have been painstakingly researched to bring us more than just the usual shots of our favourite films and it is these behind-the-scenes images that really captivate.

Pinewood has been home to some of the most renowned film series in British cinema history; all those *Carry Ons*, the *Doctor* films and the numerous big screen antics of Norman Wisdom. Then, of course, there's *Bond*. For most of the past five decades, Bond and Pinewood have been very closely linked. True, not all films made at Pinewood were *Bond*s and not all *Bond* films were made at Pinewood, but there does seem to be a tangible chemistry between these two giants. I believe that Pinewood likes to have *Bond* on site, and I believe the *Bond* production team like to be at Pinewood. Both are such well-respected names in film that they suit each other.

Every visit I have ever made to Pinewood has been a pleasurable experience. It is a Studio with a great history – one need only walk down the long corridors and view the posters of the films that have been made here since the late 1930s. There is the old mansion house and the beautiful gardens. The Studios is well cared for and looked after – as anyone or anything that is 70 years old should be. Productions both great and small are treated with equal respect. My own filming experiences – from *Casino Royale* to *Jack and Sarah*, from *The Chronicles of Riddick* to *Iris* – big budgets, small budgets, Pinewood has always made me feel at home. As you look back through this book, it is easy to see why so many actors, cast and crew, past and present, come to think of Pinewood as just that, a home.

Pinewood is 70 now – a very important milestone in British film history. This book tells us all about its interesting and colourful past and, with the glorious images and the recollections and reminiscences of the talents who have worked here over the years, I hope it will serve as a very timely reminder of why Pinewood has a place in the hearts of a filmmaking as well as a film-viewing nation.

Congratulations Pinewood. Long may the Studios continue as a place of film and television excellence.

Dame Judi Dench

INTRODUCTION

> ❝ *For me Pinewood is Number One.* ❞

It's pretty amazing to think that Pinewood is now 70 years old. I've been coming here for almost 20 of those years and I fell in love with these Studios the moment I stepped through the gates back in the late 1980s when I arrived here to make *Batman*.

When you walk through the Studios you cannot help but feel the great history of where you are working and all that has come before. You cannot help but be reminded that so

many great films have been and continue to be made at this world-famous site.

Pinewood is distinctive; it sticks out as a Studios of excellence on a whole set of levels. One of the best, from my point of view as a director, is that the Studios allows you to feel like you're shooting a movie without the feeling that you are being surrounded by studio executives all the time. Very often when you shoot in Hollywood it feels like it's just a business. At Pinewood it always feels like the art of filmmaking comes first.

Pinewood is a classic studio, I suppose because it's had so many classics produced in it. Wherever you wander around the grounds you know you're probably standing on the spot where several scenes have been shot for so many different films across the years. The gardens alone are just full of great reminiscences as you literally turn around in a 360 degree circle and recall great film moments made within feet of where you are standing – from *Dracula Has Risen From the Grave* to *Chitty Chitty Bang Bang* and the whole opening sequence of the *Bond* film *From Russia With Love*.

I have to admit, I am a bit of a *Bond* fan. Those films shoot all over the world but they wouldn't be quite the same without Pinewood, would they? I always find filming on the *Bond* stage quite thrilling – it has such an aura about it, almost a mythology in some ways. You just look at the size and shape of it and you start to recall some of the great set pieces that

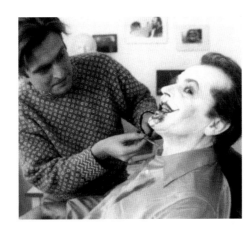

were shot there, like those magnificent submarines from *The Spy Who Loved Me*. I know that the *Bond* stage is literally only just a huge metal shed, but even so I can't help but be charmed by it.

We built the chocolate river on that stage for *Charlie and the Chocolate Factory* and, of course, the stage is so associated with the *Bond* movies that people who didn't realize that it wasn't a *Bond* that was being shot on the stage at the time were wondering just what kind of *Bond* film was being produced – with some type of weird candyland villain trying to take over the world! People genuinely thought they were shooting a *Bond* film there when I was making *Charlie and the Chocolate Factory*. It was a little

confusing for some, I recall. It was a shame that the stage burnt down again in the summer of 2006, but Pinewood is so quick and no one seemed to let it get them down that a £12 million building had to get put straight back up again. It's been pretty amazing to watch the rebuilding of one of the world's most renowned stages as we were preparing to shoot *Sweeney Todd*. I think that's part of it too, at Pinewood. None of the huge dramatics. There's a job to be done and they get on and do it – and allow us all to get on and do ours at the same time. I respect and like that.

Pinewood is a good place if you are a film fan – which you know I am. As a fan of film and as a filmmaker, both of those passions collide and I get a great energy when I work here. I first arrived back in 1988. I'd never been to Pinewood before I made *Batman*. The project had become the subject of a lot of talk and speculation in America and we felt the need to get away from the hype of it all and get down to the actual making of the film using a Studios that has always had such a tradition of having the best craftsmen – the set painters, the carpenters, the sculptors – all the arts that really get my blood flowing. Gotham City was, at the time, the biggest set to be built on Pinewood's back lot since *Cleopatra* at the end of the 1950s. That film was abandoned. Thankfully *Batman* wasn't. And I can tell

Technological advancements in filmmaking have come a long way, especially over the past few decades. Pinewood keeps up with the times yet it doesn't forget its roots and where its reputation lies – that is the tradition of set building as opposed to having everything done digitally. Some things are worth protecting and set building is one of them, possibly the most important aspect for me. I always find sets, and being in an environment on stages with sets, helps me and the actors and everybody involved, because there's a context and you're not just in a green room asking people to react to things that aren't there.

you that watching Gotham City going up was the most exciting time of my life. I would walk on to the back lot every day and see the progress of the set and watch in awe as all the artists worked. Believe me, when you are dealing with a set project as big as that one and you come to watch all these experts and dedicated professionals working to build up the vision, it is very energizing indeed. I got the same feeling when I was back at Pinewood watching the sets going up for *Charlie and the Chocolate Factory*, and it has been the same again, as the craftsmen put together all the magnificent Victorian sets for *Sweeney Todd*.

No matter what advances come along, to me the magic of making movies will always be important. That's one of the reasons that I came to film the whole of *Sweeney Todd* at Pinewood. We are not going out on location. It's an old-fashioned type of horror movie – which always have that contained feel about them – and so we decided to build all the sets and do all the filming within the Studio. And yes, shooting on stages is very helpful – we can shoot at any time in any weather.

Sweeney Todd is a story that takes place in Victorian London. So it's great to be back here in London doing it. Pinewood may be celebrating 70 years of filmmaking, but it's now coming up to my 20-year anniversary since I first came to the Studios to make a film and, after two decades, to keep being able to return on projects that are close to my heart is very meaningful to me.

The movie market is now global. Studios are cropping up everywhere and advancing technologies are joining us all together wherever we are in the world. These are exciting times for our industry – and they can be challenging times for Studios to stay on top and be successful in the face of big competition. Pinewood's age, though, does not make it aged. I think that it makes it wise as to what it needs to do to keep ahead of the game. Pinewood will stay in favour by doing what it has always done: quite simply, staying attractive for people who want to shoot here. Which it is. So Pinewood is 70 years old and here is a magnificent book to showcase its history, not just in words, but especially in pictures. Which is what Pinewood is, quite literally, a Studio in pictures.

For me, like for thousands of people who have worked here over all those years since Pinewood opened it's doors to filmmakers and filmmaking, this place is my favourite studio. I love it here. Any time I can shoot here, I will shoot here. That's the way that I feel.

" I love it here. "

Tim Burton
Director

From Mansion to Movies

TWO IMAGES OF the Heatherden Hall mansion from the early 1930s and the 1960s.

When Heatherden Hall was put up for sale in 1934, the estate agents responsible for its disposal described the manor as being "situated in the Ecclesiastical Parish of Iver Heath in the County of Buckingham" and went on to boast with some pride that the Georgian Mansion was a building on which "vast sums have been spent from time to time". The prospectus for Heatherden went on to note that the Hall was situated 200 feet above sea level – though quite why that was deemed a selling point when the nearest coast was more than 50 miles away, is anyone's guess – and that it had been built on a gravel subsoil. Potential new owners were asked to imagine what the building could next be used for: suggesting, perhaps, that it was "suitable for hotel, institution or clinic".

Heatherden was indeed to become an institution, though not perhaps the one implied in the original sales patter, evolving as it would into Pinewood Studios, one of the most renowned, famed, admired and respected sites for film production in the world.

Heatherden's history had been colourful if somewhat chequered. Early in the last century, the Canadian financier and Member of Parliament for Brentford and Chiswick, Lieutenant-Colonel Grant Morden bought the estate and set about modernizing the Victorian house. The previous owner had been a Doctor Drury Lavin, who had lived there in the late nineteenth century. Lavin frequently held lavish parties in the grounds, employing the services of the nearby Uxbridge and Hillingdon Band for afternoon tea entertainment. Lavin was a wealthy man but apparently – and seemingly without great reason – suddenly upped and left.

The next incumbent was world-famous cricketer, K. S. Ranjitsinhji, who soon tired of the British winters and sold the estate to Morden. It was Morden who added the huge ballroom, the largest indoor swimming pool in the country at that time,

a Turkish bath, squash courts and perfectly laid out gardens and lawns on the many acres of land in which his new home was situated.

Morden was a political high flier and his home, so near to the seat of British power – with Parliament less than 20 miles from the estate – became a magnet for the rich and powerful. He shot grouse and pheasant, owned Borzoi dogs and deer hounds, and seemed to live the perfect life both in public and in private. His clean living attracted senior politicians to visit and stay. International financier and film-maker Richard Norton, nicknamed "The Wicked Uncle" on account of his monocle

THE STUDIOS' ADMINISTRATION BLOCK leads out into the magnificent and beautifully maintained Pinewood gardens.

AN EARLY AERIAL SHOT of Pinewood Studios and its surrounding grounds as the site undergoes construction.

and slightly sinister expression, recalled the grandiose home of Colonel Morden: "Heatherden Hall had been built regardless of cost. It had several magnificent suites of rooms in the worst possible taste, including one with a unique marble bathroom – which is the size of my room in my Regent Street office, which was by no means small. The taps were large, gilt lions' heads, and spouted water in a splendidly Renaissance manner."

On 3rd November 1921, the Irish Free State Treaty was ratified at the Mansion, signed by Lord Birkenhead, Viscount Younger, Sir Malcolm Fraser and Morden himself. Today, the room in which the Treaty was signed is the bar adjacent to the restaurant, which used to be the Pinewood ballroom. On his return to Pinewood Studios after a 33-year absence in 1996, the late Sir Dirk Bogarde stood at the very spot that the treaty had been signed some 75 years previously, waxing far more lyrically about the history of where he was standing than any film he had ever made at the Studio as a Rank star.

Morden lavished in excess of £300,000 on his Buckinghamshire home (well over £5 million in today's money) but the economic crisis that struck in the 1930s robbed him of much of his wealth and his fortune disappeared almost overnight. On his early death in 1934 the estate was put up for sale at just a tenth of what

A PLAQUE commemorating the signing of the Irish Free State Treaty at Heatherden Hall in 1921.

Morden had spent on it. As well as the mansion itself, with the sale came almost 100 acres of grounds. For building tycoon, Charles Boot, it was too good an opportunity to miss. He snapped up Heatherden and immediately set about recouping his investment by turning the hall into a country club for the rich and famous. The ballroom was turned into a restaurant (which it continues to be to this day), and many of the smaller rooms were knocked through and joined together to make luxurious executive suites.

Yet Boot's main aim for buying Heatherden and its grounds was far more adventurous. Not so secretly, he planned to turn the land into a film studio. Boot had failed in his first attempt to start a Hollywood-style production site in Britain back in the 1920s. Now he saw this new venture as an opportunity to fulfil his dream. As well as the grounds he had bought through the sale of Morden's estate, Boot also snapped up the land on the other side of the road where he planned to build an estate of 400 homes in which to house his future studio workers.

THE EMPTY FIELDS that made up the grounds of Pinewood in the 1930s (above left) have now been developed into sound stages. The water tank to the right of this photograph is still in place some 70 years later. Above, Pinewood in the 21st century – an aerial shot of the site looking quite different from its 1930s counterpart.

ABOVE AND BELOW, pre-World War II images of Pinewood Studios' buildings and car park one. Opposite, an early image of a "star" dressing room.

While building on the Studios was underway Boot travelled to Hollywood on a fact-finding mission, and on his return brought back with him James Sloan, who was to act as the Studios' general manager and who is generally recognized as the architect behind what was to become Pinewood's design.

Until that time no Englishman had been given the opportunity to build a million-pound studios from scratch. Alexander Korda had just started building at Denham, and Boot and his colleagues kept a careful eye on Korda's progress. They were particularly keen on the latest innovation – large sound stages with electrically controlled doors, all facing inwards towards covered areas in which props and scenery could be assembled. Denham was not able to provide that type of facility: it had no covered ways connecting its sound stages, which were spread sporadically and some distance away from each other with just one long corridor connecting them. Korda's office was right at the very end of the long corridor and one day Richard Norton, on a visit to Denham and in an attempt to pull Korda's leg, borrowed a bicycle, rode along the corridor and into Korda's office puffing and panting as though he'd just been on a marathon. Korda saw the funny side of it. But it highlighted the general frustration of the way Denham had been built.

Pinewood was to be different and Sloan clearly and methodically laid out his plans for Boot and his associates. The Studio was to be constructed in symmetrical units comprising of one large stage and one small stage which had its own offices, dressing rooms and ancillary services. There were to be eight sets of stages such as these and in the middle, almost like a large courtyard, were to be the prop makers, costumiers, scene builders and general workshops. Symmetry was all very well but Sloan's plans had to be somewhat curtailed after five sets of these stages were built because the shape of the land would not allow the others to be added in the same way. Nevertheless, it was a clever plan and no attention to detail was missed – from the covered ways to protect against the inclement British weather, to the siting of electrical wiring and power cables above ground level, suspended from the ceilings of the new stages.

Construction work on Boot's dream began in November 1935. Building was quick, each stage being completed in just three weeks. Boot officially renamed Heatherden Hall Pinewood, in his own words, because: "… of the number of trees

PINEWOOD'S SOUND STAGES (above) were constructed in just 21 days in the 1930s as the Studios took shape quickly to meet the rising surge of interest in British film making facilities.

FROM ITS EARLIEST DAYS, Pinewood became renowned for the very best in props creation. Right, props for a host of productions are catalogued and stored.

**DIFFERENT ASPECTS of early Pinewood –
from the carpenter's shops for the building of
sets for films, to a theatre for viewing the daily
rushes. The portrait gallery, very much part of
the old mansion house, was said to be the
home of the Pinewood ghost.**

which grow there and because it seemed to suggest something
of the American film centre in its second syllable." Pinewood
was intended to be a prestigious studio and in an attempt to
ensure and perpetuate the level of dignity, Boot had the
former library of the ship *Mauritania* transferred to the
boardroom complete and intact, where it still resides today.
He also had a huge, hand-carved Elizabethan fireplace
removed from the old Ilam Hall in Derbyshire, which was due
for demolition, and re-positioned at Pinewood as the
entrance to the administration building, where it still holds
pride of place seven decades later.

Investing large sums into this venture, Boot was more than aware that it
would be important to bring other wealthy investors on board to ensure that this
time round his project would not collapse. He teamed up with J. Arthur Rank, the
Methodist miller and millionaire who felt that film was a medium he could exploit
to spread the word of his beliefs, and Lady Yule, the rich widow of an Anglo-Indian
jute miner, to joint-finance the project. Richard Norton, invited to lunch at the
Langham Hotel by prominent 1930s film distributor C. M. Woolf, found himself

sitting next to Charles Boot, J. Arthur Rank, and their city colleague Ronald Crammond. Norton was told

PINEWOOD'S BOARDROOM (left) originally played host to the mansion house library and is decorated with wooden panelling from the ship, the *SS Mauritania*.

of their plans for Pinewood and promptly abandoned his own plans to invest in building at Elstree studios and joined in a 50/50 partnership with the others, who were in the process of spending £1 million on creating their new dream. J. Arthur Rank impressed Norton: "During the months that followed I saw a good deal of Arthur Rank, and grew to like him more and more. Never a talkative man, what he did say was always sound Yorkshire sense, an attribute that appealed a great deal to a fellow-Yorkshireman such as myself."

Joseph Arthur Rank was born in Hull on 23 December 1888, one of six children of Joseph Rank, a prominent Yorkshire mill-owner. He went to school locally and at 17 began an apprenticeship for his father in the family's flour-milling business. Rank joined the Army at the outbreak of World War I, and served in France. By the end of the war he was a captain in the Royal Field Artillery. While a sergeant, in 1917, he married Ellen Marshall, the daughter of Lord Marshall, a former Lord Mayor of London. For a quarter of a century, from 1918 until 1943, Rank continued to work in his father's flour business. The company was big, milling and selling around 30 percent of all flour used and consumed in Britain between the wars.

The Ranks were a staunch Nonconformist family with a vigorous interest in the Methodist Church. J. Arthur's father founded the Joseph Rank Benevolent Fund and it was this practical interest in church work that led him to put up the capital for several short films on a biblical theme made for showing at Sunday school and churches. Rank found the experience a rewarding one and immediately set about entering the world of commercial film-making – a move which would ultimately lead to the development of the Rank Organisation, which was to embrace not only film production, and film distribution at home and abroad, but

SIGN WRITING – one of Pinewood's many highly skilled and respected Studio departments.

PROFILE

J. Arthur Rank

Born on 23 December 1888, Joseph Arthur Rank was one of six children of the prominent Methodist Yorkshire flourmill owner, Joseph Rank. J. Arthur served in France during the First World War.

Rank's interest in film began as a young man, believing that the good work of his church could be promoted through cinema. He formed the Religious Film Society, through which he distributed short films that he had produced for showing at cinemas before the main feature. He formed the Rank Organisation in 1937 and dominated the UK film industry in the coming years when he purchased the Odeon cinema chain, Amalgamated Studios in Elstree, the Gaumont-British Picture Company and the Shepherd's Bush Studios. By 1942, Rank owned 619 cinemas.

In 1957 J. Arthur Rank was elevated to the Peerage, becoming Baron Rank of Sutton Scotney in the County of Hampshire.

Rank remained a man of great faith throughout his life. He once said: "If I could recall to you some of my various adventures in the film world, it would, I think, be as plain to you as it is to me that I was being led by God."

Lord Rank died on 29 March 1972.

also catering, leisure activities and a wide field of manufacturing interests and would, at its height, employ more than 30,000 people.

One of the early Rank religious film writers was Peter Rogers, future producer of the long-running *Carry On* comedy film series, all 31 of which were to be made at Pinewood Studios. Rank employed Rogers to write on *Thought for the Week*, a religious slot that was slipped into the cinema schedules ahead of the main feature on Sunday evenings. The premise behind *Thought for the Week* was to use a fictional character, Doctor Goodfellow, who would lean over a garden gate and talk to the cinema audience. Rogers took Rank's religious tracts and translated them into everyday language: "They weren't all very well received but we did our best and J. Arthur was a good man on a mission. There are some who used to say that there was Methodism in his madness."

In October 1934, J. Arthur Rank set up British National Films. He initially wanted to produce a cinematic version of *The Pilgrim's Progress* but the project never took off. He then turned his attention to a novel about the rivalry between two Yorkshire fishing families whose feuding is brought to an end by a marriage. *The Turn of the Tide* starred Geraldine Fitzgerald, Wilfrid Lawson and Moore Marriott. The film was well received, described by writer Graham Greene as "an unpretentious and truthful film", and was the project that saw Rank dip his toes into a business which he now knew had religious possibilities.

While Rank was impressed with film, he was less impressed with the British and Dominions Studios at Elstree, where the interiors for *The Turn of the Tide* were shot. The studios felt cramped to him and as a businessman whose success was based on quick and efficient turnaround of a product, he couldn't tolerate filming being held up while sets had to be taken down and rebuilt between takes. He knew that if British films were ever to compare to Hollywood, film production would have to step up a notch or two. With this in mind he was attracted to the Pinewood project with its planned large stages and Americanized methods of production. Ironically as Pinewood's first brick was being laid in late January 1936 a further

J. ARTHUR RANK, founder of Pinewood Studios, in his office.

injection of capital came to the project from Richard Norton and British and Dominions, following an insurance pay-out on a fire which had destroyed their facilities at Elstree. As part of the deal, Norton was to become Pinewood's first managing director

From the outset it wasn't all plain sailing for the different characters on the board and before long, Lady Yule tired of films and sold out her share to Rank who became Chairman while Norton remained as managing director. Rank was by this time tied in with film distributor C. M. Woolf who had first organized the lunch that had brought British and Dominions and Norton to the table. From the outset Norton and Woolf did not hit it off and their rivalry continued to grow. As Norton recalled: "I had a flat furnished for myself in the buildings at Pinewood, and settled down to enjoy myself making pictures and having rows with C. M. Woolf." On one occasion when Norton was escorting C. M. Woolf around the studios, both men were stopped in their tracks by a piece of graffiti etched on a wall which read: "The Honourable Richard Norton is a shit". Norton's father had died a few days before, elevating Norton to the peerage. Norton picked up a piece of chalk, scribbled out the words "The Honourable" and replaced them with "Lord Grantley".

Rank's teaming up with C. M. Woolf led to the formation of General Film Distributors, which was the first company to use the "man with the gong" as its symbol. The first man to beat the gong was silent film star Karl Dane, followed by former heavyweight boxer, Bombardier Billy Wells, then in later years by wrestlers Phil Nieman and Ken Richmond. GFD immediately bought into Universal Pictures, a stable if not major Hollywood brand at the time and Rank soon bought out Gaumont Screens in Britain. This meant that he had a studio to film in, connections in Hollywood and a distribution network at home and abroad, to set him on track to become one of the most powerful men in British cinema history.

The completion of building at Pinewood was fast and the Studios were opened officially on 30 September 1936, when Charles Boot handed over the opening key to the Parliamentary Secretary to the Board of Trade, Dr Leslie Burgin, in front of more than 1,000 guests on sound stage "D". As Richard Norton recalled: "To celebrate the opening, the Board gave a lunch-party to over a thousand people. I made a halting speech, in the wake of the Cabinet

PROFILE

Billy Wells

William Thomas Wells, who later was to become known as Billy "Bombardier" Wells, was born on 31 August 1889. Billy was a big chap – measuring six foot three inches and weighing around 190lbs. Hardly surprising then, that he was a very successful heavyweight boxer, becoming both the British and the British Empire champion for eight years between 1911 and 1919. He fought his last fight in 1925. Billy was described as a "good mover in the ring, a good hitter and owning an excellent jab".

After hanging up his gloves, Billy took over as the Rank Gong Man from original striker, Karl Dane. He remained the gong hitter until after the Second World War, when the post was taken on by movie extra Phil Nieman for seven years. He was to be succeeded by the fourth and last gong man, Ken Richmond, an Olympic bronze medallist at the 1952 Helsinki games, who was also a prolific film extra.

In his later years Billy Wells owned a pub at the Piccadilly end of Park Lane, London. Though four decades have now passed since Bombardier Wells died, in June 1967, his reputation still lives on. On 23 September 2006 a contestant on ITV's quiz show *Who Wants to be a Millionaire?* correctly identified Billy Wells as the former gong man who was a heavyweight boxing champion. It was the million pound question.

representative and Mr Rank. There followed what must be a unique event. Dr Gregory, a senior member of the Methodist Church, said a prayer to bless the new studios." A blessing that welcomed the birth of a new Studio and a new era in British filmmaking.

The doors of Pinewood may have opened to the world of filmmaking at the end of September 1936 but production was already underway while the finishing touches were being put to the Studios. Indeed, guests who attended the inaugural event on 30 September were treated to a visit around the set of Herbert Wilcox's *London Melody*, which had begun filming elsewhere and ended up at Pinewood for completion. Wilcox's wife, actress Anna Neagle, starred in the romantic musical drama in which a diplomat falls for a dancer. Released in 1937, it is generally recognized as being the first film to have been completed at Pinewood Studios.

Production got off to a flying start, *London Melody* being one of eight productions shot at Pinewood within months of its doors opening. Carol Reed made

RANK HAD FOUR MEN beating their gongs across the decades: Danish silent film star Karl Dane, heavyweight boxing champion Billy "Bombardier" Wells, wrestler Phil Neiman, and fellow wrestler and film extra Ken Richmond.

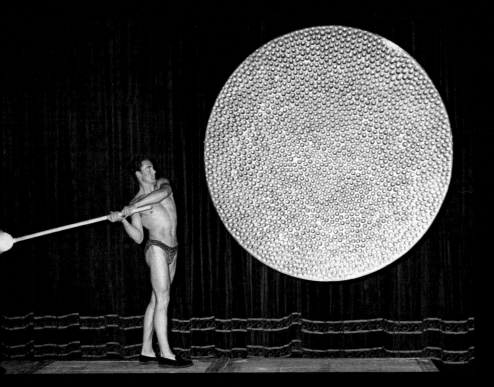

Talk of the Devil (1936), a drama of double cross and crooked deals, notable less for its cast and production values than for being the first film that was both started and completed at Pinewood. Wally Patch and Wifrid Hyde-White starred in Paramount's *The Scarab Murder Mystery* and a young Margaret Lockwood appeared in Maurice Elvey's *Melody and Romance*. Within months of it's opening, Pinewood had become the busiest studios in the country, yet other studios, such as Elstree and Denham, which technically had more sound stages than Pinewood, were not idle at Pinewood's expense.

The reason for the surge in demand for studio space lay fairly and squarely at the foot of The Cinematograph Films Act of 1927. The Act had been brought in by Parliament at the end of the 1920s in an attempt to breathe life into a dying film industry, which faced constant pressure from American imports. The USA had plenty of studio capacity and was churning out vast numbers of films in double quick time, flooding British markets with their musicals, gangster movies and melodramas. The advent of sound had just fuelled the rush. The Government was trying to help when it brought in The Cinematograph Films Act. The Act dictated that an increasing number of British films should be made and released on a sliding scale over a ten-year period and that by the end of the 1930s, the number of British productions should total at least 20 per cent of all films produced. The Act also laid out terms for the numbers of staff who needed to be employed on a production that had to be of British origin. British film producers saw this as an opportunity to knock out films quickly and cheaply – after all they had a Government-imposed quota to fill. These films became known as "quota quickies".

The Act was successful in that it did a great deal to stabilize and ultimately increase the rate of British film production. However, these cheap and often not-so-cheerful flicks did little to improve the industry's reputation. Under the law, the definition of "British" extended to anywhere within the Empire. From the far ends of British colonial rule came productions that were all but un-watchable. They were costed by length of film not by quality of production. Some silent offerings from India came in at just £500.

The majority of the "quota quickies" did not make a profit – they were never really intended to – and several made a small loss. But the sheer number produced

THE ENTRANCE to the Studios administration building (opposite) is the magnificent sixteenth-century Elizabethan hand-carved solid oak fireplace, which originally resided at Ham Hall in Derbyshire.

WAVING FAREWELL to Pinewood after making a film test for the Rank Organisation, Dorothy Moreau who had recently been elected Miss Canada 1956.

OPPOSITE, EARLY SHOTS of the tank with backdrop (above), and a camera car (below) rigged up for the filming of moving and driving sequences.

offset worries of a huge financial disaster. Additionally, and far more importantly, they were a good training ground for up-and-coming actors, writers, technicians, producers and directors.

The Act also had an additional benefit of encouraging American studios to set up operations in Britain to feed their own home markets by producing films cheaply over here for visual consumption over there. The Act certainly helped kick-start the almost stagnant British film industry of the 1920s, but by the time Pinewood had opened its doors, British films had developed a bad reputation, and cinemas screening quota quickies were shunned in favour of those showing the lavish Hollywood offerings – the Rogers and Astaire musicals, the Marx Brothers' comedies, classical adventures such as *Mutiny on the Bounty*, the latest adventures of Laurel and Hardy, and so on.

In 1937, Pinewood saw 24 films made within its Studios. Several were quota quickies, which the Studios' management did not object to as they could be filmed in between other larger productions and so kept workers employed consistently throughout the year. Busy with productions great and small, Pinewood became a home to directors and producers from all filming backgrounds. Some had just a few weeks' experience in the industry; others had many years of experience behind them. And there were new faces just entering the business who were to become the big filmmaking names in years to come – Alexander Mackendrick, the future Ealing comedies director, Freddie Francis, award-winning cinematographer and horror film director, Roger Macdougall, future renowned playwright, and Carol Reed, film maker of classics such as *The Third Man* and *Oliver!* Pinewood truly was a melting pot of talent.

Pinewood's lavish surroundings attracted the Americans. It was very typically British and very untypically what they perceived as a film studio. They were attracted to the grounds, the old mansion house and its history. The Studios continued to see refurbishment and improvements to the old mansion house that became the centrepiece of attraction at the site. The former gun room – the room in which the Irish Free State Treaty was signed – was now converted into a small but opulent cocktail bar and the ballroom that adjoined it now served as a spacious wood-panelled restaurant in which diners could sit, eat and relax while looking out onto the well-groomed lawns outside. In the gardens, fresh vegetables were grown for serving at lunch. The mansion house had its own art gallery and billiards room, as well as several suites ornately fitted with marble bathrooms. The Studios had an air about it, which made it different from the other studios in the country. It felt very special, probably because there was what had been a home, sitting at the very heart of it and visitors who came to make films at Pinewood felt very pampered and special indeed.

Pinewood and Denham studios opened within a year of each other, with a great sense of optimism for their own futures and for the future of the British film industry. Much of the enthusiasm had been whipped up by Alexander Korda who, following the success of his film *The Private Life of Henry VIII* in 1933, had used his Hungarian charm to elicit large sums of capital out of City institutions to invest in studios and filmmaking. He received £1 million to build Denham studios and such was the belief from investors that British films could hit it big across the Atlantic, that a further £3 million was handed over in 1936 alone.

Yet among all its quota quickies, few precious cinematic treasures were to be found and it soon became obvious that while Korda could talk the talk, he couldn't deliver the prestige productions that would satisfy audiences and more importantly see investors recoup their huge loans. The death knell was ringing for The Cinematograph Films Act, which was coming to the end of its ten-year life span anyway and Pinewood's managing director, Richard Norton, was in talks with the Government as to the way forward: "For a long time I was occupied with negotiations over the new Quota Bill, due in 1938. The original Act, which had first protected British pictures, was only for a ten-year period. We started the British Film Producers' Association, to speak for the industry in discussions with the Government, and I became its Chairman. When the Act was finally passed by Parliament there was set up the Cinematograph Films Council, of which I was appointed a member, to advise the Government on matters of film policy. To guard

J. ARTHUR RANK spends some time, in between filming sequences, with Miss Great Britain and 1950s starlet, Anne Heywood.

against the worst quota quickies, the new Act laid down that a film would not qualify for quota purposes under a certain minimum cost: but it was decided that an under-cost film should not be penalized for economy if reputable judges considered its quality satisfactory. A sub-committee was set up to consider films of this kind, consisting of Miss Plumer, sister of Field Marshall Lord Plumer, producer Philip Guedalla, myself and two others. 'I cannot think of any precedent,' Philip protested, 'for the merits of putative entertainment being decided by four just men and a statutory woman'."

For a while, the new law actually made matters worse. Twickenham Studios went into receivership, unable to afford the increase in costs that the new minimum standards imposed. Korda began to suffer and pay cuts were levied at Denham. Gaumont-British saw their overdraft soar and their subsidiary company, Gainsborough Pictures, based at Islington Studios, was losing money hand over fist. Gaumont closed their studios at Shepherd's Bush and Gaumont-British Distributors was wound up, moving its feature distribution arm to Rank's General Film Distributors – making GFD the largest British renter in the market and placing it on par with its American counterparts. In return for its risk, while allowing a few films to continue to be produced at Islington, all other film production was to be transferred across to Pinewood. There followed a period of great activity at Pinewood, and while other studios flagged, films continued to roll off the production line at the Buckinghamshire site, including two musicals *Gangway* and *Sailing Along*, with audience favourite Jessie Matthews, and the much admired murder mystery *Young and Innocent*, a low budget but high thrills minor entry by the man who would become the world's favourite thriller maker, Alfred Hitchcock. It was to be another 35 years before Hitchcock would return to Pinewood to made one of his last thrillers, *Frenzy*, in 1972.

The frenzied activity at Pinewood in the late 1930s wasn't to last. The depression, which was hitting the British film industry in general, now had its sights firmly set on Pinewood. Things were not helped by the difficult atmosphere, which had developed on the Board of Directors between C. M. Woolf and Richard Norton. Woolf, a former leading name in film distribution who had become great friends with J. Arthur Rank, continued, as he had previously, to make it quite clear that he felt the monocoled Etonian did not serve the Studios nor the Board well and had no reason to be involved in the film business. Woolf was not to be underestimated. Indeed, it was generally felt that if it hadn't have been for his early death in 1941, the subsequent history of the Rank Organisation may well have been vastly different. For now, at boardroom level, the arguments continued. Norton fought back. He knew that while the arguing continued, Pinewood was beginning to slip away. He set up Pinebrook Ltd, to try and make films on a co-operative basis. As Norton recalls: "Loud arguments with C. M. Woolf went on, of course: they were almost as regular as my calls on the National Provincial Bank. He told me I was crazy when I started Pinebrook Ltd. I told him that I had to keep the Studios going somehow. Woolf said that he would not mind if the Studios fell down; I retorted that he had better ask Arthur Rank about that, as Arthur was one of its owners. Then Woolf got mad at what was probably my patronizing tone; and, after further shrieking at each other, we would then proceed to lunch together at the Embassy Club, in the greatest of harmony."

Even though facing large financial crises at Pinewood, Norton and Rank worked with Alexander Korda, ably assisted by the Prudential Bank, on a scheme to buy Korda's Denham Studios, allowing Korda to concentrate on making films. Norton rebuffed critics who questioned what Pinewood thought it was doing getting involved with Denham when it has its own monetary crisis to deal with: "In big money, you are often better off with a large liability than a small one; and with the borrowing powers of Denham added to Pinewood, I was able to work various new ways of raising liquid capital."

For a while Pinebrook Ltd managed to make and release films, thereby tentatively contributing to keeping Pinewood afloat. There was an expert farce, *A Spot of Bother* starring Robertson Hare, a taut thriller *This Man is News*, starring Valerie Hobson and Alastair Sim, and an early attempt by Carol Reed to produce a musical, *Climbing High*, starring Jessie Matthews and Michael Redgrave. *Climbing High* was fraught with problems from the moment it went into production. Telling the story of a wealthy man pretending to be a male model in order to win over a girl, the original casting of the male lead had gone to American actor Kent Taylor, who quit the project after the film's production start was

A SCENE FROM ONE OF PINEWOOD'S earliest films, the 1938 Religious Films' production *Beyond Our Horizon*.

POSTER ARTWORK from the 1938 version of *The Mikado* (opposite page), which was to be Pinewood's first Technicolor film.

BELOW, POSTER ARTWORK for a 1938 classic Pinewood thriller.

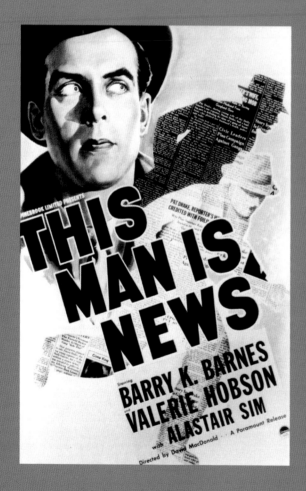

delayed. Jessie Matthews disliked many of the songs in the film and had them taken out, severely reducing the length of the film to a mere 78 minutes.

For the then 13-year-old child actor, Leslie Phillips, the whole experience of making the film was extraordinary: "Many people don't realize I've been making films for almost 70 years. I started off in films as a child. One of my first films was *Climbing High*. There was some funny goings on. I remember Carol Reed being an exceptionally good director and I seem to remember us filming a custard pie fight, but I'm not sure if that ever made it into the final version. It's quite funny really but a few years ago I was sitting with some colleagues and everyone was talking about how long they'd been in the business. I waited until the very end and then mentioned that I'd been acting for 70 years. You should have seen their faces. Yes, I remember working at Pinewood in its early days. It filled me with awe working with the likes of Michael Redgrave and Alastair Sim. That's an awfully long time ago now isn't it?"

Although some of the films performed well at the box office – *This Man is News* costing £12,000 and, according to Norton, grossing £58,000 – the financial crisis across the industry was now hitting Pinewood hard and it was becoming increasingly difficult for staff costs to be met. To stem the outflow of money, Pinebrook introduced a scheme that encouraged staff to take a smaller salary giving them instead a slice of the action. If a film performed well, as, say, did *This Man is News*, workers could earn themselves a reasonable amount in addition to their basic lower salary. Norton also enforced his own idea for cutting costs on a film. Known at the time as "The Norton Formula", the essence was quite simple: to cut down on the number of re-takes that a director called for. As Norton recalls: "I laid down the rule that (except for technical faults) there could never be more than three takes of any scene without permission from Tony Havelock-Allan, or more than four without permission from myself. Since Tony was tough, and my offices were miles away from the studio floor, the economy effected was quite considerable."

For a short time the new arrangements seemed to keep management and workforce happy. Among the poorly performing quota quickies there were to be some successful productions of good reputation. Remembered as much for its title song as the film itself, *The Lambeth Walk* (1938) was the big-screen version of a popular musical play which became a nationwide hit and – revived over 50 years later on stage as *Me and My Girl* – remains popular to this day. The 1938 Pinewood film version starred Lupino Lane, Sally Gray and Wilfred Hyde-White, and was directed by Albert de Courville.

Gordon Harker reprised his dour police inspector role made famous on pre-war radio for three cinema outings in the late 1930s and early 1940s. The first outing, *Inspector Hornleigh*, also starring Alastair Sim, was made at Pinewood in 1938. Gilbert and Sullivan's *The Mikado* was the first film at Pinewood to be made in colour. The process of making colour films in those days was cumbersome – a larger than usual camera was required, which exposed three separate rolls of film at the same time which then had to be matted together. The Technicolor production required a considerably higher budget, the increased costs emanating not just from the process but also from the additional lighting required to bring out the colour. The production's 750 costumes did much to increase the budget further. *The Mikado* was not a huge success but in terms of its production values and with some of the D'Oyly Carte Company's most recognized cast members taking the major roles, and with the music performed by the Royal Symphony Orchestra, the film remains a very watchable and useful reminder of two great musical institutions.

Like his Hungarian counterpart, Alexander Korda, producer Gabriel Pascal had the gift of the gab and could be incredibly persuasive when he needed to be. Having made many quota quickies of the 1930s, Pascal was determined to break out of the rut and make his mark in more respected

WENDY HILLER as Eliza Doolittle and Leslie Howard as the definitive Professor Henry Higgins, in Gabriel Pascal's famed production of Shaw's *Pygmalion*, directed by Anthony Asquith at Pinewood in 1938.

cinema. With true style and a considerable degree of cheek, Pascal cornered the writer George Bernard Shaw as he was about to enter his apartment in London and, after a long meeting, came away with the rights to film Shaw's *Pygmalion*. Shaw was sceptical about cinema – a poorly made version of his play *How He Lied to Her Husband* had bombed at the box office and Shaw was naturally sceptical about allowing one of his most cherished works to be given the big screen treatment again.

Quite how Pascal persuaded Shaw to hand over the rights for *Pygmalion* is unknown. Richard Norton, whom Pascal approached for funding, was equally bemused: "Why Shaw gave one of his plays to Pascal, after having refused many other producers, was a mystery to some people. One explanation given is that Shaw asked Pascal how much money he had, and Pascal took half a crown out of his pocket; Shaw being so delighted by his frankness that everything went smoothly thereafter. At any rate I think it is true, because I heard the story from both of them, that their interview ended with Gaby borrowing money from Shaw to pay off his taxi."

Norton took the idea to the Board at Pinewood, which, with the exception of C. M. Woolf, was glad to proceed with the idea, which was just as well, as *Pygmalion* proved a huge hit. Starring Leslie Howard as Henry Higgins and Wendy Hiller as Eliza Doolittle, the story of a professor of phonetics who accepts a bet that he can pass off a Cockney flower girl as a Duchess, won four Oscars including one for Shaw himself. On hearing the news of the award the playwright declared: "It's an insult. It's perfect nonsense. My position as a playwright is known throughout the world. To offer an award of this sort is an insult, as if they had not heard of me before – and it's very likely they never had." One can only imagine what Shaw's comments would have been if he had lived to witness the eight Academy Awards bestowed on the musical version of the play, *My Fair Lady*, almost 30 years later. *Pygmalion* did go over budget during production but it was a big box-office success on both sides of the Atlantic. For the first time since *The Private Life of Henry VIII*, queues formed to see the film in New York.

Back in England, Pinewood's future was not looking good. The problems at Denham had grown worse. Korda's overspending on projects, which performed badly at the cinema, saw debts continue to rise almost out of control. It was time to call in the debts and in an effort to consolidate the situation the decision was taken to add Pinewood's liabilities to those of Denham. Production could only continue at one or other of the Studios. It was no longer viable to keep both operations open if at least one of the Studios was to survive. J. Arthur Rank decided that production should continue at Denham and on Christmas Eve 1938, Pinewood's doors closed to film production.

Ironically, as Pinewood's fortunes fell, J. Arthur Rank's continued to rise. He joined the board of Odeon Theatres, injecting much-needed capital into the cinema circuit chain. "Odeon" stood for Oscar Deutsch Entertains Our Nation, and with Rank's investment in his company, Deutsch was able to expand his cinema chain which had stood at some 200 screens even before Rank had taken his position on the board. With more sound stages at his disposal, further expanded exhibition interests, and now leasing studio space to the Ministry of Works for storage, Rank had become the biggest player in the British film industry, in the space of just four years.

Yet Pinewood was out of the industry. Requisitioned by the Government for storage, its great sound stages became home to mountains of sugar, flour and other much-needed wartime supplies. In great secrecy, the Royal Mint moved in, producing millions of copper coins. And the joke went round that for the first time since it had been built, Pinewood wasn't making films anymore but was finally making money.

Less Light but Still
Cameras and Action
2

As war descended on Britain, a site of almost 100 acres, close to the capital, peppered with empty sound stages the size of huge warehouses, was an opportunity to good to be missed by the Government. Already occupied by the Royal Mint, other important industries were soon to enjoy being evacuated to Pinewood, particularly Lloyd's of London which moved into the Studios just days before hostilities broke out in September 1939.

While the Royal Mint occupied a sound stage – the heavy clanking noises emanating from the pounding of the metal presses subdued by the soundproofing around them – Lloyd's, along with 500 of its workers, moved into the mansion house and administration building. Daily buses were laid on for staff to get too and from the Studios and for those who preferred to live locally, accommodation was provided in nearby homes. Pinewood Green residents gave up rooms to

THE INSIGNIA OF the Army Film and Photographic Unit (above), which was stationed at Pinewood from 1941. On the right, Hugh Stewart (third from the left), during filming for the AFPU. Stewart went on to produce many of Norman Wisdom's big-screen outings in the 1950s.

AN AFPU ANIMATOR (opposite page) at work at the Studios. The output from the AFPU was an extremely important part of the war effort.

FILM PRODUCTION UN
Nº1
R.A.F.

THE ROYAL AIR FORCE FILM PRODUCTION UNIT (above) prepares for another mission. In the centre of the picture on the right is film director John Boulting, who was responsible for the influential wartime films *Desert Victory* (1943) and *Burma Victory* (1945).

accommodate staff for Lloyd's and other companies from the City who, of necessity, and to keep the financial boat afloat, needed to be moved out from the middle of London, where it was expected that, if the war became a very serious affair, the Germans would target the financial heart of the country to try and bring Britain to its knees.

Earlier in the year, on 30 June, Pinewood's managing director Richard Norton had literally been brought to his own knees. Rank had decided to make a film of Compton Mackenzie's romantic novel *Carnival* and the

" I WISH THE FELLOWS BACK AT THE STUDIO COULD SEE ME NOW . . BACK AT THE STUDIO"

A WARTIME CARTOON lampooning the stresses and strains of filming during the hostilities.

producers felt that some of the shots could be filmed on the sands in Cornwall. Norton knew the area well and offered to take the film's production manager on a trip to study the location. The two were near Ilminster, by Yeovil, when they were involved in a car crash. Norton recalled the events: "I was driving, with my chauffeur in front with me: Galperson [the production manager], who mercifully was rather fat, was in the back with one of the girls on each side of him. It was about 1.30 a.m. and I was going round a slight bend at a very reasonable speed of 50 miles an hour, when we came on a bridge with two stationary lorries completely blocking the way. There was no escape from a collision unless I plunged over the bridge. So I shouted to the others to duck, and put the brakes on so hard that the back tyres came off. All would have been moderately well but for the fact that the lorry ahead of us turned out to be a horse-box, with an overhanging part which stuck out behind just above the height of my car bonnet. It crashed through the windscreen, with unfortunate results to myself."

The chauffeur was miraculously unhurt. The production manager came away with a broken leg. Norton was not so lucky. Pinewood's MD suffered, among other injuries, a broken kneecap, two smashed hands, a smashed arm, a smashed face

OUT ON VERY REAL LOCATIONS (left) gathering images for the Army Film Unit, which would then be sent back to Pinewood for processing and editing for wartime newsreels, documentaries and films.

THREE MEMBERS OF THE ARMY FILM UNIT (right) prepare to leave Pinewood for yet another expedition into a dangerous war zone.

PROFILE

The Boulting Brothers

Twin brothers John and Roy Boulting were born on 21 December 1913 at Bray in Buckinghamshire, just a few miles from what would later become Pinewood Studios. They became renowned throughout the film industry for the way in which they alternated the producing and directing of their own films.

They set up Charter films in 1937 making several short features before the highly regarded *Pastor Hall* in 1940, in which a German preacher refuses to bend in the face of Nazi bullying. Roy Boulting joined the Army Film Unit in 1941 where he directed the much respected *Desert Victory* in 1943 and *Burma Victory* two years later. John Boulting joined the RAF Film Unit directing a young Richard Attenborough who was stationed at Pinewood Studios during the war. Attenborough also worked with the Boultings on *Brighton Rock*, and *The Guinea Pig*, both in 1948, as well as in their later social comedies.

In the late 1950s the Boultings brought biting satire to the big screen. The films took swipes at this country's "great" institutions – mocking the Church, the Army, the Civil Service and both the Unions and the Upper Classes in the widely acclaimed and highly regarded *I'm Alright Jack* (1959).

It was their down-to-earth attitude that made them attractive to a new board of directors at Shepperton, who were looking for impressive independent filmmaking talent. John Boulting was to eventually become MD of Shepperton in the late 1960s. The Boultings continued to make challenging films, such as the comedy of marital difficulties *The Family Way* (1966) and the troubling psychological thriller *Twisted Nerve* (1968), both starring Hywel Bennett and Hayley Mills, whom Roy Boulting married in 1971.

John Boulting died on 17 June 1985 and Roy on 5 November 2001.

FILMING FROM THE AIR –
another hazardous sortie for the
RAF film unit.

and a collapsed lung. Norton was hospitalized for two months. The film was put on hold and eventually made in 1944, and released almost two years later. Norton was convalescing at the Palace Hotel in Torquay over the first weekend of September and it was there that he heard Prime Minister Chamberlain's speech announcing the declaration of war.

Having been out of action for several months and with Pinewood effectively closed for filming, Norton started to worry about his job: "My contract was running out and the future was indefinite, as nobody knew what the war was going to do to film production. I had plenty of enemies in the film world, notably C. M. Woolf. The circumstances of my car accident – driving to Cornwall in company with two highly proper girls – could easily be presented in a way to antagonize Arthur Rank (and Woolf presented it very easily). Advantage had been taken of my absence to spread round a story that my Pinebrook Ltd films had been losing money."

IN THE CUTTING ROOMS AT PINEWOOD (left), the editing process gets underway, following the processing of the footage shot by the various film units and their cameramen while abroad in war-torn Europe.

Norton's doctors insisted he should stay away from London, so he went to stay with friends who owned a house near the Studios, accompanied by his sister. After a while, he started returning to his office at Pinewood for a few hours at a time and worked on plucking up the courage to tackle Rank on the issue of renewing his contract. Eventually, Rank himself called on Norton to go and see him and had apparently been dreading the meeting as much as Norton had. The upshot was that the Board decided there was no new contract for Norton and he was offered instead a part-time post as a technical adviser to Rank's film arm, a post he continued to hold throughout the war.

Being so close to London, Pinewood was always considered a likely target for bombing. Much of the site was surrounded by dense woodland. It wasn't difficult therefore for much of the Studios to be easily camouflaged, which ensured that Pinewood remained, unlike other studios such as Shepperton, relatively bomb-free throughout the war. Pinewood's nearest bomb, a V2, landed in a field just south of the gardens and, apart from a large hole in the ground, caused little damage.

Production on film was revived with the arrival of the Crown Film Unit, the Army Film and Photographic Unit and the Royal Air Force Film Unit, to the

COUNTING THEM OUT AND COUNTING THEM BACK IN AGAIN – keeping a tally of flying missions and bombs dropped on the side of the aircraft.

Studios in 1941. The Polish Air Force Film Unit joined them. Former editor's assistant at Pinewood before the war, Dick Best, recalls the return of filming to the Studios: "I returned to Pinewood in 1940 as a member of the Army Film and Photographic Unit having been transferred from the Royal Berkshire Regiment. To return in uniform to a place where one had worked as a civilian four years before must be a kind of record. A wire fence had been placed diagonally from the vaults across the car park and down the middle of the road past the administration block, separating the house and gardens from the production area. The wire fence did not prevent a certain amount of fraternization … especially when the American film servicemen arrived sometime later!

"Regular roll-call parades took place in the car park each morning. Afterwards, army boots and gaiters were changed to civilian shoes for normal production work. These parades offered some amusement to the Lloyd's staff, which would be arriving for work on the other side of the fence. It was quite amusing to have to salute Lieutenant Tony Keys [future acclaimed film producer Anthony Nelson Keys], when he often took the roll-call parade. As civilians, we had both worked on the same productions at Pinewood."

To keep the servicemen fit, Pinewood's ample grounds were utilized for cross country runs, much to the delight of the ladies of Lloyd's whose attention was often distracted as another troop of ablebodied men came rushing past their windows. The dressing rooms in blocks "A" to "D" were converted into billets for the officers and men who didn't live close enough to be able to return home nightly. The art department became the Army pay parade and in the same block was also situated the orderly room and the Officers' Mess. The Sergeants' Mess was upstairs at the side of the covered way and a general canteen was hastily erected to the back of the old cutting room block. As the Studios were to become busier again, particularly with the arrival of American editors (following the country's entry to the war in 1942) additional cutting rooms were added along the corridor which led from the dubbing theatres to the administration building.

At lunch times, to break the monotony, there would be musical recitals organized by the chief of sound with the Crown Film Unit, Ken Cameron. John Boulting put on a pantomime on one of the stages, casting his show from members of the RAF and Army Units. And Princess Marina, the Duchess of Kent, paid a special visit to the Studios to encourage the men and see how they were coping with the rigours of war. Certainly, the atmosphere at Pinewood was not as dreaded as elsewhere but none of the Units took their work as being anything less than very important to the war effort. The service cameramen and army film units knew they had a very important part to play in producing shorts and films as well as working on the "rushes" and reels of footage sent in from around the world for editing to show all aspects of life behind the lines and at the front. One cameraman arrived at a Pinewood cutting room just three days after D-Day with rushes of the first landings in Normandy. In the 21st-century digital age when pictures are beamed across the world literally as they happen, that may not seem much of an achievement, but it was a huge feat for such material to make its way so quickly across war-ravaged Europe.

Several distinguished composers and writers worked for the Army Film Unit. The novelist J. L. Hodson wrote the narration for the 1943 Ministry of Information film, *Desert Victory*. This classic war documentary tells of Montgomery's army chasing the Nazis through Tripoli. *Variety* described *Desert Victory* as: "The greatest battle film of the war ... it puts the audience right in the middle ... Americans who see this film will be anxiously waiting for the next – and a US equivalent." The *Daily Telegraph* called the film "the finest factual film ever made." *Desert Victory* won an Oscar for best documentary feature.

While the film units tried to stay true to their subjects and use genuine footage from the war fronts wherever possible, there were to be occasions when just a few shots had to be reconstructed at Pinewood. During the editing of *Desert Victory*, Roy Boulting organized the excavation of a huge ditch at the Studios to simulate a desert wadi, in order to film a night crossing under fire. This was an essential scene for the film and the events did happen, but it would have been impossible to have successfully shot the material when it had actually taken place at night in the desert.

The composer William Alwyn composed the score for *Desert Victory*, Alan Rawsthorne composed the score for *Burma Victory* and Sir Arnold Bax composed the score for *Malta GC*. There were also many young craftsmen starting off in the

THE BRITISH MINISTRY OF INFORMATION'S *Desert Victory* won the Oscar for best documentary feature for 1943 (opposite). While most of the film was shot on location, a few scenes were reconstructed at Pinewood.

EDWARD G. ROBINSON AND RICHARD ATTENBOROUGH, above, in John Boulting's 1945 film *Journey Together*, about trainee pilots going on their first bombing mission.

ON THE SEA AS WELL AS IN THE AIR, moving pictures were required to show wartime hostilities, opposite. These images were used as stock material for wartime information films as well as newsreel footage.

business who would later make their names in feature film production, among them Gil Taylor, John Howell, Johnny Guthridge, Bob Verral, Ernie Walters, Harry Waxman, John Aldred and Frank Clarke. Producer and director talents serving in the film units included Jack Lee, Pat Jackson, Jack Holmes and Humphrey Jennings. David Macdonald led the Army cameramen overseas in the Western Desert, Tunisia, Burma and later in Europe, ably accompanied by Hugh Stewart, who had started his film career as an assistant editor for Alfred Hitchcock in the 1930s and who would return to Pinewood after the war to produce many Rank film favourites, including several of the Norman Wisdom outings of the 1950s and 1960s and the three Morecambe and Wise big screen features. And, of course, there were the twin brother interposable producing/directing team, Roy and John Boulting – Roy was in the Army and John in the RAF.

It was at this time that a 20-year-old aspiring actor joined up for service with the RAF and found himself billeted at Pinewood Studios. Richard Attenborough had already appeared uncredited in Noel Coward's wartime classic, *In Which We Serve* in 1942. Under the wing of John Boulting, he was about to land himself his first lead role. As Lord Attenborough remembers: "I was in the Air Force from 1943 to 1946. Though I was never to be classified as a "Rank baby", Pinewood will always hold a very special place for me because that was where the RAF film unit was based and it was where I was stationed. I lived in the Studios – the dressing rooms were turned into bedrooms and that's where we stayed for the duration. I played in *Journey Together* with Edward G. Robinson in a movie that was made by the RAF film Unit, directed by Flight Lieutenant John Boulting. It was down to that film that when I came out of the air force I did the movie version of *Brighton Rock* for the Boultings."

Journey Together tells the story of three trainee pilots learning to fly in England and America before being sent out on their first bombing missions. The screenplay was written by Terence Rattigan and the young pilots, Richard Attenborough, Jack Watling and David Tomlinson, played opposite American star name Edward G. Robinson. The semi-documentary was well received, declared by the *News Chronicle* to be: "One of the most realistic and brilliant films of the war in the air."

PROFILE

Earl St. John

The larger than life Earl St. John, was born on 14th June 1892 in Baton Rouge, Louisiana. He was a First World War doughboy who became general manager in charge of Paramount's film circuit in England. He was taken on by J. Arthur Rank and became the producer in overall charge of film production at Pinewood Studios from 1950 until 1964.

Under the stewardship of the then Pinewood Managing Director John Davis, St. John's official title was Executive Producer, and the two of them were tasked with bringing down the crippling losses being suffered by the film production arm of the Rank Organisation. St. John ensured that location filming was cut back to a minimum and enforced Davis's rule that no film should have a budget of more than £150,000 (around £2 million at today's rates). As a result, many films from the Rank stable were accused of being bland and samey. Nevertheless, a few classics did emerge during St. John's tenure at the top, such as *Reach for the Sky* (1955) and *A Night to Remember* (1957). It was also Earl St. John who shelved *Genevieve* for 18 months in 1952, claiming that no one would want to go and see a film about old cars!

Opinions about Earl St. John were mixed; *Carry On* producer Peter Rogers described him as "a large Texan type who strolled around like John Wayne". But generally St. John was well liked and there is no doubt that while he was at the Pinewood helm he brought some great films to the screen in time and in budget.

Earl St. John died on 26 February 1968.

Once America had entered the war, many American film servicemen came to Pinewood to work with their British counterparts, particularly on the making of Frank Capra's *Tunisian Victory* (1944) and Carol Reed's *The True Glory* (1945).

Sadly, for some, the safety of the Studios gave way to the dangers of being on the frontline collecting images for the wartime productions, and a number of service cameramen lost their lives in action. Today, a plaque still hangs at Pinewood commemorating the memory of the 38 members of the Army and Royal Air Force Film Units who lost their lives in the Second World War.

There is a misconception that Pinewood Studios played host to the making of just a handful of training films during World War II. This is a myth, which many who served there during the war know to be untrue. Many great film-making talents worked at Pinewood between 1939 and 1945, producing some of the classic war documentaries of all time, which reflected life in wartime Britain – both civilian and military, at home and abroad.

The fortunes of J. Arthur Rank continued to rise during the war years. Oscar Deutsch of the Odeon Group died in 1941 as did C. M. Woolf. Rank now ran both the Odeon and the Gaumont-British cinema circuits. The Government became troubled by the increasing control that Rank appeared to hold over the industry and set up the Palache Committee in 1944, which recommended legislation preventing Rank from merging further with other industry chains. At the same time, the Government recognized that the British film industry needed to be robust enough to be able to stand a takeover onslaught from the Americans – which many both inside and outside the industry feared. It suggested that a Government body be set up akin the to National Film Finance Corporation – which had plumbed money into the industry during the 1930s – to oversee matters.

The report stated: "A cinematograph film represents something more than a mere commodity to be bartered against others. Already the screen has great influence, both politically and culturally, over the minds of the people. Its potentialities are vast, as a vehicle for expression of national life, ideals and tradition, as a dramatic and artistic medium, and as an instrument for propaganda." Few who had witnessed the output of the various British and other film units during the war, could argue with that last sentiment.

ITALIAN-BORN PRODUCER Filippo del Giudice, who had a penchant for big-budget films that rarely made back their money for the Rank Organisation.

Though Rank continued to buy out interests held by others in studios such as Elstree – meaning he was now receiving income from the three largest studios in the country – he was no megalomaniac. From the outset, Rank had always been passionate about the film industry and wanted British films to be shown and respected across the globe, proving the equal of the output from Hollywood. That was his dream and only the war had got in the way of that.

To enable him to achieve his goals, Rank had taken on two men who would become established and important figures within the Rank empire. The first was Earl St. John, an infantryman in World War I who had stayed in Britain and become the general manager of the Paramount film circuit between the wars. The second was a young accountant, John Davis, who had been brought in by Rank to try and work through the troubled Odeon's books. From very early on, Davis established himself as a man of brilliant financial ability in a host of different jobs. He also pleased Rank by being one of the very few people in the industry whom he witnessed arriving at his desk at the crack of dawn and still being there when others had long since left the studios for the day.

A third person who had a powerful influence on J. Arthur Rank during the war and in the years immediately afterwards was Italian refugee, Filippo del Giudice. "Del", as he was known, had arrived in Britain in the 1930s, without money or the ability to speak English. He made ends meet by giving Italian lessons to the children of waiters in the restaurants of London's West End. With the money he saved up, he started a small film company Two Cities (referencing London and Rome). When the war started he was interned but was released in September 1940.

Del approached Noel Coward to join him in making a film about the Navy. After some persuasion and the offer of a free artistic rein over the production, Coward agreed to the idea. Del didn't have the money and approached C. M. Woolf, who after first offering a distribution contract, recanted, leaving the film partly made on borrowed money at Rank's studios in Denham. British Lion stepped in and though the costs spiralled – as they would on most of Del's films – *In Which We Serve* became one of the most successful war films ever made, and gave a great start to the cinematic careers of a host of names, including Richard Attenborough, David Lean and Ronald Neame. Many felt that J. Arthur Rank

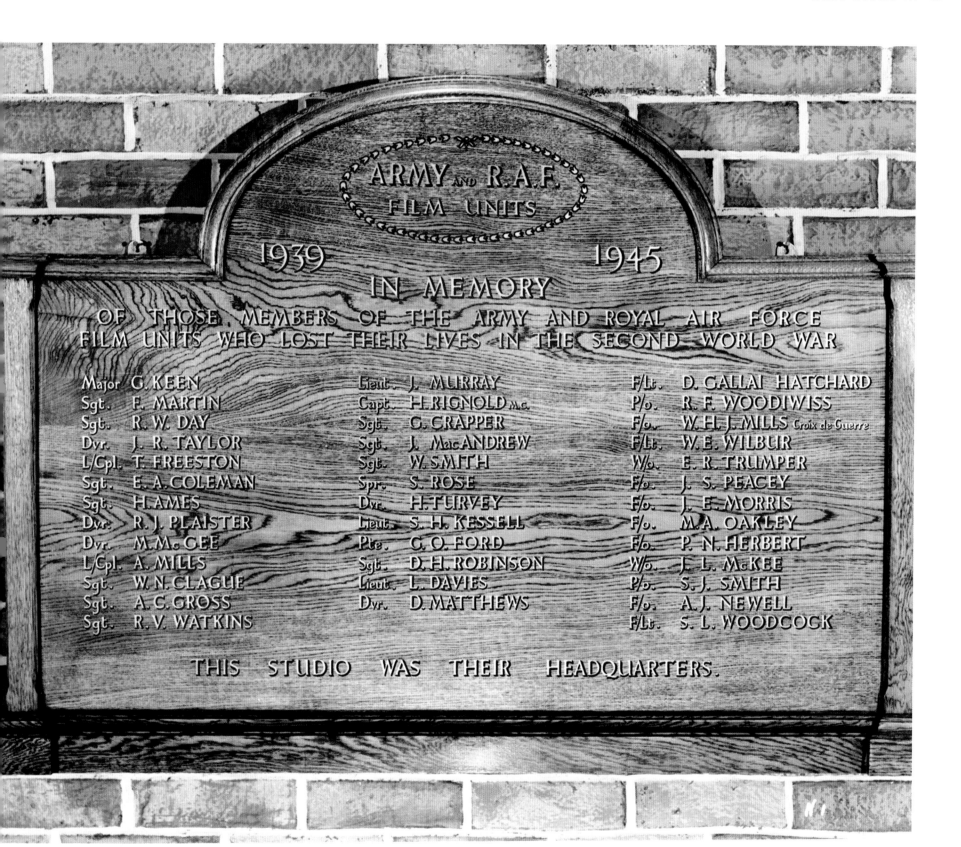

FILM UNIT MEMBERS being trained at Pinewood before being sent out to cover the war on camera.

would have been more wary of Del Giudice's penchant for high spending on films if C. M. Woolf had lived longer, but following his death, Del was given power and influence by Rank and he initiated several expensive productions – many of which never had any chance of making their money back, let alone a profit.

Still recovering from his crash, the now partially out of work and former Pinewood MD, Richard Norton, was approached by Rank to work at Two Cities to keep any eye on Del Giudice. By that time Rank had put vast sums of money into the company and Two Cities had, in effect, become part of the Rank Organisation. Norton recalls: "I had a talk to Arthur, who said it would be most useful to have someone like myself to give occasional conservative advice to Del Giudice; and I agreed to do so on condition that I was working directly for the Rank Organisation. Del had for some obscure reason a great affection for me. I suppose I was some use as a "Don't do it" man, although I never honestly felt I was earning my money."

Others felt they were earning their money and with less interference from Rank than might have been imagined. J. Arthur had created a company called Independent Producers Ltd, bringing together both distinguished as well as up-

LESS LIGHT ...   61

and-coming producers and directors of the time, freeing them up from the shackles of external pressures of film production to allow them to use their time and energy creatively and make great films. Co-operation was the buzzword; with Rank offering them the facilities they needed to get their films off the ground and also a cut in any profits to plumb back into film production.

Among those who were members of IP Ltd – which operated from 1944 to 1947 – were Ronald Neame, Leslie Howard, Frank Launder and Sidney Gilliat, Michael Powell and Emeric Pressburger, and David Lean. Lean spoke highly of Rank's efforts: "I doubt if any other group of filmmakers anywhere in the world can claim as much freedom. We of Independent Producers can make any subject we wish, with as much money as we think that subject should have spent on it. We can cast whatever actors we choose, and we have no interference at all in the way the film is made. No one sees the films until they are finished, and no cuts are made without the consent of the director or producer, and, what's more, not one of us is bound by any form of contract. We are there because we want to be there. Such is the enviable position of British filmmakers today, and such are the conditions which have at last given our films a style and nationality of their own."

Viewers of Lean's early Pinewood-made classics – *Great Expectations* and *Oliver Twist* – which were to be made in the immediate years after the war, when the Studios were finally to be re-opened, would come to know that these words and thoughts were indeed, no exaggeration.

Early Classics

POSTER ARTWORK FOR THE HIGHLY ACCLAIMED 1946 thriller, *Green for Danger,* **starring Alastair Sim.**

The first film to be made at the newly re-opened Pinewood Studios after the war had come to an end came from one of Rank's Independent Producer teams, Frank Launder and Sidney Gilliat. *Green for Danger* became an instant classic. Starring Alastair Sim, Trevor Howard and Leo Genn, the film told the story of a murderer preying on victims on the operating tables of an emergency hospital during wartime. The film was a clever thriller with heaps of black comedy thrown in with its wartime setting, allowing audiences the time to sit back and be thrilled as well as given an opportunity to laugh at wartime situations – something they hadn't been able to do for a while. The film was described by the *Daily Telegraph* as "slick, witty and entertaining". *The Times* declared: "Launder and Gilliat have told an exciting story, excitingly."

Alas, the same could not be said for the team's next Pinewood offering, *Captain Boycott*, which went into production immediately after *Green for Danger*. A lavish cast, including Stewart Granger, Kathleen Ryan and Robert Donat played out the story of Irish farmers rebelling against their English landlords near the end of the nineteenth century. Many years later, Sidney Gilliat said of making the film: "It is said that no actor can survive playing opposite a child or a dog. Let me add here that it is just as lethal playing with the Abbey Players. Apart from being able to act you off the stage, they can also drink you under the table." *Captain Boycott* did not perform well and was a failure at the box office. But that didn't stop the enthusiasm for what appeared to be a resurgence in the fortunes of the British film industry in general and a revitalized Pinewood in particular, which was now seeing large sums invested into the site to bring the studios up to post-war specifications.

Ronald Neame directed the excellent Hitchcock-style thriller *Take My Life*, produced by Anthony Havelock-Allan's company Cineguild in 1946. The two worked together again for Havelock-Allan's classic adaptation of *Great Expectations* the same year. This time, Neame worked on the screenplay and it was to be fellow IP member David Lean who would direct. *Great Expectations* originally started production at Denham but the sequences that involved the paddleboats trailing through the water were too large for Denham and so the production moved to Pinewood, which, with its large water tank, was ideal for the sequences and film.

Shooting began in early 1947. John Mills, who played Pip in the film, recalled working on *Great Expectations*: "We started shooting in January. Three months later David had completed what was arguably one of the best films ever turned out of a British studio. The casting was perfect, and there were some memorable performances, particularly from an actor who was making his first appearance on the screen – Alec Guinness, whose Herbert Pocket was a delight; Francis L. Sullivan as Mr Jaggers, Bernard Miles as Joe Gargery, Valerie Hobson as Estella and Martita Hunt as Miss Havisham were all excellent. Estella as a child was played by an enchanting young actress, Jean Simmons."

Great Expectations was very well received on both sides of the Atlantic. Critics sang the film's praises. *Great Expectations* picked up two Oscars, for best cinematography and best art direction. Yet at the time, Ronald Neame recalled David Lean's uncertainty over taking on the project: "I asked David if he would direct *Great Expectations* and I can remember walking around the studios together and David saying, 'You're one of the top cameramen in the country and it's true I've directed, but are you sure this is a good idea?' I said, 'in my opinion, David, you're going to be one of the great directors and it would be an honour for me to produce a film if you'd direct it'."

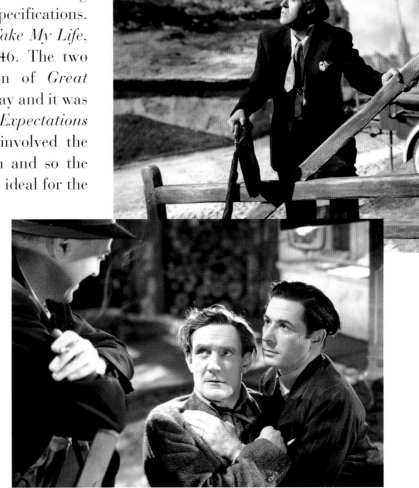

TWO SCENES from the atmospheric 1940s post-war British thriller, *Green for Danger*, with Alastair Sim as Inspector Cockrill, Trevor Howard as Dr Barney Barnes and Leo Genn as Mr Eden.

JOHN MILLS is Pip, with Martita Hunt as Miss Havisham and Valerie Hobson as Estella in David Lean's 1946 Oscar-winning adaptation of *Great Expectations*.

PROFILE

David Lean

Born in Croydon on 25 March 1908, David Lean had a strictly Quaker upbringing and as a child wasn't allowed to visit the cinema. He considered becoming an accountant before taking on a series of menial studio jobs in 1927, working his way up from tea boy, to clapper boy, then on to become a newsreel cutter before being given the chance to cut his teeth as a film editor for the likes of Anthony Asquith and Michael Powell. By the end of the 1930s he had established himself as a top film editor.

Noel Coward gave Lean his first directing break, inviting him to co-direct the wartime flag-waver *In Which We Serve*. Following the film's great success, Lean teamed up with cinematographer Ronald Neame and producer Anthony Havelock-Allan to form the production company Cineguild, going on to direct three Coward plays – *This Happy Breed* (1944), *Blithe Spirit* (1945) and *Brief Encounter* (1946). From filming Coward, Lean went on to film Dickens and directed *Great Expectations* at Pinewood in 1946 and *Oliver Twist* the following year. He is recognized as one of the world's greatest film directors – bringing many breathtaking epic stories, such as *Lawrence of Arabia* (1962) and *Dr Zhivago* (1965) to the screen across a cinematic career spanning 40 years.

Of filming, Lean once commented: "I think people remember pictures not dialogue. That's why I like pictures."

MADE AT PINEWOOD in 1947, Michael Powell and Emeric Pressburger's visually striking production, *Black Narcissus,* went on to win two Oscars for Best Cinematography and Best Art Direction.

BLACK NARCISSUS (1947), based on the book by Rumer Godden, became a classic film and is still highly regarded by film enthusiasts for its taut emotional and sexual tension.

MOIRA SHEARER plays dancing protégé Victoria Page in *The Red Shoes*, made at Pinewood in 1947.

At the same Academy Awards ceremony, Powell and Pressburger's story of British nuns in the Himalayas struggling against the desire for worldly things, *Black Narcissus*, also walked away with two Oscars. Just as *Great Expectations* had won for cinematography and for art direction for a film made in black and white, *Black Narcissus* went on to win the exact same awards for a film in colour.

Though *Great Expectations* and *Black Narcissus* were well-received, financial problems both with these films and others were beginning to emerge. Budgets were being overstretched and there was no certainty that however popular a film was proving to be, the spiralling costs on some productions could be made back. *Great Expectations*, for example, cost around £375,000 to make and though Rank was able to circuit this and other films both in this country and abroad the returns were not proving to be as healthy as he would have hoped.

Losses on films began to build. Rank ordered budgets to be capped. But that wasn't always possible. Powell and Pressburger's 1947 classic story of a great ballet dancer torn between love and her work, *The Red Shoes*, posed such a problem. Starring Anton Walbrook and Moira Shearer, this early British Technicolor film offering originally had a budget of £380,000 (more than £6 million in today's money). Rank would only give permission for the film to be made if the budget was cut by 20 per cent. Powell and Pressburger agreed, but once filming was underway, it soon became

MERVYN JOHNS AND CECIL PARKER in *Captain Boycott* (1946), and, below, poster artwork from the film, which starred Stewart Granger and Kathleen Ryan.

J. ARTHUR RANK presents

STEWART GRANGER
KATHLEEN RYAN

Captain Boycott

ALASTAIR SIM · MERVYN JOHNS · NOEL PURCELL
and CECIL PARKER as Captain Boycott

AN INDIVIDUAL PICTURE
Produced by
SIDNEY GILLIAT and FRANK LAUNDER
Directed by FRANK LAUNDER
Screen play by
FRANK LAUNDER and WOLFGANG WILHELM
EAGLE-LION DISTRIBUTION

RICHARD ATTENBOROUGH AND ARTHUR LOWE in *London Belongs to Me* (1947). A youthful Attenborough played Percy Boon, a young man who gets mixed up with gangsters and murder.

evident that the sum allowed for was clearly not going to be enough. The choice was either to pull the plug on *The Red Shoes* or carry on with the filming. There was such confidence in the film that shooting continued, though Rank's accountants, such as John Davis, watched on nervously. *The Red Shoes* finally came in at more than £500,000 but at the same time became the highest grossing British film to be screened in America of that era. The film was rewarded with two Oscars, for best art direction and best score and picked up nominations in a further three categories, including best picture.

The second classic film to be made at Pinewood in 1947 was *Oliver Twist*. Following on from his directorial success with *Great Expectations*, David Lean turned his hand to another Dickens' novel to great effect. Pleased with Alec Guinness's performance as Herbert Pocket in *Great Expectations*, the actor was offered the much larger role of Fagin. Such was the power of his performance that the film was banned in America amid claims that the film and specifically Guinness's portrayal was anti-Semitic. Concerns were expressed during the making of the film that it may be construed in this way but Lean was given carte blanche to tell the story how he felt it should be shown, even though in doing so, the film lost valuable income at the American box office. This too added to the financial woes that were besetting Rank, but still people's minds were fixed firmly on producing high quality films, with withering finances playing second fiddle. Though not for much longer.

While *Oliver Twist* lost out in America, the film was not short of interest and plaudits wherever it was shown. The cast comprised old acting stalwarts and fresh

A BESPECTACLED DIRK BOGARDE on set with Kathleen Ryan during the making of *Esther Waters* in 1947.

new talent. Robert Newton was a memorably villainous Bill Sikes, while Francis L. Sullivan's Mr Bumble was highly acclaimed. Among the young actors making early but notable appearances was Anthony Newley as the Artful Dodger and Britain's blonde bombshell of the 1950s and 1960s, Diana Dors, in her second film appearance, aged just 16. The title role of Oliver was played by John Howard Davies who in years to come would step behind the camera to become one of BBC television's most respected sitcom directors. *Time* magazine called *Oliver Twist*, "a brilliant, fascinating movie, no less a classic than the Dickens novel which it brings to life."

Rank continued to invest vast sums in different aspects of an emerging post-war British film industry, though not all his investments were successful. There was an attempt to produce a regular monthly news magazine to be played before the main feature. The Americans had their series *The March of Time*; Rank felt Britain should have something similar and pushed ahead with his regular two-reelers, *This Modern Age*. The 20-minute featurettes were professionally made and bore high journalistic standards, but it wasn't really what people wanted to see when they went to the cinema and the project lost him £500,000.

Slightly more successful was Rank's venture into grooming acting talent for his future productions. Rank bought a small studio in Highbury, London, and founded a "Charm School" to train up-and-coming actors. Some of the actors were just in their teens and all were paid £20 a week, whether they worked or not. They were taught the art of screen performance and primed for parts in forthcoming productions. In return, Rank took 50 per cent of the profits that an actor made

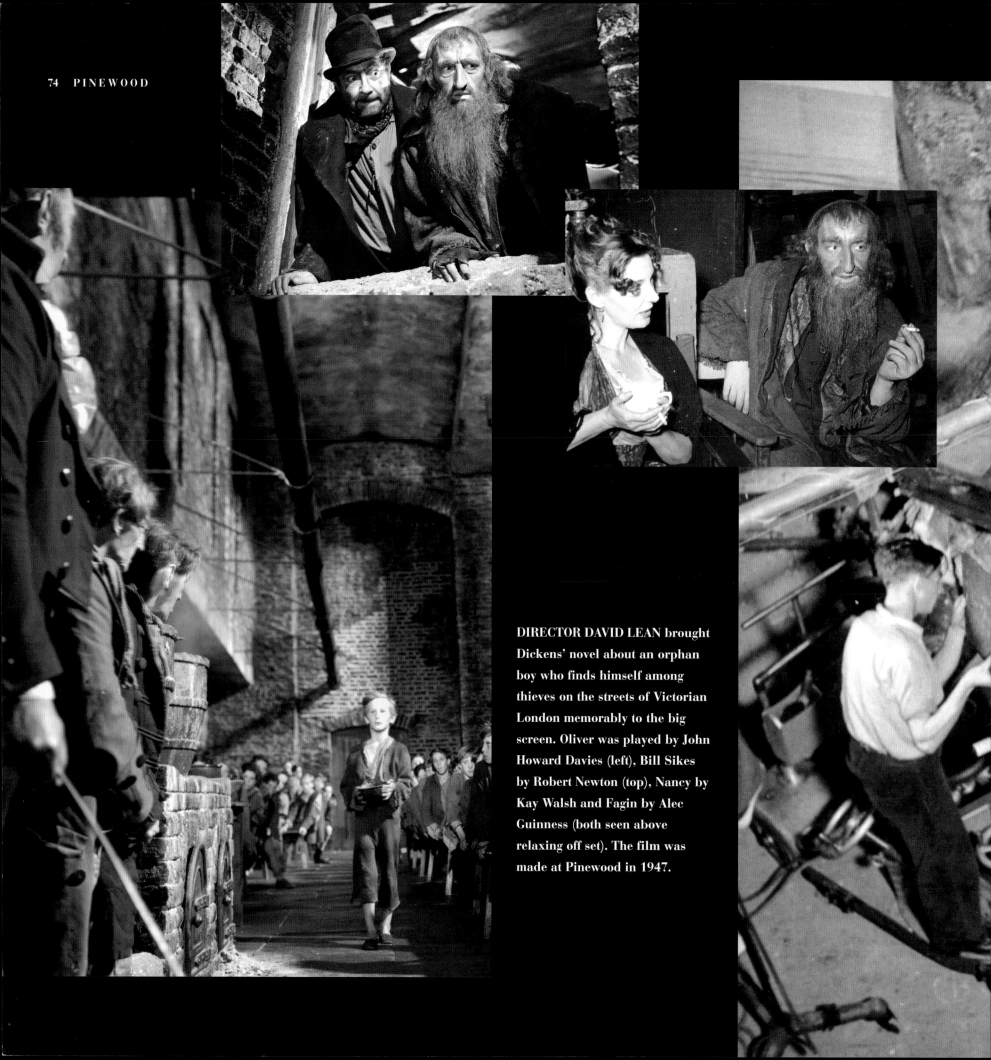

DIRECTOR DAVID LEAN brought Dickens' novel about an orphan boy who finds himself among thieves on the streets of Victorian London memorably to the big screen. Oliver was played by John Howard Davies (left), Bill Sikes by Robert Newton (top), Nancy by Kay Walsh and Fagin by Alec Guinness (both seen above relaxing off set). The film was made at Pinewood in 1947.

ELEANOR SUMMERFIELD AND BRYAN FORBES, above right, in *All Over Town* **(1948).**

JEAN SIMMONS AND DONALD HOUSTON, above, in *The Blue Lagoon* **(1948).**

whether on screen in a film or off screen at, say, a public event where they were paid an appearance fee. Among those who attended Rank's Charm School were Dirk Bogarde, Roger Moore, Joan Collins and Christopher Lee.

Rank continued to buy into the film industry both at home and abroad. From the Winter Gardens in New York to circuits in Canada, Australia and New Zealand. Yet throughout the years immediately after the War, he was to be constantly haunted by the high cost and low returns on his lavish films. When the figures for 1946 were published, everyone across the industry was shocked. The losses on his productions for that year were estimated to be over £1.5 million – more than £20 million today. And it soon became clear that before things would become better, they were set to get much much worse.

John Davis, having joined Rank in 1939, was to become managing director in 1948, his cool head under the burden of the heavy financial pressures that were now facing the organisation, making him regarded as the ideal man to get Rank out of the mess that they were faced with. Immediately Davis wielded the knife on

DIRK BOGARDE AND GLYNIS JOHNS rehearsing a domestic fight scene on the Pinewood set of *Dear Mr Prohack* (1948).

both unprofitable arms of the company as well as producers and filmmakers for whom profligacy was now too high a price for Rank to pay. Filippo Del Giudice had already been given his marching orders. Now it was the turn of some big names to go and their leaving sent shock waves through the industry.

The Box family were highly renowned and even more highly respected in British film. Sydney and Muriel Box were husband and wife. He was a writer and producer who ran Gainsborough Studios. She was a successful director, producer and screenwriter who after failing to become a professional actress, turned first to documentary production in the 1940s before moving on to feature films in the 1950s. Sydney's sister Betty Box also joined the industry and was his assistant for several years at Gainsborough before branching out into film production – at Pinewood – in her

PROFILE

Richard Attenborough

Born in 1923, acting was in Richard Attenborough's blood from the start: "I always wanted to be an actor. I never wanted to be a director. I had only really ever wanted to appear on the stage."

During WWII Attenborough joined the air force and was seconded to the RAF Film Unit based at Pinewood. In the 1940s and 1950s, Attenborough appeared in over 30 films, but he began to tire of playing the spivs and below-deck naval officer roles. By 1959, he decided he'd had enough and formed a production company, Beaver films, with Bryan Forbes – their first cinema outing to be one of the most important British films, *The Angry Silence* (1959).

Over the next 20 years he worked in films as an actor, producer and director. Among his acting highlights were: *The League of Gentlemen* (1960), *The Great Escape* (1963), *Loot* (1970), and *10 Rillington Place* (1971). His directing credits included: *Oh! What a Lovely War* (1969), *Young Winston* (1972) and *A Bridge too Far* (1977).

The worldwide acclaim for *Gandhi* (1980), allowed him to continue to produce and direct handpicked projects over the following years, including, *Cry Freedom* (1987), *Chaplin* (1992) and *Shadowlands* (1993).

Elevated to the peerage in 1993, as well as continuing in film production, Lord Attenborough has chaired many cultural and charitable bodies, including Channel 4 Television and the British Film Institute.

own right. As part of Davis's cost-cutting measures several of Rank's filmmaking sites were closed. They included studios at Shepherds Bush and, sadly for the Box family, the Gainsborough Studios at Islington.

Production was curtailed at Denham with Earl St. John, who had been running it, brought across to run Pinewood. Other heads rolled including Denham's manager Joseph Somlo and George Archibald who had been in control of Rank's Independent Producers company at Pinewood.

Some of the production teams, those thought of as being able to assist in helping to revive the ailing business, were invited across to work at Pinewood when Gainsborough and Shepherds Bush closed. Some came across – but with trepidation. Betty Box moved to Pinewood but was saddened by what had been happening. Her brother Sydney Box "decided to take a year's sabbatical" as producer Peter Rogers once described the time off that was enforced upon him by Davis. Betty Box insisted that her brother "was instructed by his doctor to take a long holiday or risk being ill". Either way, he left Gainsborough and didn't move across to Pinewood, choosing instead to tour America in a caravan for a year. Betty Box's move to Pinewood was made that much more pleasant by the studios' beautiful surroundings, as she recalled: "When I moved to Pinewood Studios I had no idea that it was to be my 'home' for over 30 years. The contrast between the shabbiness of Islington Studios and the grand and beautiful surroundings at Pinewood was enormous. The stately home formed the administration centre of Rank Films, housing the elite filmmakers David Lean, Anthony Havelock-Allan, John and Roy Boulting etc., all with beautiful offices. The house was surrounded by immaculately kept gardens (used in countless movies) with half a dozen huge sound-stages, cutting rooms, viewing theatres, carpenters', plasterers' and painters' shops, property and scenery bays – all built on Pinewood's many acres of fields and paddocks. My office (as pleasant as the rest of Pinewood) was on the third floor, looking over the gardens, directly above the large, paved terrace onto which the French windows of the ground floor opened."

Davis next set about cutting costs of productions being made at Pinewood. He

TWO SCENES FROM DAVID LEAN'S
Passionate Friends, **made at Pinewood in 1948 and starring the director's bride-to-be, Ann Todd.**

slapped a limit of £150,000 on films and made it quite clear that any film with a budget above that limit would not be made. For those who had made it past the first set of redundancies and closures, this new rule added to their woes, and several long-serving players decided it was time to get out. An enforced 10 per cent cut to salaries cemented those decisions. There were many departures, though always with generous handshakes. Davis was considered hard, but fair. His main aim was to streamline operations within Pinewood and fill up cinemas with films that people would pay to go and see. This he believed was the only realistic way of saving both the Rank Organisation and Pinewood Studios. Davis was less interested in the lavish productions that may be considered classics in years to come and more with the common sense of trying to keep Pinewood afloat and people in jobs.

It naturally followed that with smaller budgets came less lavish and more workmanlike productions. Cheaper (to make), populist entertainment was the order of the day at Pinewood. The Rank board once again set about bringing production and directing talent together, mixing and matching until it came up with good working teams. Pinewood had its own story department where

DIRK BOGARDE STARS as Bill Fox in the 1948 melodrama *Once a Jolly Swagman*, alongside Thora Hird as Bill's mother.

CLASSIC CHARACTER ACTOR ROBERT NEWTON, below, in *Obsession*, 1948.

FILM IDOL Stewart Grainger in *Blanche Fury* (1947).

DIRECTOR DAVID LEAN and his new bride, actress Ann Todd, receiving a wedding gift from cast and crew, on the set of the film *Madeleine* in 1949.

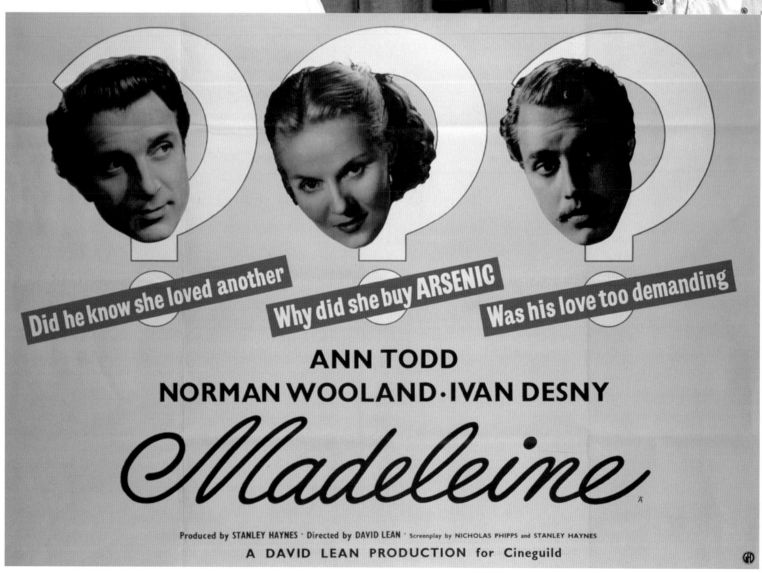

Did he know she loved another

Why did she buy ARSENIC

Was his love too demanding

ANN TODD
NORMAN WOOLAND · IVAN DESNY

Madeleine

Produced by STANLEY HAYNES · Directed by DAVID LEAN · Screenplay by NICHOLAS PHIPPS and STANLEY HAYNES

A DAVID LEAN PRODUCTION for Cineguild

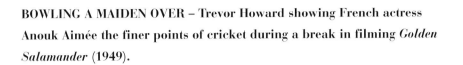

BOWLING A MAIDEN OVER – Trevor Howard showing French actress Anouk Aimée the finer points of cricket during a break in filming *Golden Salamander* (1949).

IN THE THICK OF IT – director Ronald Neame, setting up the next shot for his 1949 crime adventure, *Golden Salamander*.

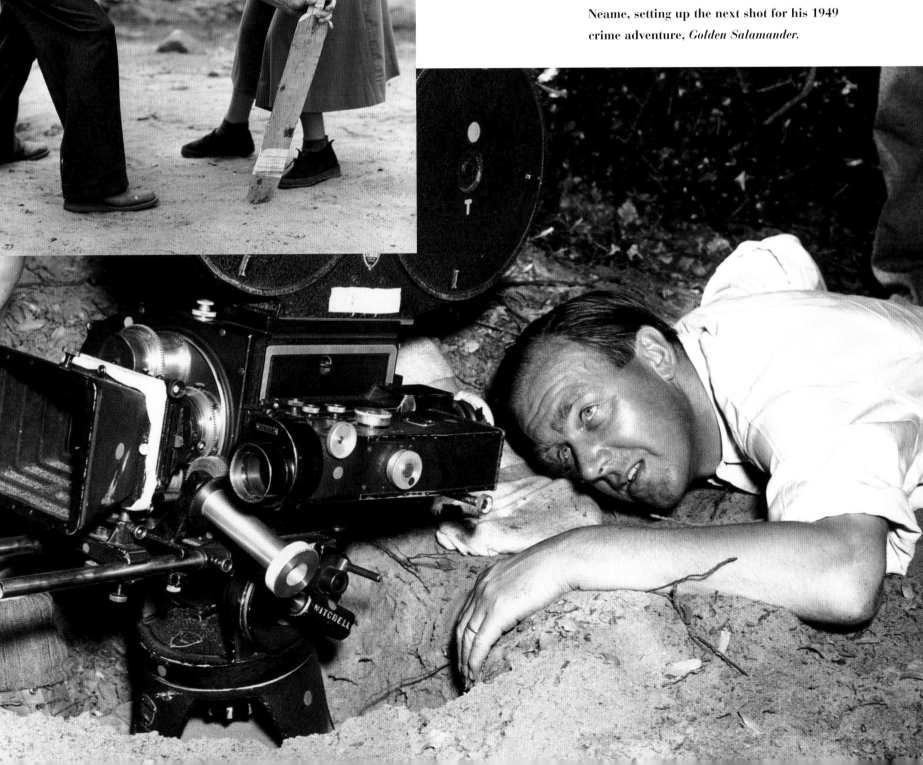

FAMED BRITISH CHARACTER ACTRESS Joyce Grenfell puts in an early film appearance in the 1949 Rank comedy, *Poet's Pub*.

IN ANOTHER SCENE from *Poet's Pub*, James Robertson Justice plays Professor Benbow and Derek Bond is Saturday Keith – an Oxford don who tries his hand at running a country pub.

EARL ST. JOHN, far left, at a music conference for
Trottie True (1949), with (l to r) music arranger
Carol Gibbons, actress Jean Kent and producer
Hugh Stewart.

producers could go for ideas. Several teams were put together. Very few survived. The most remembered and successful of these teams was to be that of Betty Box and Ralph Thomas. Betty remembers how the 30 year partnership began: "I first met Ralph Thomas when he was making the trailers for all the Rank films and he came to Islington to see the first cut of *Miranda* (1947). He later directed several films for brother Sydney – it's amazing how many British film directors were given a first chance by him. When Sydney was instructed by his doctor to take a long holiday or risk being very ill, *The Clouded Yellow* was one of the titles he was contemplating making and he generously suggested that Ralph and I take it over. In the first half of 1950, *The Clouded Yellow* was the only film being made in England."

ON THE SET OF *BLACKMAILED* (1950) are (l to r) director Marc Allegret, actress Fay Compton, Earl St. John and actor Harold Huth.

Starring Trevor Howard as a sacked secret service agent who becomes embroiled in a murder plot while tending a butterfly collection, *The Clouded Yellow*, was the first film to be made at Pinewood under the new financial restrictions. But the film, which also starred Jean Simmons and a young and relatively unknown Kenneth More, had high production values and with its Hitchcock-style chase sequences, hit the right buttons with the public, and even if not quite a classic, it did do well at the box office. So well in fact, that while some producers were looking over their shoulders to see if they were next in John Davis's firing line, Betty Box's place at Pinewood was secured, as was her working relationship with Ralph Thomas which would last for 30 years and over 30 films.

Rank may well have been smarting at the exit of some of Pinewood's great filmmaking talent who had jumped ship to join Alexander Korda at Shepperton, but John Davis believed that his was the only way forward for J. Arthur Rank Productions' survival. It meant that the number of films made at Pinewood through the late 1940s and early 1950s to be regarded as classics were few and far between. Under Davis's care, Rank's overdraft fell by almost £4 million in the first year. No one on the board seemed too troubled that they weren't making films like *Great Expectations* or *Oliver Twist* anymore.

Director Anthony Asquith, who had returned to the fold, went on to show that a film that was cheap to make did not make it a cheap film. His production of Terence Rattigan's play, *The Browning Version*, was made in 1950 under the same financial constraints as all other films in Pinewood at that time. Yet the story of a retiring classics master seemingly hated by all around him, was indeed a smooth production, thanks in no small part to excellent casting of Michael Redgrave as the teacher, Jean Kent as his unfaithful wife and Nigel Patrick as her lover.

Asquith's next Pinewood outing still remains a classic to this day, not just because of its production values, but also due to the quality of the acting. *The Importance of Being Earnest* was both written and directed by Asquith. The story was based on the play by Oscar Wilde, in which two wealthy and eligible Victorian bachelors try to find suitable suitors for marriage. The films feels stagey – it is effectively a straight filming of a stage play – yet what lifts the production to a more classic status is the first class performances from all the leads, including

Michael Redgrave, Michael Denison, Joan Greenwood, Margaret Rutherford and the finest and most definitive portrayal of Lady Bracknell you're ever likely to see, by the wonderfully over-the-top, Edith Evans. For a young 24-year-old actress, Dorothy Tutin, playing the part of Cecily, the whole experience of working on the film was a delight: "I was playing Princess Katherine in *Henry V* and Michael Redgrave saw me and recommended me to Anthony Asquith. We did the whole play in sequence, which is very rare in filming, and it was wonderful for a stage-trained actress. The sets were superbly designed and I thought the costumes were wonderful. The whole house and garden was a fantastically beautiful set. I totally believed I was in the country. Margaret Rutherford was perfection. To be on the set when she was doing that scene with her handbag was such a privilege. She did it in two takes, both of which were wonderful and I was practically in tears."

Pinewood's biggest early and probably most affectionately remembered classic film during its first 20 years was a film which, in the best traditions of these

A MEETING OF Rank Organisation executives and board members, who met regularly at Pinewood to monitor the progress of the company and ensure that strictly imposed production budgets – which had been capped at £150,000 during the early 1950s – were not being breached.

JOHN GREGSON AND DINAH SHERIDAN pit their driving wits against
Kenneth More and Kay Kendall in the 1953 classic comedy, *Genevieve*.

DIRECTOR HENRY CORNELIUS, during the making of *Genevieve*.

sorts of stories, almost never made it to the big screen even though it had been filmed. Henry Cornelius, the director of post-war comedy greats *Passport to Pimlico* (1949) and *The Galloping Major* (1951) had decided to leave the Ealing stable and strike out as an independent. Cornelius had been working on an idea with William Rose for a story of a veteran car rally to Brighton and the incidents and accidents that befall the owners of two of the vehicles, along the way. Ealing's boss, Michael Balcon, rather liked the idea, which he thought had the right feel for the sort of product his studios was making very successfully at that time. Yet Balcon was not pleased that Cornelius had decided to leave and decided against reorganizing his busy studios' schedules to allow Cornelius back in to make the film. Magnanimous as he was, Balcon sent Cornelius to see Earl St. John who was running Pinewood. St. John didn't seem quite as keen on the idea but was persuaded to allow it to go into production, since a considerable amount of the cost of the film was to be met by the National Film Finance Corporation. The film was *Genevieve* and starred John Gregson and Dinah Sheridan as the happily married McKims, Kenneth More as Ambrose Claverhouse and Kay Kendall as his feisty girlfriend Rosalind Peters.

In the film, the two couples engage in a race on the way back from the London to Brighton veteran car rally. Dinah Sheridan remembers being offered the role: "I had three scripts drop through the front door in the same post. The first two were a bit yawn-worthy. The third was for *Genevieve*. I was on a film set with Dirk Bogarde the day I was leaving to go for the audition. He asked where I was off to and I said I was going to talk to someone about a script I'd just read called *Genevieve*. He said, 'If you get the chance to, grab it. That's the best script I've read on the first run through.' That was the reaction I got too."

What Bogarde didn't tell Dinah Sheridan was how he'd come to have read the script already. Bogarde had in fact been offered the role of one of the Edwardian car owners, Alan McKim, but had turned it down. Bogarde was concerned at the number of whimsical film leads he was being offered and though he thought *Genevieve* might be a pleasant film he wasn't sure what it might do to his rising star status. Indeed, none of the stars who appeared in the film's four lead roles had been the first choices of studio bosses, who would have preferred to have seen more established players in the movie. Dinah Sheridan only found out afterwards that Claire Bloom was mooted for her role of Wendy, and Earl St. John's feelings about Kenneth More not being a big enough name outside of the south east of England were vocalized to many, including More himself, who knew that he wasn't the preferred choice for Ambrose Claverhouse. Producer Peter Rogers had had a similar problem when trying to cast Kenneth More in his early 1950s naval comedy *You Know What Sailors Are!* just a few months earlier. Rogers had cast More in the lead role. Earl St John refused. Rogers had a word with More who agreed to take the second lead. Again Earl St. John refused. Even when Kenneth More said he was prepared to take the third lead, St. John still said no. Rogers had no choice but to look elsewhere and in the end chose the new up-and-coming Rank star, Donald Sinden, for his film.

With the knowledge that Rank didn't really want to make the film and that the cast were not the first choice to play the lead roles, the atmosphere was a little frosty. So was shooting, taking place as it did in October and November of 1952. As Dinah Sheridan recalled: "We had a moment towards the end of the film – it was the end of October – and we arrived behind another bush in Bucks and the prop man had a little tray with four little glasses of brandy. Henry Cornelius said, 'I don't mind if you're cold but I do mind if your photograph blue, so drink up.' From then on we had a glass of brandy at the start of shooting every morning."

The tight budgetary restraints still in place meant that although the plot dictated a series of events taking place between London and Brighton and back again, most of the filming was undertaken within a 10 mile radius of Pinewood Studios in Buckinghamshire. The start of the race was filmed at Hyde Park; there was some filming in London and a one-day trip with overnight stay for cast and crew to Brighton to film the end of the race sequences.

Even so, the costs rose slightly as director Henry Cornelius insisted that all the shots of the cars being driven should be done on the open roads and not in a studio using

FACING TROUBLE – Rosalind (Kay Kendall) has a heart-to-heart with Ambrose (Kenneth More). Meanwhile, below, The McKims (John Gregson and Dinah Sheridan) are off the road again.

an artificial back drop. Replicas of the cars were built and mounted on to low-loaders to look as though they were being driven, which proved just as well as it was only as production got underway that the cast and crew were shocked to discover that John Gregson couldn't drive – he didn't even have a driving licence. Cornelius continued, apparently without concern, and had to re-mortgage his home to ensure there was enough money in place to make his film.

It wasn't all hard going and there was a lot of laughter on the set. Dinah Sheridan remembers the larger than life Kay Kendall: "They needed extra dressing rooms. Kay Kendall came into the dressing room. She said that's no fun. If I'm bunking down with anyone I'm bunking down with Kenny. Which she did. Kay was huge fun."

Once the shooting was in the can, Cornelius approached the famed American harmonica player Larry Adler to compose the music for this very British film: "I was in America and a friend asked me to drive his new Cadillac from New York to Long Island for him. I got caught in a terrible traffic jam. Suddenly the first eight bars of *Genevieve* came to me. I pulled over and pulled out my wallet, which had manuscript paper in it. I wrote down the first eight bars which I never had to change. It took me another two months to come up with the middle section."

The final cut of *Genevieve* was shown to Rank and Earl St. John in early 1953. They thought the film a huge failure. J. Arthur Rank found the film unfunny and Earl St. John insisted that nobody would go to see it other than a "few car cranks" in England. He decided it was unshowable, even suggesting that *Genevieve* be cut down to 60 minutes and shown as a second feature. In the end, the film was literally put on the shelf.

Towards the end of 1953, a year after the film had been made, *Genevieve* was finally to get a showing, more out of another film's misfortune than a sudden resurgence of belief in it's cinematic quality. A picture was running at the Odeon Leicester Square, in London's West End, that was due for a six-week show. The film was an unmitigated disaster and was pulled after just a few days of poor business. The only other film that Rank had available which didn't have commitments for showing and distribution elsewhere was *Genevieve*. Earl St. John went to the first showing of the film and was taken aback by the audience

reception. There was laughter throughout the auditorium and within days word had spread that *Genevieve* was the film to see. It went on to win the Bafta for Best British film in 1954, and Kenneth More was nominated for Best British actor.

The film wasn't released on the American circuits until February 1954. It performed well in the USA too and was rewarded with two Oscar nominations, for best screenplay and best score. Larry Adler, who was blacklisted in America, saw his name removed from the prints shown in the US cinemas, the nomination going to the arranger Muir Mathieson instead. Adler had the last laugh. The fee he was offered to write the music had been so low that he finally agreed a two and a half per cent share of the profits instead. *Genevieve*, became one of the kindliest remembered of all Pinewood's classics and gave Rank an unexpected financial windfall. Larry Adler didn't do too badly out of it either.

THE FINAL SEQUENCE from *Genevieve* (above left), as the classic cars arrive in London. Inset, composer Larry Adler works on his fondly remembered score for the film.

Gerry Anderson

PRODUCER

I started my professional life at Gainsborough Pictures and was then called up for National Service after the war, after which I was sent to Pinewood and started work in the cutting room. I worked on pictures such as *The Clouded Yellow* (1950) for Betty Box. I then went to work in the cutting rooms at Shepperton for a while, coming back to Pinewood to make 26 episodes of *UFO* (1970), which was made on "J" and "K" stages in the 1970s. I made *Space 1999* (1973), and that ran to 52 episodes. Most recently I took the top floor of the Kubrick building to make a new CGI version of *Captain Scarlett*.

I was no scholar when I was young and ended up going to building school. The only thing I was ever any good at was plastering. But I suffered with dermatitis and was told I couldn't become a plasterer. About this time I met with a friend at Pathe's labs and when I saw the all the reels of film, I knew I wanted to be in film. I walked from studio to studio asking for work. After writing many letters I got a reply from the Colonial Film Unit based in Soho Square. It was a part of the Ministry of Information and I worked in their cutting rooms.

I became sound editor on *So Long at the Fair* (1949), my first Pinewood film. The sound recording technique was very different in those days. Basically, the sound was recorded photographically – which means a slit of light was focussed on the side of the film and as it went through a sound camera it would modulate according to the voice it was recording. When the editor had finished cutting the picture, we had a cutting copy and the soundtrack comprised mainly of the voice of the artists. Sometimes the sound was good, sometimes there was traffic or other noise in the background and it was unusable.

The first thing we had to do was re-record the actors' voices where necessary and that was achieved by making a loop of the picture for the section we were hoping to replace. It would go round and round and the actor would hear themselves saying the same thing and then would repeat it until we felt we had the right fit to the lip movement. In order to make the sound synchronize properly with the lips, my speciality was actually cutting through the track with scissors to reduce vowels. That way I was able to lip synch the sound. Then we had to lay the sound effects.

As the years passed, photographic recording came to an end and magnetic film was introduced. Then we were able to record cleaner sound but I couldn't see the modulation as before. The next part of the evolution was when digital formats were invented. Today when I go into the dubbing theatre I no longer have to hump reels of film across the Studios, all the information is contained in a little box just a few inches big, which has all the tracks and effects on it. People say things are much faster now. No they are not. They take just as long but the result is a hundred times better.

I got fed up working on films. I was very critical of sound and the way some films used it. I got together with some friends and we formed a production company – in the days when it was really something to do so. It was called AP – my partner Arthur Provis said it was named after him. I insisted it meant Anderson Productions. We went through many quiet months of sitting in a little ballroom in a mansion house near Maidenhead, which was to double as our production stage. At the end of six months we were about to shut shop, when along came Roberta Lee and Susan Warner, who offered us 52 15-minute scripts for TV. We were delighted. Then Roberta used those immortal words: "They're with puppets." I almost threw up. But we were short of money. I tried to emulate live action with puppets because I thought, naively, that somebody would say this guy is wasting his time and should be making live action. The opposite happened and my success caused me to be typecast.

I worked for Lew Grade, a wonderful man. I miss him still and so does the industry. I had got into science fiction with the puppets. Lew called me and asked me to make some live action shows and so I came back to Pinewood to make *UFO*. I had been working at ABPC at Elstree and we had started shooting *UFO* there, but the studio announced it was going to close down and there were pickets on the gate preventing anything from being taken in or out. I told our team to pack everything in their cars, keep it all covered, and when we left Elstree "to go home", we actually came to Pinewood, which was very quiet at the time. Sadly, we were classified as strike breakers and so Pinewood workers went on strike. We explained we were just trying to keep

people in jobs; Elstree was closing regardless of us. The unions agreed and Pinewood went back to work.

I've always felt there is something special about Pinewood. The reason I like the Studios is because of the old mansion house and the wonderful gardens, and it's a joy to drive to through the countryside every day. This Studios was always loyal to its permanent staff, so when people returned to make films, the staff always knew who we were and what we liked and disliked. It wasn't friendly for the sake of it. It was about efficiency, and the people at Pinewood wanted to help to make things right – and this contributed to making good pictures. I hope this tradition is kept up. It does make a difference.

Pinewood's been on a rollercoaster for years. Its success always felt like it linked to the rise and fall of the dollar. In recent years the Studios has been revived. Painting, refurbishing and so on. The corridors are cleaner than a hospital! Now with Shepperton and Teddington the facilities are bigger and better than ever. It certainly feels the strongest it has ever been since I have been here.

I call myself a producer because I can't find any other title. I'm not a producer in the traditional sense – buying the rights to books and scouring the world for the right directors, then raising the money, sitting in a nice office and either praising or firing people to get the production through. I am very much hands on. I don't do all that. I create my own ideas. I find it difficult to find writers who can write my stuff. I try to control everything – because I need it to be done the correct way. "Creator" is the word that probably sums me up best.

How do I feel coming into Pinewood after all these years? I can't wait to finish breakfast and get in my car to come to Pinewood to work. As a filmmaker it's like coming through the gates of heaven.

Saved by Laughter

KAY KENDALL AND DIRK BOGARDE in *Doctor in the House* (1953).

THE OLDEST BUNCH of medical students in town, right – as (l to r) Donald Sinden, Donald Houston Kenneth More, Suzanne Cloutier and Dirk Bogarde tuck into a chip supper in the classic comedy, *Doctor in the House*, made at Pinewood in 1953.

Comedy proved to be a very serious business indeed for both the Rank Organisation and Pinewood Studios. The financial constraints placed on filmmakers at Pinewood had begun to work within a few years of their introduction and, although films made in the early 1950s were often accused of being bland, there was no doubt to the money men that thriftiness and sticking to the carefully laid out rules about what could and could not be spent on film production at Pinewood was beginning to show results. John Davis's tight rein had already seen a not unsizable £4 million lopped off Rank's £16 million overdraft during his first year of as the financial head of the flagship company. As the 1950s progressed he was to reduce that even further to a £4 million overdraft.

There were several reasons for the continuing falling back in Rank's financial woes, not least a run of highly successful film comedies that ensured that even though audience numbers at cinemas were dropping – due in large part to the advent and increasing success of commercial television from 1955 – the films people did go to see in large numbers were coming from just a small handful of producers. Indeed in the seven years from 1954 to 1960, five of the top moneymaking films made in Britain were made at Pinewood. More interestingly, four out of those five were medical film comedies, *Doctor in the House* (1954), *Doctor at Large* (1957), *Carry On Nurse* (1959) and *Doctor in Love* (1960). The films were made separately by husband and wife couple, Betty Box and Peter Rogers. The non-comedy Pinewood film to have topped the box office charts in Britain in 1956 was the war actioner based on the exploits of Douglas Bader, *Reach for the Sky*, starring Kenneth More. More – who just a few years earlier had not been deemed a big enough star by Earl St. John to allow him a lead in any Pinewood film and who saw *Genevieve*, in which he starred, shelved for over a year – was now in two top films in three years, also having starred in *Doctor in the House*, for which he won the Bafta for Best British Actor.

Doctor in the House was to be the first of seven medical outings produced by Betty Box, from the ideas and stories of real-life medic Richard Gordon. The "series" ran intermittently from 1954 to 1970. The first film told of the exploits of a bunch of medical students making their way through their studies, encountering all the trials and tribulations of life at college as each try to graduate. Betty Box

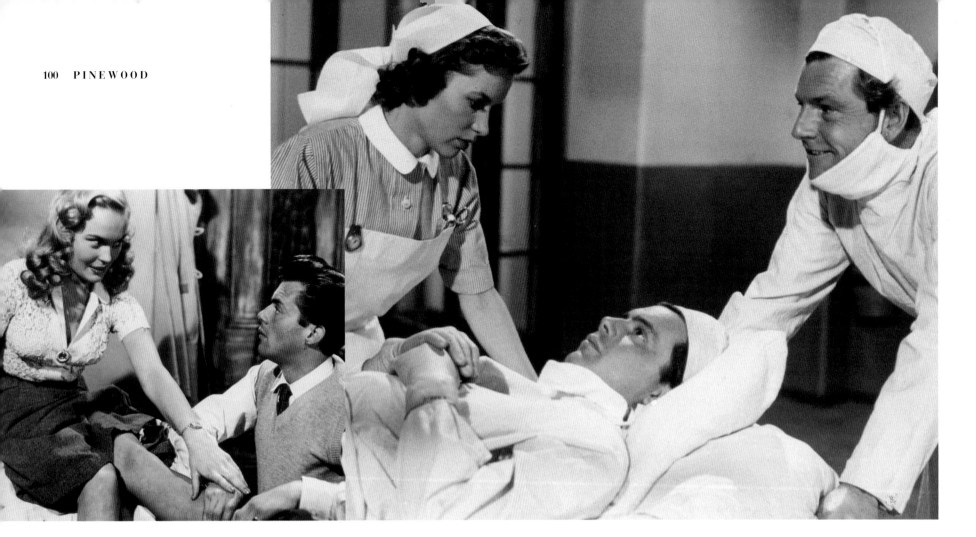

ACTRESS SHIRLEY EATON (above) in her first credited film role, asks trainee medico Dirk Bogarde for a helping hand.

MURIEL PAVLOW, DIRK BOGARDE AND KENNETH MORE (above right) in *Doctor in the House* (1953).

remembers casting the film: "We'd hoped to use young unknowns for the four students in *Doctor in the House* but, unable to find a suitable age-matched quartet, abandoned the idea. We'd already worked with Kenny More and knew that he was ideal casting for Grimsdyke, the perennial student – the one who intended to delay becoming a fully-fledged medico for as long as his inheritance lasted out. I'd worked only briefly with Dirk Bogarde (*So Long at the Fair*), but I knew he was a more versatile screen actor than he'd yet been able to prove. I wanted him for Simon Sparrow. Donald Sinden, already under contract to Rank, was right for the amorous, girl-crazy Benskin, and for the rugger-playing student we opted for Donald Houston, a star since his juvenile lead with Jean Simmons in *The Blue Lagoon*."

Betty Box was surprised to encounter strong opposition to the casting of Bogarde from Rank's executive producer, Earl St. John. He openly doubted the actor's ability and capacity for comedy. Betty persuaded St. John to allow Bogarde

PROFILE

Betty Box & Ralph Thomas

Betty Box and Ralph Thomas are still regarded as one of the Rank Organisation's most successful teams, which was formed when a scheme was introduced at Pinewood after the Second World War to pair producers and directors together. While other such pairings fell by the way side, Betty Box and Ralph Thomas continued to work together for 30 years.

Betty Box (1915–1999) entered the film industry in 1942, joining her brother and his wife, Sydney and Muriel Box, at Verity films, where she helped produce propaganda shorts during the war. She became head of Islington Studios in 1946, learning early on to produce films on tight shooting schedules and even tighter budgets. In 1949 she moved to Pinewood Studios where she was teamed up with film editor Ralph Thomas (1915–2001), and so began a collaboration on 30 films across the next three decades, some of which were the highest earners of their time. Their most notable Pinewood productions were the *Doctor* film series (1954-1970), *A Tale of Two Cities* (1957), *The 39 Steps* (1958), *Conspiracy of Hearts* (1959) and *No Love for Johnnie* (1961). Several actors, such as Dirk Bogarde, Kenneth More and Leslie Phillips, worked for them many times – all speaking of the couple with high regard. Such was the financial success of the Box/Thomas films that, within the industry, Betty was nicknamed "Betty Box-Office". She was awarded an OBE in 1958.

Betty Box married fellow producer and *Carry On* creator Peter Rogers in 1948. Ralph Thomas's brother, Gerald, after a stint as a film editor, also became a successful director, teaming up with Peter Rogers for more than 30 years. Ralph Thomas's son is acclaimed producer Jeremy Thomas. Betty Box and Peter Rogers, who remained childless, became godparents to both Ralph's son, Jeremy, and to Donald Sinden's son, Marc. For a while, Pinewood really did feel like a family affair with Box, Rogers and Thomas churning out around 100 productions between them.

PINEWOOD

IRENE HANDL, JANET MAHONEY AND ROBERT MORLEY, right, in *Doctor in Trouble* (1970).

DONALD SINDEN, MURIEL PAVLOW AND DIRK BOGARDE, below, in *Doctor in the House* (1954).

the chance to read the script and then discuss how he felt about the actor's performance and ability after that. It was not the first time that Earl St. John had used these tactics. He had tried to dissuade her from working again with her director-partner Ralph Thomas simply, it seemed to Betty, because he had made a success of films like *The Clouded Yellow* and St. John was nervous that Thomas would be typecast as a "juvenile Hitchcock". As she so often did with great success, Betty Box dug her heels in and won the battle.

The scripts for *Doctor in the House* were sent out to the actors to read. Within hours of them being delivered, Betty's phone was already ringing: "'It's Mr Bogarde calling,' I was told. Dirk liked the script very much, he said, and would like to play young Simon Sparrow. There was just one thing. Kenny More's part seemed to him to have more screen time, so he felt we should give him at least one extra scene. 'We'll talk about it. I'm sure we can work it out,' I told him. 'You do your piece with Earl – I've told him we want you.' My other phone was already ringing. It was Kenny More. 'What a lovely script,' he was saying. 'But Dirk's part is bigger. I'll do it if you'll decide to give me another scene or two.' I smiled and decided not to tell

PRINCE CHARLES, above left, with James Robertson Justice during a Royal visit to Pinewood Studios in 1962. The young Prince visited the sets of both *Doctor in Distress* and *Carry On Cabby*.

THE IRASCIBLE JAMES ROBERTSON JUSTICE as Sir Lancelot Spratt, above, in the sixth Doctor film in the series, *Doctor in Clover* (1966).

FRENCH MODEL TURNED ACTRESS Brigitte Bardot with producer Betty Box, *Doctor* film lead Dirk Bogarde and director Ralph Thomas. The four worked together on *Doctor at Sea* at Pinewood in 1955. It was Brigitte Bardot's first British film. Bogarde claimed in later years that it was he who had brought Bardot over to star in the film and introduced her to a British audience.

him of the previous call." Donald Sinden and Donald Houston both accepted their parts as written, and Betty Box turned her attention to casting the rest of the roles. Donald Sinden was pleased to be working with Bogarde on the film: "Dirk was a dear fellow. Very solitary chap. Oddly enough we were brought up in two small villages adjacent to each other and our parents knew each other but Dirk and I never met until 1953 on the set of *Doctor in the House*. We had a thoroughly enjoyable time making it."

The first choice for the bombastic but eminently lovable surgeon, Sir Lancelot Spratt, had been Robert Morley but, according to Betty Box, the price his agent had demanded was so ridiculously inflated that she and Ralph Thomas went straight to their second choice, James Robertson Justice. It was somewhat ironic that Justice

went on to play the character through all seven movies in the series but when ill health prevented him from playing a larger role in the last film, *Doctor in Trouble* (1970), the character's "brother", George Spratt, was brought into the plot and was played by an obviously by then less expensive, Robert Morley.

Betty Box was very aware of every penny when it came to making all of her films but most importantly, with the warnings she had received from Earl St. John and for her first venture into colour, she knew she had to get the budget for *Doctor in the House* right: "The day we started shooting our movie, having had a thumbs-down reaction on *Genevieve*, and with Sir Michael Balcon (also on the Rank Production Board) unenthusiastic about our *Doctor* script, I had a call to say 'Keep your costs down. (They were already almost sub-zero.) Try to cut the budget.

BRIGITTE BARDOT as Helene Colbert and Dirk Bogarde as Simon Sparrow, in *Doctor at Sea* (1955).

FILMING NEXT TO THE ELEPHANTS, left, are (with his back to the camera) James Robertson Justice, Michael Medwin. Dirk Bogarde and Muriel Pavlow, on location in central London shooting *Doctor at Large* (1957).

TAKING SOME TIME OUT of filming *Doctor at Large* on the French Riviera, above, are Muriel Pavlow, producer Betty Box and Dirk Bogarde.

**STILL IN HER TEENS, Shirley Eaton, above,
at a Pinewood photo shoot for *Doctor* films
publicity material.**

**LEAD ACTOR Michael Craig, above right, with
his son, as they "audition" cars in a London
park. The successful car was to be used in the
fourth *Doctor* film, *Doctor in Love* (1960).**

You're only making a film with a limited audience potential.' That
was how we started on the biggest moneymaker the Rank
Organisation had for years." Betty Box said nothing about this to
her cast or crew.

Theirs was an enthusiastic team. The leading cast members
became good friends with Betty Box, Peter Rogers and Ralph and
Joy Thomas. One Sunday during filming, Kenneth More and his then wife, Billy,
invited Betty and Ralph, along with fellow *Genevieve* actors, John Gregson, Dinah
Sheridan, Kay Kendall and a dozen or so more, to a party in their penthouse
overlooking Hyde Park. As the guests were about to leave – the cast had to be on
set early the next morning – Kay Kendall was kissing goodbye to the Kenneth and
Billy More. Betty Box takes up the story: "Suddenly, one of the guests went berserk.
She was the wife of one of the actors from another movie and what triggered her
off none of us knew, but suddenly she was shrieking and screaming and she

DIRK BOGARDE WELCOMES Donald Sinden's two children, Jeremy (centre) and Marc (right) on to the set of *Doctor at Large* (1957).

reached out and savagely scratched Kenny's face, long, deep scratches so that the blood was running down his face and dripping onto his shirt collar. Kenny's immediate reaction was completely professional. 'How bad does it look?' he asked us. 'You need me first shot tomorrow. Can we cover it with make-up?' We could and we did, and saved the close-ups until the livid scratches had healed."

One of the most fondly remembered scenes in *Doctor in the House* involved a students' rag and the kidnapping of the rugby team mascot, Gilbert, a huge stuffed gorilla. The scene in which a fracas was created as bags of flour and soot were liberally thrown around as the students fought in the streets to recapture the mascot turned a usually quiet residential square in London into a war zone. Kenneth More was dressed as a nurse and all the cast threw themselves into the mock fight with gusto. By the end of shooting that scene, three extras became casualties themselves: one with a broken arm, one with a gashed leg and the other with a suspected concussion. A watching journalist reported: "Miss Box's battalion

PROFILE

Leslie Phillips

One of this country's most cherished actors, Leslie Phillips was born in 1924. He was pushed into acting to help pay the family bills following the illness and premature death of his father. Phillips first appeared at Pinewood as an 11-year-old in *Sailing Along* (1937) alongside Michael Redgrave and Jessie Matthews.

His good looks and upper-class accent saw Phillips selected for officer training during the war and he was commissioned as a second lieutenant, though illness prevented him from active service.

Phillips, who has remained a workaholic throughout his life, became a familiar face on stage and screen across the 1950s. He was a hit in the long-running BBC radio series, *The Navy Lark*, and became one of the founding lights of the *Carry On* series. He left the *Carry Ons* after three early outings, not wanting to be typecast, and took the lead roles in three *Doctor* films. The success of *Carry On Nurse* and *Doctor in Love* – the highest grossing films of 1959 and 1960 respectively, established Phillips as a household name.

Phillips' career took on a new direction when he appeared in *The Cherry Orchard* and two further plays for the Royal Shakespeare Company. Roles in *Out of Africa*, *Empire of the Sun* and *Scandal*, and television dramas such as *Chancer* and *Rumpole of the Bailey*, cemented his place in the hearts of the British viewing public. Most recently, he was nominated for a BAFTA for his role opposite Peter O'Toole in the award-winning *Venus*. He has also found new status among Harry Potter fans, appearing as the voice of the Sorting Hat.

Leslie Phillips was awarded the OBE in 1998 and lives in west London with his wife, actress Angela Scoular.

of stars staged a students' rag and before it finished a £6,000 limousine was concertinaed by a furniture van (there was so much to look at on the other side of the Square) and an errand boy on a bike, badly knocked about, was retrieved from a window at the rear of a baker's van. Not one of Betty Box's embryo medicos proved very professional at first-aid treatment."

Donald Sinden remembers filming that scene very well – and the ambulance chase afterwards, which required some high speed driving through the streets of the capital. "Donald Huston and I had to drive this ambulance around. One of the most frightening moments was going down Gower Street in the heart of London. The police were controlling the traffic lights. Betty ensured that all the cars going down Gower Street when we were filming this scene were film unit cars, so they knew what they were doing. All the cars streaming across Gower Street were just normal drivers going about their business. Now all was going very well. We were driving down Gower Street and were supposed to come to a set of red lights, which, in the film, we drive through. Of course the normal drivers were being held on red on the roads that cut across Gower Street so they were stationery as we jumped the lights. We shot down Gower Street at something like 60mph when the policeman in charge of the lights pushed the wrong button and instead of changing our lights to red, changed the others on the roads cutting across Gower Street to green and suddenly we had all this West End traffic coming across us. To this day I don't know how we missed them."

Richard Gordon (real name Gordon Ostlere), the author of the *Doctor* books, as well as being the medical adviser on the *Doctor* series of films, played the part of an anaesthetist during operation scenes, a cameo he continued throughout the series. Accomplished comedy actress Joan Sims, in an early film role, played Rigor Mortis, the nurse whose name gave away her attitude to sex. Joan went on to play in cameos in six of the seven *Doctor* films as well as 24 of Peter Rogers' 31 *Carry On* films, becoming, alongside Hattie Jacques, one of this country's most respected and highly regarded comediennes.

Joan recalls the role of Rigor Mortis with great affection: "I had just one scene in *Doctor in the House*, but since that scene was with the dreamboat to end all dreamboats, Dirk Bogarde, playing the handsome Dr Simon Sparrow, my pre-

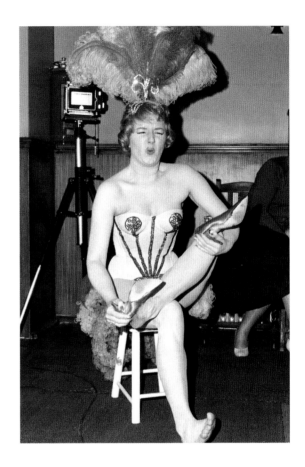

FEELING THE PINCH – comedy actress Joan Sims finds her "exotic dancer" costume a little pressing, in a moment away from filming *Doctor in Love*. (1960)

THE APTLY NAMED DOCTORS BURKE AND HARE (Leslie Phillips and Michael Craig), above, entertain two patients at a Flu Remedy Clinic, nightclub dancers Leonora (Liz Fraser, left) and Dawn (Joan Sims, right) in the 1960 hit comedy *Doctor in Love*.

NICHOLAS PARSONS, LESLIE PHILLIPS AND MICHAEL CRAIG, above right, in *Doctor in Love (1960)*.

DR. BURKE (Leslie Phillips) shows Kitten Strudwick (Carole Lesley) a few moves, opposite, in a scene from the highest grossing British film of 1960, *Doctor in Love*.

filming nerves were even more taut than usual – which Dirk promptly sensed. Just before we started filming, he presented me with a large box of Black Magic chocolates. This charming gesture increased rather than calmed my palpitations but I managed to control myself sufficiently to play the scene."

At just 16, blonde starlet Shirley Eaton played the landlady's daughter, who continuously dreamt up illnesses that enabled her to expose her sexy shape to the disinterested lodging student, Sparrow. Shirley, too, went onto appear in a further *Doctor* outing as well as becoming the first *Carry On* "girl", playing the love interest in the early films of the series' long run. Perhaps Shirley is best remembered for playing Jill Masterson whose gold-plated death in the Bond film *Goldfinger* remains to this day one of the most iconic cinematic images of the twentieth century.

One of the great television comics of the twentieth century was Tommy Cooper. He filmed a scene for *Doctor in the House* in which he performed his "sawing a lady in half" magic act, which ended with a mock disaster and Cooper crying out, "Is there a doctor in the house?" The scene was funny but unfortunately the film was over-running quite considerably and since it was a

THE LEAD CAST of *Doctor in Love* (1960) – (back) Michael Craig and Leslie Phillips, with (front) Virginia Maskell, James Robertson Justice and Carole Lesley. Both the lead actresses suffered personal frustrations in their careers, and sadly both were to take their own lives in the coming years.

stand-alone scene that could be excised without affecting the continuity of the plot, Betty Box decided that Tommy Cooper's scene would be consigned to the cutting room floor. "I wrote and told him," she recalled. "I try always to tell an artiste if his work is cut. I've known an actor go to the cinema with a party of friends only to find his scene has been 'left on the cutting room floor' and I can imagine how let down he must feel."

The first inkling of the success that *Doctor in the House* was to prove to be, came with a "sneak preview" of the film. Occasionally, at the last moment, a film would be shown in a cinema in place of the published movie – the idea being to test the reaction of the average filmgoer without the audience being told in advance that they are attending a preview. The new title was literally slotted in, with a small notice displayed outside the cinema just minutes before the film started. For Betty Box and Ralph Thomas, who knew so much was resting on this film, it was a nerve-wracking time: "We are just helpless onlookers while our brainchild is being tested – later we sometimes perform remedial surgery, according to how the audience reacts. We usually tape-recorded the whole performance to test the size and length of laughs. This time I quickly lost my shaking nerves. From the first scene to the last the audience was with us and the laughter was non-stop. Afterwards I stood outside and listened to people's comments as they left and, believe me, there are few pleasures sweeter than knowing that, for a short while at least, you've given people enjoyment."

Doctor in the House opened to "standing room only" business and the critics' reception was equally satisfying. The *Daily Telegraph* called it, "The best British comedy for years." C. A. Lejeune declared: "Not on screen five minutes before house rose to it with a roar – destined to be one of the biggest popular hits." Of Kenneth More, one critic declared: "Plays civilized naughty comedy better than

DIRECTOR RALPH THOMAS, lifting the barbells off the floor, shows how he wants the next scene to run, on set at Pinewood, making *Doctor in Distress* in 1962.

GOOD FRIENDS – actor John Mills visiting director Ralph Thomas on set at Pinewood during filming of *Doctor in Trouble* in 1969.

CAPTAIN GEORGE SPRATT, Robert Morley (left) looking on in shock as cruise liner passenger Llewellyn Wendover (Harry Secombe) takes the instruction to dress for dinner "in black tie only", a little too far, in *Doctor in Trouble* (1970).

GRAHAM STARK AND LESLIE PHILLIPS in *Doctor in Trouble* (1970).

LEGENDARY FARCEUR Leslie Phillips (below) is more than happy to get dragged up for the last *Doctor* film in the series, *Doctor in Trouble*. Acting alongside him is Angela Scoular. Over a decade later, the two were to get married.

PROFILE

Dirk Bogarde

Dirk Bogarde was born in 1921, son of Ulric Van Den Bogaerde, art editor of *The Times*, and former actress Margaret Niven. He served in the army during the Second World War, reaching the rank of Captain, and was one of the first Allied officers to liberate the Bergen Belsen concentration camp in Germany – an experience that had a profound effect on him throughout his life.

His good looks ensured an early contract with the Rank Organisation and while his appearance in the 1950 thriller *The Blue Lamp*, brought him to prominence, it was to be as medical student Simon Sparrow in *Doctor in the House* four years later, that Bogarde was to find matinée idol fame. Throughout the 1950s, he continued to make films for Rank at Pinewood, including three more *Doctor* film appearances, *A Tale of Two Cities* (1957), *The Wind Cannot Read* (1957), and *The Singer Not the Song* (1960). Bogarde's last Pinewood film was *Doctor in Distress* in 1963. The actor didn't return to the Studios until 1996, when a commemorative plaque was unveiled in honour of the *Doctor* films and their producer/director team Betty Box and Ralph Thomas.

Away from Pinewood, Bogarde abandoned his heartthrob image and took on more challenging roles, such as the gay barrister in *Victim* (1961), the put upon valet Barrett in *The Servant* (1963), and television journalist Robert Gold in the award-winning *Darling* (1965).

Bogarde left England to live with his manager, Tony Forwood, in France. He continued to make films and in latter years embarked on a highly successful writing career – his several volumes of autobiography and novels, proving witty, literate and very popular. He died in 1999 aged 78.

any British screen actor I know. Rare gift of being light and sincere at the same time." Of Dirk Bogarde – who had turned down *Genevieve* just a year before because he had wanted to get away from playing light comedy, the critics were equally praising. The *Morning Advertiser* exclaimed: "Dirk must feel on top of the world – turned in a stunning show in comedy on a par with *Genevieve*", and *The Times* said: "Shines in part unlike those to which … normally condemned." Dirk Bogarde was very clear as to why he thought the film was such a success. Speaking to the author of this book in 1996, he said: "*Doctor in the House* was different because it was the first time that hospitals were shown in a kinder way. People were scared of hospitals. They had seen family or friends going in with something or another and never coming out again. This film demystified hospitals a bit. It was also different from all those warry films that had been running endlessly since the end of the war. I worked with Betty and Ralph several times. We didn't always see eye-to-eye but it was always a pleasure making a film with them."

Bogarde's last Pinewood film was indeed to be another *Doctor* film, *Doctor in Distress* in 1963, returning after a six-year break for one last appearance as Simon Sparrow. Bogarde then left Pinewood to return just one last time 33 years later, in April 1996, to be re-united with Betty Box and Ralph Thomas for the unveiling of a plaque commemorating and celebrating both the series and its makers.

The second *Doctor* film, *Doctor at Sea*, went into production in 1955. It was based on Richard Gordon's second book, which was based on his observations as a ship's doctor during time out he had taken from hospital work. Betty Box was not a fan of sequels: "I have never really been a believer in sequels and/or series films – perhaps due to a distaste for repetition, a need for pastures new – although my husband, Peter Rogers, has broken the world record for a feature film series with over 30 *Carry On* films, each one on a completely different subject. And so it was with *Doctor at Sea*, not truly a sequel. Any actor could have played the doctor and all the other characters were different from those in *Doctor in the House*. But I was delighted to be working again with Dirk Bogarde, who had readily agreed to play our lead. Maybe the casting of Brigitte Bardot helped him to decide!"

In years ahead, Brigitte Bardot was to become the world's top sex symbol, but just starting off in the mid-1950s when she was told she would have to appear

JOAN SIMS WAS RENOWNED for bringing laughter to a film set and regularly burst into giggles during shooting. Here she can be seen "corpsing" with fellow comedy actor Arthur Haynes, during the making of *Doctor in Clover* at Pinewood in 1965.

nude in a shower sequence in the doctor's cabin, the French actress recoiled: "We will 'ave to see how well Dirk and I get to know one another. I'm not sure I want to do eet." The day arrived when the scene needed to be shot at Pinewood, and all around the sound stage a flurry of assistants gathered, adorned with bath towels, flesh-coloured bras and briefs – the typical costume used by British actresses on set when asked to strip down in those days. Suddenly the actress took off her bathrobe and stood quite unselfconsciously in the tiniest of briefs in front of the director, Ralph Thomas: "You can tell me Ralph when I goes into the shower, when I am to take off my knickairs, OK?" And she took them off, without a word, and the scene was shot and in the can. Aware of potential censorship concerns, a second shot was also filmed through a semi-transparent shower curtain – the shot that made it into the final print.

Doctor at Sea – which was largely filmed aboard a real ship travelling around Greece and its islands, with the interior scenes filmed back at Pinewood – did equally good business as its predecessor and it was only a matter of time before a third film would be made. That time came in 1957. Richard Gordon had by now written a third book of stories about medical life and, with the first two *Doctor* films being huge financial successes, Rank was more than keen for a third film to go into production.

In *Doctor at Large*, Dirk Bogarde returned once again and was re-joined by Donald Sinden, back on terra firma. The film wasn't hugely exciting, this time the accident-prone Simon Sparrow escaping a city hospital for the more tranquil life of a doctor at a country practice. One of the film's best performances came from accomplished character actor Lionel Jeffries, whose small role received very good reviews. As the actor recalls: "I remember working on *Doctor at Large*. It was a small role. I only had a couple of days at Pinewood to do on it. I played Dr Hackett, a skinflint of a local GP who comes back from some night visits to find his wife embracing the locum, who was played by Dirk Bogarde, at the top of the stairs. I got great notices for a bit part actor."

The fourth *Doctor* film – *Doctor in Love* – was to be different from the first three. It was still to be based on the light-hearted stories of Richard Gordon but the times were changing, the novelty of the first films was wearing off, and there were

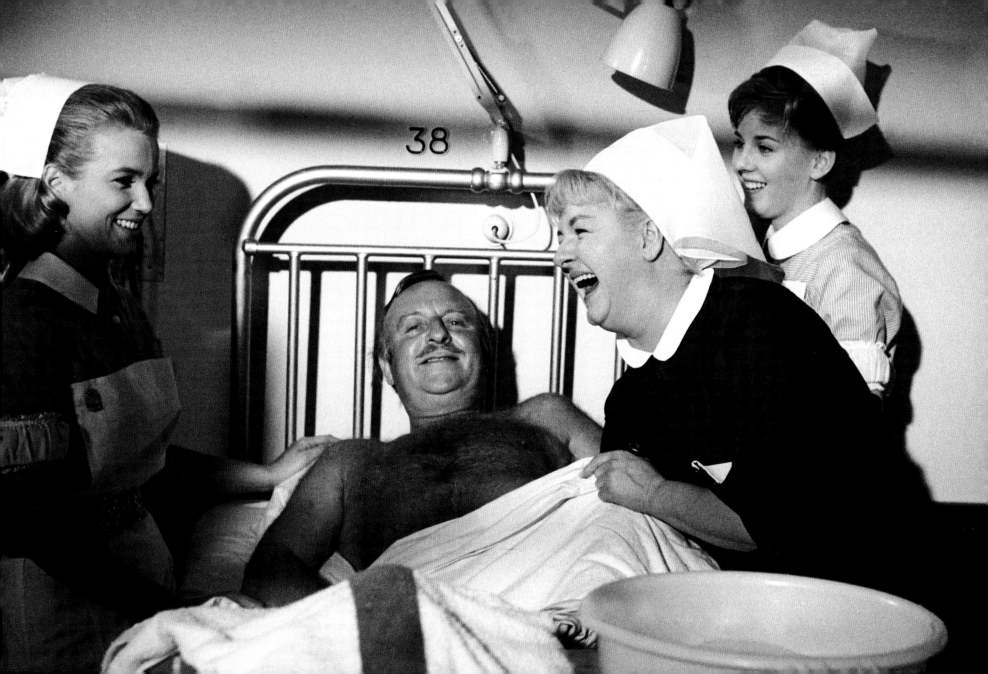

to be changes in the cast. Bogarde had turned down reprising the role of Simon Sparrow once again and even if he hadn't, his fee for films was now so great that it would have totalled almost the entire cast budget for *Doctor in Love*.

The old character names were dropped and new ones brought in. Michael Craig and Leslie Phillips played Dr Burke and Dr Hare. Craig, who was signed up to Rank, didn't have much choice in the decision to appear in the film and did so somewhat reluctantly. Phillips, on the other hand, jumped at the chance, fresh from the huge success of *Carry On Nurse* (1959), in which he had played one of the lead roles and received great reviews. The cast comprised classic comedy favourites including Joan Sims and Liz Fraser as a couple of variety strippers, Irene Handl, Fenella Fielding and Warren Mitchell. The beautiful Virginia Maskell, who tragically committed suicide in 1968, aged just 31, played the love interest. The other pretty actress in the film was Carole Lesley – who also sadly committed suicide in later years.

James Robertson Justice was back as Sir Lancelot Spratt, although in this storyline the boot was on the other foot, with his character having to go under the surgeon's knife. In that scene, Leslie Phillips has to administer the pre-med injection. When they were shooting it, JRJ refused to wear anything under his operating gown costume, "I don't under the kilt!" he exclaimed. So there he lay, virtually naked on set. The line he barks out as the anaesthetist tries to inject him is: "Prick me, don't skewer me. I'm not a shish kebab." To which the cameraman was heard to say, a little too loudly, "Well, if you stay like that you'll look like one on screen. We only need the skewer." Cast and crew all broke up with laughter and filming stopped until they regained their composure.

Leslie Phillips recalls working with James Robertson Justice: "I did about seven films with James. He was exceedingly irascible but he became a great friend of mine. That was rare. He didn't make friends with a lot of actors. He was a one off. He wasn't an actor in the true sense you see. James was a fantastic personality. In his life he had been a paid soldier, a smuggler and a professor. And he hated learning lines. I hate learning lines, though I still do it. But he used to write them all over the place on set and wander round during a scene as though it was part of the action so that he could find out what his next line was. We all got used to that."

Doctor in Love repeated the success of the earlier films in the series and was the highest grossing British film of 1960. Betty Box and Ralph Thomas decided that that was probably enough and turned their attention away from matters medical. However, three years later, they returned to make *Doctor in Distress*, which saw Dirk Bogarde back for one last outing as Simon Sparrow. As part of a bigger deal in which he was making other films for Betty Box and Ralph Thomas, and also with his film career slightly on the wane, Bogarde's services were employed for less than he had previously called for. He was affordable again and Betty Box was delighted to get him back on screen as everyone's favourite medico.

Bogarde recalls working on the *Doctor* films: "I did four of the *Doctor* films and Betty in particular fought for me to be in them, although the studio didn't want me. I had been noted by critics but I hadn't become the major star Rank had hoped I'd be. Betty and Ralph had seen me in a couple of plays and realized that I could play comedy. The studio believed I could only play spivs and Cockneys, but Betty and Ralph put me in tweeds and let me speak in my own voice, and the rest is history. I changed my character's name to Simon Sparrow because I thought it was funnier and so it stayed. The one stipulation I made was that I had to be a real doctor. I would do things that were funny, but would never instigate anything funny. We had two doctors always on the set; if any of us had to perform an operation or some medical procedure, there was always someone there to explain exactly how to do it. I wouldn't put a stethoscope to a body until I knew exactly how it was done and what I would have said."

DIRK BOGARDE AND BRIGITTE BARDOT
in *Doctor at Sea* (1955).

KENNETH MORE AND
LAURENCE OLIVIER (left)
rehearsing their lines for their
parts in hosting a Bafta ceremony
in the mid-1950s.

BETTY BOX SURROUNDED by
favoured cast members –
including Peter Finch, Leslie
Phillips, Dirk Bogarde, Dora
Bryan and director Ralph
Thomas – at a film festival in the
early 1960s.

After *Doctor in Distress*, Dirk Bogarde said "no more", and so when it came to making the sixth film, *Doctor in Clover* in 1965, Leslie Phillips was brought back to lead the increasingly slapstick proceedings. Indeed it's the comedy performances of Phillips that kept both *Doctor in Clover* and *Doctor in Trouble* (another aboard-ship medical outing, made in 1969) afloat.

Doctor in Trouble was aptly named. There were problems from the outset. The screenplay had been written to allow James Robertson Justice to play two roles: Sir Lancelot Spratt and his twin brother George, the captain of a cruise liner, both of which were variations on the roles he had played in *Doctor in the House* and *Doctor at Sea*, some 15 years earlier. Sadly and unexpectedly, JRJ suffered a cerebral stroke and was rushed from his home in Inverness to Aberdeen for serious brain surgery. Betty Box takes up the story: "When we eventually saw him, only a matter of days before shooting was due to start and with the sets already built, we knew there was no way we could put him through the ordeal of such a heavy assignment, even though he courageously insisted that he could do it. Although he tried to hide it, he had an uncontrollable tremor in his right arm, which would make shooting anything other than close ups a very tricky proposition. So we compromised and got Robert Morley to play the far larger part of the ship's captain, and James eventually got through the few days required for the Sir Lancelot part. It must have taken every ounce of energy he possessed to do it. We knew he needed the money and paid him for both parts – he certainly deserved it for long and loyal service. James was the only star to appear in all the *Doctor* films, and with him they died."

Betty Box and Ralph Thomas continued to make films into the 1970s, including two adult comedies about the first man in the world to undergo a penis transplant, *Percy* in 1971 and *Percy's Progress* in 1974. The producer/director team worked together for three decades and made more than 30 films together – most of them at Pinewood – but it is likely that they will be most fondly remembered for tickling the ribcages and reaching the funny bones of millions of viewers across the world, in their series of medical comedies, the *Doctor* films.

Bryan Forbes

ACTOR AND SCREENWRITER

I started in the industry as an actor and when I came out of the army I starred in an ill-fated play put on by Sam Goldwyn, Jnr. I was spotted by one of Rank's casting people and I asked to go to Pinewood for an interview with Ian Dalrymple, who ran Wessex Films in those days. Much to my amazement he gave me a job, with a role in *All Over the Town* (1949). It was an agreeable comedy film with a cast of Pinewood regulars, such as Norman Wooland and Sarah Churchill. Subsequently, a woman called Joyce Briggs – who was something akin to the script supervisor at Pinewood – gave me a job as a screenwriter at £100 a week, which enabled me to buy my first car. Her partner was my agent, Olive Harding. They lived together in what today would be described as an "arrangement". I became a sort of script doctor – without credit – I would help to get screenplays up and filmed. I was a fairly fast writer. I think I was given the contract because of my work on *Cockleshell Heroes* (1955) for Cubby Broccoli.

Very often the original writer didn't even know I was working on it. I'd give the pages straight to the producer who had asked me to look at the script. My own work was doctored for a time. It was the name of the game. I wrote or re-wrote material for *An Alligator Named Daisy* (1955), *The Black Night* (1953), *The Small Victory* (which was never

made), *The House of Secrets* (1956) and *The Captain's Table* (1958), to name a few. I was acting in a lot of films at the same time.

I originally wrote *The League of Gentlemen* (1959) for Cary Grant, after being commissioned by Carl Foreman. Much to my amazement when I went in to get a copy of the script from Carl's office, my name wasn't on it. His was. Foreman explained that Cary Grant wouldn't have known me and so wouldn't have even looked at the script, but he knew Carl. Naively I accepted this. Cary Grant said "no" and the film lapsed and wasn't made, until one day my agent called with good news that *The League of Gentlemen* had been bought by Basil Dearden. I knew Basil and rang him that night to tell him how thrilled I was. Basil was always very straight to the point: "What's it got to do with you?" I told him I'd written it. "No you didn't. Do you think I would pay £18,000 [around £250,000 in today's money] for a Bryan Forbes script? This is a Carl Foreman script." We went and faced Carl Foreman together and he had to back down. Shortly after, we formed Allied Film Makers.

The idea for *The League of Gentlemen* came from a novel and I was commissioned to write the screenplay. I changed a lot of it and used a lot of my own army experiences. I was very *au fait* at the time with the way the army operated. The film was ahead of its time in that I turned things on their head, particularly casting Jack Hawkins as the errant major. Normally he would be "up on the bridge" and very stiff upper

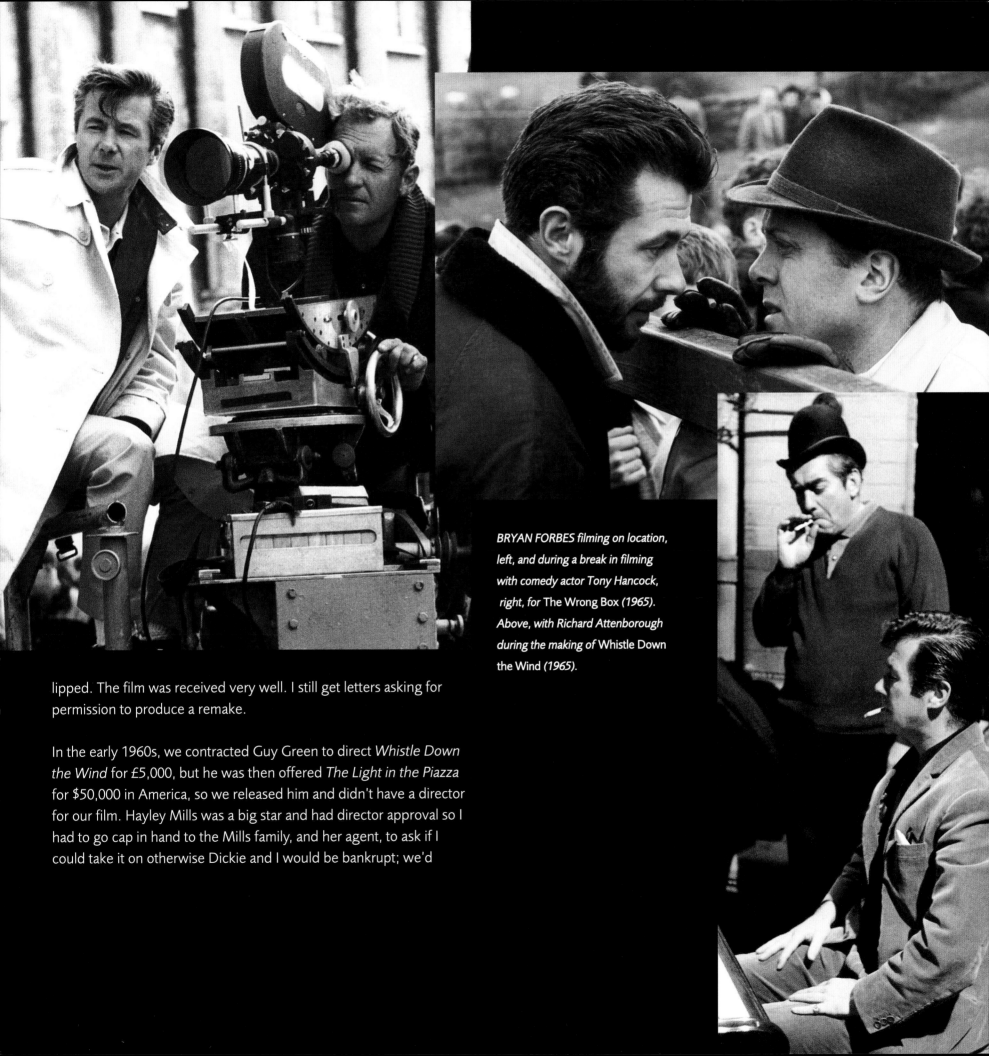

BRYAN FORBES *filming on location, left, and during a break in filming with comedy actor Tony Hancock, right, for* The Wrong Box *(1965). Above, with Richard Attenborough during the making of* Whistle Down the Wind *(1965).*

lipped. The film was received very well. I still get letters asking for permission to produce a remake.

In the early 1960s, we contracted Guy Green to direct *Whistle Down the Wind* for £5,000, but he was then offered *The Light in the Piazza* for $50,000 in America, so we released him and didn't have a director for our film. Hayley Mills was a big star and had director approval so I had to go cap in hand to the Mills family, and her agent, to ask if I could take it on otherwise Dickie and I would be bankrupt; we'd

invested all our money in the film – and we couldn't afford the preferred directors on Hayley's list, such as David Lean. All we could afford was me. Which is how I got *Whistle Down the Wind*. The film, made in 1961, cost just £140,000 – much of which went to Hayley.

I was in and out of Pinewood in the 1960s, working again with Dickie on *Séance on a Wet Afternoon* (1963) and *The Wrong Box* (1965), which was a favourite of mine. We had such a wonderful cast with Ralph Richardson, John Mills, my wife Nanette, Peter Cook and Dudley Moore, and Peter Sellers funnier than I have ever seen him. Michael Caine was in *The Wrong Box*, too. I then made *The Whisperers* (1966). I liked working at Pinewood even as an independent.

After *Deadfall* (1967) – also with Michael Caine – I left England to make *The Mad Woman of Chaillot* (1969). I returned in the mid-1970s to make *The Slipper and the Rose* (1975). It had a £5 million budget, which was big for me at the time.

Pinewood has always felt like home, probably because it's the Studio in which I worked as an actor, writer, producer and director. You just knew everybody at the Studios – cast, directors and writers, most of them in the bar at lunchtime. The main house has always been lovely. Pinewood never felt like a factory, it always felt like a Studio.

I've been a writer/director for most of my career and there's no greater pleasure than working with great actors and suddenly you look at your words in the dailies and they've come to life. As I have said before, I've always thought of myself as a writer who became an actor who became a screenwriter who became a film director. Writing has been my life since aged 16 and I have been very lucky to have that second string to my bow as a director. I've had a chequered but very lucky career I suppose.

A TOP-NOTCH CAST OF ACTING GREATS,
above left, for Bryan Forbes' The Mad Woman of
Chaillot *(1969). Below left, off set shots from*
Deadfall, *starring Michael Caine, made in 1967.*

ON LOCATION for Whistle Down the Wind,
right, made in 1961.

Norman!

Whether or not you are a fan of Norman Wisdom, there is no disputing the popularity of one of this country's favourite clowns. And with the advent of multi-channel television, sell-through video and DVD and all the opportunities they bring for repeat showings of his work, it is difficult to believe that Norman, who turned 90 in February 2005 made his last Pinewood film some 40 years ago, after fulfilling a highly successful contract as a Rank "star". Yet the comedian very nearly didn't make it in the film business at all.

Norman Wisdom was born on 4 February 1915 and started the musical side of his career in the Army, to which he enlisted as a very small 14-year-old. It was while serving in the forces that Norman, outsized and outweighed by most of those around him, began to develop the "Gump" character that was to become his trademark throughout his long career in showbusiness. The persona of the happy little bloke who was as honest as the day is long and who was the last man on any girl's list of suitors but who would eventually win her over nonetheless, found huge appeal. Mixed with his great physical agility and verbal dexterity, as well as a talent for music that saw him play many instruments, Norman was fast becoming an act to contend with as the war years came to an end and he began to travel the music halls with his stand-up act. His first appearance on BBC television at the end of the 1940s was a huge success, thrusting him into the limelight and prompting critics to draw comparisons between the fledgling comedy actor and Charlie Chaplin. Yet still, now in his 30s, Norman hadn't made it into the world of film, something he was desperate to do. He felt he had a great deal to offer the medium and was frustrated that he couldn't break through.

In 1952, Wisdom was appearing in the revue "Paris to Piccadilly" at the Prince of Wales theatre in London's West End. The Rank Organisation talent scouts were, as usual, out in action across theatreland, scouring the shows and stages for potential new stars for their films. Wisdom had been seen on television a few weeks before in a seasonal special called *A Christmas Party*, by Earl St. John, who was impressed by his appearance alongside established

NORMAN WISDOM PROVES a big hit with the Moscow State Folk Dance Company during their 1950s visit to Pinewood Studios.

entertainment names including Petula Clark, Terry-Thomas, Jimmy Jewel and Ben Warris. St. John sent his "boys" out to see if Wisdom was as good in "real life" as he'd come across on the small screen. The West End show was a big hit and the huge crowds that went to see the show each night during its run regularly cheered Wisdom's performances. That was good enough for Earl St. John, who immediately approached Wisdom's agent, Billy Marsh, to discuss plans to sign the comedian up to a seven-year contract. Marsh shrewdly pointed out that he was, at that time, already in discussions with Associated British Cinemas about Norman signing up with them. Thus, without the mandatory screen test expected of all actors and actresses before a contract was signed, an agreement was struck within 24 hours.

Wisdom's deal with Rank stated that he would film exclusively with them for seven years. The Organisation guaranteed that he would have three films in the first two years of the life of the contract, the first of which he would be paid £5,000 to appear in – around £80,000 in today's money. No sooner had the ink dried on the contract than it became clear that in the great rush to sign up Norman Wisdom, no one had any film ideas for the actor to start work on. As Norman recalls: "They had no films lined up for me. No story outlines. Nothing. They didn't even want

AWAY FROM THE BUSY schedules of film making, Norman relaxes at home.

WITH AN UNERRING ABILITY to raise a laugh, Norman shone in front of the camera – be it film or stills – as he shows in these seasonal publicity shots.

me to do a screen test until after I'd signed the contract. By which time, if I'd turned out to have a stutter and a nervous tic every time I saw a camera lens pointing at me, it would have been too late."

As mentioned earlier, the fortunes of the Rank Organisation and Pinewood Studios in the early 1950s, were precarious to say the least. John Davis had started to turn the oil tanker but progress was slow and even though he had managed to reduce the company's overdraft by several million pounds, the company had strict budgets to meet and maintain in all areas of its business, especially filmmaking. Signing up future stars and doing nothing with them was not an option and the word came from on high that if Wisdom had signed a contract, it was time he was put to work.

A screen test was hastily organized on one of Pinewood's smaller sound stages. The director of the film was to be cinematographer-turned-director, Ronald Neame, who had had several successes at Pinewood producing films such as *Great Expectations* and *Oliver Twist* in the post-war years. At the allotted hour Wisdom turned up for his screen test, went through make up and was taken onto the set. Neame and singer/actress Petula Clarke, with whom Wisdom was to share a domestic scene, met him. Norman read the dialogue, looked up slightly worried at Neame, looked down at the dialogue again, looked into Petula Clarke's eyes and said, with all the comedy gusto he could muster: "Your eyes are as light as gossamer …" The line wasn't funny. The situation wasn't funny and Wisdom found himself floundering. The actor was paid off for his first film and the project was abandoned.

It was not a good start for Wisdom's film career and it did not appear to bode well. It wasn't long before the press began to ask questions. Wisdom's signing for Rank had been much trumpeted but now all had gone silent and some journalists wanted to know what had happened to this up-and-coming star. In August 1952, *Picturegoer* magazine wrote: "It has been three months since the perky little clown with the clever line in poignant comedy signed his first film contract. Now decision time is at hand. After months of worrying about Norman Wisdom's debut, the Rank studio chiefs have reduced the field to three or four possible scripts. But let's be blunt, the odds are dead against him in this new venture." There was some truth

NORMAN WISDOM'S "GUMP" CHARACTER first made it to the big screen in his cinema debut under Rank contract, *Trouble in Store*, in 1953. Wisdom won a British Academy Award that year for Best Newcomer to film. He was 37.

PROFILE

Hugh Stewart

Born in Falmouth on 14 December 1910, Hugh Stewart entered the film business in the early 1930s at Gaumont-British, training as a film editor and first working on the film *Marry Me* in 1932. He graduated to editing, soon showing his skills to good effect on many well-known films of the time including Hitchcock's *The Man Who Knew Too Much* in 1934.

During World War II, Stewart was enlisted to the army film unit, shooting in Algeria and Tunisia. After the hostilities were over, he joined the Rank Organisation to produce films, his first being *Trottie True* in 1949. Stewart continued to make films at Pinewood for the next 20 years, producing 10 of Norman Wisdom's 12 Pinewood big-screen outings. Stewart's great height compared to Wisdom's smaller stature was always a source of amusement to them both, but some of the difficulties they experienced as Wisdom attempted to gain more control over his own material in the 1960s were less pleasing to them.

Stewart also made the trilogy of comedy films by Morecambe & Wise in their mid-1960s attempts to take their humour from the small screen to the large. The films were not wholly successful but, as with much of Stewart's work, are worth revisiting for the smiles if not the huge laughs they bring on further viewings.

By the late 1960s, Stewart had moved towards retirement, teaching English but also producing a few films for the Children's Film Foundation.

WITH *TROUBLE IN STORE*
co-star, Lana Morris, who would
appear with Norman again in
Man of the Moment, two years
later, in 1955.

in this unkindness and no one could have been more
frustrated than Wisdom himself. A hard worker all his
life, he wasn't one who wanted to be paid for doing
nothing. More importantly, as a performer he craved a
repeat of the success on screen that he was experiencing
each night on stage in the West End.

At Pinewood there was equal discomfort. *Genevieve*
had just been made and then shelved, and it was still
some months before Betty Box was to hit it big with
Doctor in the House. Earl St. John needed a big comedy
success and turned to writer Jill Craigie for solace. Jill –
the wife of the Member of Parliament, Michael Foot, who
would go on to become the leader of his party in the 1980s – ensconced herself in
her Hampstead home and turned her attentions to producing a storyline that was
worthy of Wisdom's very specialized talents. Six weeks later she presented her ideas
to both Wisdom (who loved them) and Earl St. John (who did not). Craigie
described her storyline for *Trouble in Store* as "a satire on a big store in a
Chaplinesque vein, with plenty of scope for slapstick". St. John wanted more work
on the script. There was a falling out between him and Craigie and she asked for
her name to be removed from the project's credits. Writer and director John Paddy
Carstairs was brought in to work with Wisdom on the script for *Trouble in Store*.
Another writer, Ted Willis, and producer, Maurice Cowan, were also brought on
board. Wisdom hit it off immediately with his new team, especially Carstairs, with

FAMED BRITISH CHARACTER ACTRESS
Margaret Rutherford, who appeared as
the lovable roguish shoplifter, Miss Bacon,
in *Trouble in Store*. She appeared in
another Norman Wisdom comedy, *Just My
Luck*, in 1957.

NORMAN VISITS THE SET of *As Long As They're Happy*, **above, while making** *One Good Turn* **at the Studios in 1954, and meets up with (left to right) Susan Stephen, Brenda de Banzie and Janette Scott.**

THORA HIRD AND NORMAN, above right, ambling through Pinewood while making *One Good Turn* **in 1954. Thora's daughter, actress Janette Scott (seen above), was also filming at the Studios at that time.**

whom the actor struck a good working and personal friendship. Almost cut from the same humour mould, the two set about turning Jill Craigie's ideas into a workable script. The film's plot was basic. Wisdom played a stock assistant in a large department store and caused equal measure of havoc and mayhem while foiling a gang of crooks intent on robbing the store – and winning the girl of his dreams at the same time. Wisdom's character was called Norman, as it was to be in all his Pinewood films, a clever blurring of the man and the much-loved character he created. He was surrounded by a sterling cast of British talent including Lana Morris, as love interest Sally, Margaret Rutherford as a fiendishly clever shoplifter, admired character actors Joan Sims and Derek Bond and everyone's favourite straight man, Jerry Desmonde.

Shooting the film was nervewracking as Norman recalls; "In those early days of shooting, everyone was as tense as a bowstring, from the director down to the clapper boy. The atmosphere on the set was electric. I don't mind admitting that I was scared stiff every time I stepped out there, especially in the first week – though I wouldn't let anyone see it. I was given dressing room number eight – my lucky number – and I would insist on it for every film I made at Pinewood afterwards."

On the first day of filming, Wisdom pulled Carstairs to one side and whispered in his ear: "I've got to tell you, Paddy, I'm really nervous." Back came the reply: "If it's any consolation to you, Norman, so am I." Wisdom then felt more at ease.

John Paddy Carstairs had the sort of temper which, rather than let angst and frustration build up for long periods of time, would explode into a rage quickly, get it out of his system, and move on. The first time he lost his temper on the set of *Trouble in Store* was just a few days into filming. Shooting was taking place of a scene in which Norman carries out a crate of crockery to the shop window, which he thinks he's been asked to dress. This humble assistant is thrilled at the – mistaken – sudden promotion from dogsbody to window dresser and performs his newfound role with relish, if not ease. He soon falls out with a fellow window dresser and it's not long before the crockery is flying. A custard pie fight without the custard takes place in the front of the store for onlookers to watch with horror and glee in equal measure. Carstairs felt that there was enough slapstick in the scene to get the required laughs and insisted that Wisdom played the scene straight. Wisdom disagreed. Carstairs flew into a rage and left the set. He was back a few minutes later, calmer and ready to shoot. The two compromised and the scene was filmed both ways. One look in the rushes the next day showed who was right. Wisdom won the day, and the respect of Carstairs, and theirs was to be a long and enduring friendship that saw the pair work on six consecutive films.

The days were long during the making of *Trouble in Store*, and when shooting at Pinewood came to an end, Wisdom was whisked off by car for his twice-nightly performances of "Paris to Piccadilly" in the West End. He'd finish the shows around 11 p.m. and would have to be back on set at Pinewood the next morning ready for filming by 8 a.m. But Norman didn't complain. This is what he had been waiting for and he was loving every long and tiring minute of it. Wisdom even managed to get a song he had written into the film. *Don't Laugh At Me* became Norman Wisdom's signature tune, even making it to the top of the charts briefly before dropping back in the top ten where it stayed for many months.

CLASSIC COMEDY STRAIGHT MAN Jerry Desmonde (top), who appeared with Norman Wisdom in seven films between 1953 and 1965. Above, John Paddy Carstairs – who directed Norman Wisdom's first six Rank appearances between 1953 and 1958 – with the actor, during the filming of *Up in the World* (1956).

JOKING ABOUT FOR FOR A PUBLICITY SHOT taken at Pinewood during filming of *One Good Turn* (1954).

Rank bosses were nervous: they were unsure whether audiences would laugh at Norman Wisdom or not. So, as they had with many of their film outings, such as *Doctor in the House*, they decided to give *Trouble in Store* a sneak preview at the Gaumont in Camden Town on 25 November 1953. As with all sneak previews, the audience wasn't told until the last minute that there was to be a change in the film they had come to see. Audiences that night were expecting to sit down to watch Bernard Braden and Barbara Kelly in the light comedy *Love in Pawn*.

It was a difficult evening for Norman: "The Rank Organisation and all the producers were frightened out of their lives putting me into the film, because they didn't know whether it was going to work or not. They had a sneak preview for the film when it was finished. I remember standing in the foyer before the film started, and John Davis and Earl St. John passed me, saying, 'Good luck, Mr Wisdom.' I was terribly nervous. When the film started I didn't watch it. I watched the audience's faces and they were screaming with laughter. Then I stood in the same spot in the foyer as everyone came out. And they were all saying, 'Oh darling, you were wonderful!' It's called the bullshit of showbusiness."

Earl St. John didn't hang about. It was Christmas time and he wanted the film out as a family must-see for the 1953 yuletide season. There was no West End showcase, where the film would normally have expected a six-week run before being sent out across the regions. It was immediately ordered to be put out on the Odeon circuit throughout the country. *Trouble in Store* broke the records in more than 50 of the 67 cinemas in which it played. The critics heaped praise on it. The *Daily Mail* wrote: "What rich deep joy it is to find a master of really top-grade slapstick. Norman Wisdom hits the bull in one and gives the impression that he was born for the cinema." The *Evening Standard* declared: "It is impossible to avoid comparisons with the early Chaplin, for there is much in common between them. It establishes Norman Wisdom as potentially the greatest living comedian of the screen." Wisdom's crowning moment of glory came just a few months later at the British Film Academy Awards where, at the age of 37, Norman Wisdom was awarded the Bafta for Most Promising Newcomer.

Confident now of Wisdom's success and box-office appeal, production speedily got underway for his second film under contract at Pinewood for Rank. In

THE MEN FROM THE MINISTRY – humble civil servant "Norman" rises through the ranks in another comedy of confused identities, *Man of the Moment*, made in 1954.

One Good Turn Norman played an orphan who stays on at the orphanage as an odd job man once he's grown up and recounts his efforts to raise money to buy an old car. Written and directed by the same team who made *Trouble in Store*, the film was a poor imitation of its predecessor, relying heavily on pathos for the humour and falling somewhat short of the expected comic mark. But there are some nice pieces in the film and if points were awarded for giving it your best shot on screen, Norman Wisdom would once again score 10 out of 10.

Norman liked the storyline behind the film from the word go. It also afforded him another opportunity to write and perform a song, hot on the heels of the success of *Don't Laugh at Me*, which was still high in the charts when *One Good Turn* was being made. It also allowed Wisdom to continue to undertake his own stunts – something he had persuaded John Paddy Carstairs to allow him to do early on, during the making of their first film together. In the film a sequence entailed Wisdom driving through an underground drainpipe in a toy car. The set was built

TAKING A BREAK IN FILMING on location for
Man of the Moment (1954).

on a Pinewood soundstage and Carstairs was confident that Wisdom could perform the stunt at some speed without injury. The actor, with great confidence, decided a dummy run to test the length of the drainpipe wasn't necessary and, when Carstairs called "Action", went for the take at full speed. What Wisdom hadn't allowed for was that the floor of the tunnel wasn't flat but curved and as he shot down it at top speed the car turned over and Wisdom found himself sliding along the set with the car on top of him, until they both came to a painful halt.

Carstairs' immediate reaction was to call for an ambulance. Wisdom looked completely out for the count but then finally, having realized that the crew genuinely believed he had injured himself, he started to laugh. The turnover had looked a lot worse than it actually was and Wisdom's physical dexterity had protected him from major harm. Carstairs, more out of relief than anger, lunged at Wisdom when he realized they had all been taken for a ride. Literally. "Don't *ever* pull a gag like that again," Carstairs barked as he stormed off the set.

ON THEIR WAY TO THE SOUND STAGE for the filming of *Man of the Moment* 1954. Jerry Desmonde and Norman (right). Desmonde and Wisdom are seen again (centre) with producer Hugh Stewart and director John Paddy Carstairs. Below, Carstairs in a quiet moment on set.

Wisdom's co-star on the film was Thora Hird, who played the cook at the orphanage. Thora found working with Wisdom one of the happiest of her career: "In this business there are some people who only have to look at you and you laugh. One of my favourites has always been Norman Wisdom. He is such a physical comedian and I used to think he made all his falls look so easy. But anyone in the business will tell you how hard Norman worked to get those movements just right. In *One Good Turn* we had some very funny business to do together, particularly a scene in a railway carriage where a wasp sets upon Norman, and a scene in the kitchen where we are peeling onions and both of us start out crying but end up in hysterics. If you watch the film you would think we weren't acting. Well, I can tell you, we weren't. We really were laughing. Norman just set me off and we went on for ages. We had to re-shoot a couple of times and though John Paddy Carstairs started off looking a little angry,

While making the film, Wisdom tried to give up smoking. So did Thora and the two made a pact to help each other through the difficult times. Both were stressed out filming at Pinewood by day and on stage in shows at night, but they were determined to get through the cravings and give up the cigarettes. Thora thought they'd both cracked it and was feeling quite proud until someone caught Wisdom having a drag between scenes at the back of the set. Thora's revenge was swift: "I went to Pinewood props and asked them to make me up a huge chocolate box and tipped the cleaners to gather together all the cigarette butts they could find from the studio floor that day. I packed them into this chocolate box, tied it with ribbon and had it sent to the London Palladium where Norman was appearing in the evenings. He came on set the next morning boasting about this present, which he assumed was from an adoring fan. It wasn't until he opened it, saw the contents and read the message I had

THE LONG AND THE SHORT OF IT – Norman Wisdom with Hugh Stewart who produced 10 of the star's 12 films made at Pinewood between 1953 and 1966.

written – which I won't repeat here – that he realized he had been rumbled. But even then we shared a laugh. And we have done every time I have seen him since." Thora Hird and Norman Wisdom were reunited at Pinewood more than 40 years later, when a plaque celebrating Wisdom's 50 years in showbusiness was unveiled in his honour in June 1997.

More films were to follow at the rate of one a year and soon working 18 hours days while also trying to raise a family began to take its toll. During the making of *Man of the Moment* in August 1954 Wisdom fell ill. He had, as previously, been filming at Pinewood by day and was on stage at the London Palladium by night. The last show would finish at 11 p.m. and, after changing and the mandatory autographs at the stage door, he would not get back to his home in Arkley, north

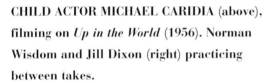

CHILD ACTOR MICHAEL CARIDIA (above), filming on *Up in the World* (1956). Norman Wisdom and Jill Dixon (right) practicing between takes.

west of London, and asleep until the early hours. It was back up again at 5.30 a.m. to get ready and back to Pinewood for make up at 7.30 a.m. and on set by 8 o'clock. Out came the rash of boils – the first sign that all was not well. He carried on filming in great pain for several weeks but once work at Pinewood on *Man of the Moment* was over, admitted himself into St. Stephen's Hospital, where he was diagnosed as suffering from malnutrition. Wisdom had never been late for work but his attention to eating had been far from perfect. There just hadn't been the time to eat and drink properly and the daily punishment he had been putting himself through finally took its toll: "From that time onwards I have always had three square meals a day."

Man of the Moment once again teamed Wisdom with Lana Morris and Jerry Desmonde, with the plot this time revolving around a government filing clerk who

finds himself having to impersonate a high ranking diplomat at an International conference in Geneva. It was the usual mix of slapstick and pathos for which Wisdom was becoming renowned and once again the audiences came out in their droves to see this latest offering.

JOHN PADDY CARSTAIRS in pensive mood, (far left), and discussing the script with Norman, left. Above, Jerry Desmonde and Maureen Swanson during the filming of *Up in the World* (1956).

A new addition to the Wisdom filmmaking team was producer Hugh Stewart. Before World War II, Stewart had been an editor for Gaumont-British and, at Denham Studios, had worked for some top directors, including Michael Powell and Alfred Hitchcock on his first version of *The Man Who Knew Too Much* (1934). Stewart spent most of the war working for the Army Film Unit and was based at Pinewood. He spent some time out in Africa and on his return co-directed the highly regarded *Tunisian Victory* with Roy Boulting in 1944. After the war, Hugh Stewart began producing films, first the 1949 musical *Trottie True*, and set up his own production company, Europa, under the auspices of the Rank Organisation.

Stewart had throughout his early years been a great admirer of silent comedy, particularly the likes of Charlie Chaplin and Buster Keaton and he was therefore

A PUBLICITY SHOT of a relaxed Norman Wisdom, taken during the making of *A Stitch in Time* (1963).

delighted to land the job of producing *Man of the Moment*, the first of 10 Wisdom films he would be involved with over the coming decade, as well as the three Morecambe and Wise big-screen outings of the mid 1960s, which were also made at Pinewood: "I'd always adored the Laurel and Hardy, Keystone cops comedy. I didn't realize it until a certain time, but instinctively it had always been my ambition to get back to making films with a minimum of dialogue. Norman Wisdom was a great popular success because he represents a very special kind of indomitable spirit that says, 'I'm as good as you lot, I have a bath every Saturday.' It's childish but he does represent something uncrushable."

Stewart was a great encourager. Wisdom needed assurance that his work would be a success. He had hit the ground running with *Trouble in Store* and was keen to ensure repeated success. But with any classic clown comes some doubt and Stewart was there to help assuage the insecurities; "The first thing I had to do was convince him that the thing was OK; he'd start off deeply suspicious. He was very insecure. He'd done everything on his own. He'd started from scratch; all his achievements were entirely his own effort and he needed a lot of convincing."

Stewart assembled a team he could work with. Wisdom's films were either directed by John Paddy Carstairs, or, later, Bob Asher. Stewart recognized that Wisdom and Carstairs had a bond, a mutual understanding of each other's talents. The same instinct was not present with Bob Asher, but that didn't matter, because Asher was, according to Stewart: "… a brooding, Jewish talent, terrified of lots of things. He was a mass of inhibitions. Very good for comedy! He understood Norman and Norman liked him."

It seemed like the scene was set for a raft of successful films from the Rank/Stewart/Wisdom stable. And indeed it was. *Up in the World*, the story of a window cleaner who forms a friendship with a wealthy but unhappy boy, followed in 1956 and *Just My Luck*, with Wisdom as a jeweller's assistant who gets involved in horse racing, came along in 1957. Neither were classics but they kept the audiences rolling in. It was while making *Just My Luck* that Norman Wisdom met Marilyn Monroe, who was at Pinewood filming *The Prince and the Showgirl* with Laurence Olivier: "I was introduced to Marilyn, though she didn't really know who I was. Then one day she came onto the set of my film and watched me and I could

NORMAN WISDON SHOWING
AN ARRAY of "talents" during
his 1956 comedy *Up in the World*.

PROFILE

J. P. Carstairs

John Paddy Carstairs was born in 1910, son of the silent screen comic actor Nelson Keys and brother of producer Anthony Nelson Keys. After beginning his career as an assistant cameraman, he graduated to film direction with several pre-Second World War offerings including *Holiday's End*, which was made at Pinewood during the Studios' first year of production in 1937. Carstairs directed a further pre-war Pinewood film, *Night Ride*, the same year.

After the war, Carstairs found himself directing middle-budget crowd pleasers such as *The Chiltern Hundreds* (1949). In 1953, he was given charge of Norman Wisdom's first star vehicle under Rank, *Trouble in Store*. The film was a huge hit and Carstairs gained the reputation of being able to steer young comedy talent to box-office success. He continued to work with Wisdom and also early comedy vehicles for the likes of Frankie Howerd, Tommy Steele, Charlie Drake and Bob Monkhouse. Carstairs' relationship with Wisdom was often fraught, with the two talents at loggerheads on set as well as off. Eventually, after making *The Square Peg* in 1958, Carstairs turned his back on making further films with Wisdom.

A talented artist, Carstairs also wrote humorous novels, and quit filmmaking in 1962 to concentrate on his writing and painting. He also produced shows for television including episodes of *The Saint*, and the pilot episode of the 1963 BBC sitcom hit, *Meet the Wife*. He died in 1970 at the age of 60.

hear her screaming with laughter. A couple of days later, I was walking down through Pinewood from my dressing room and she was coming the other way. When she saw me, she dashed over, grabbed my arm and kissed me. Did my reputation the world of good that did."

Wisdom's next film, his sixth in as many years since he signed his contract, was to be his last with director John Paddy Carstairs. Ironically it was to be a big hit for all concerned even though it meant the parting of the ways for Carstairs and Wisdom. *The Square Peg* was written by Jack Davies and starred Norman as an incompetent army recruit who finds that he is the double of a prominent German general. The film was made at Pinewood in 1958 and was to be the first occasion that Wisdom took a dual role in one of his films. It was also the first film in which Edward Chapman starred as Norman's frustrated boss, Mr Grimsdale.

When Carstairs heard that Davies's script called on Wisdom to play the German officer too, he flatly refused, insisting that the role of the officer should be an acting one and not played for comedy. Davies knew Wisdom was the man for the part and went over the director's head to producer Hugh Stewart who liked the idea and overruled his director. Carstairs didn't say a word. Neither did he say much on set when they came to film the scene a few weeks later. Carstairs called "Action" and walked away, making a point of staying behind the camera. Wisdom continued delivering his lines with the comedic German accent. The director called "Cut", walked up to Wisdom, put his arms around him and kissed him on the cheek. No words of apology were uttered, they didn't need to be.

Hugh Stewart was relieved that director and lead actor were friends again. He knew how demanding both could be and knew that's where their respective talents came from: "My main problem was to curb Norman's enthusiasm, and keep the script to the right length. He was a great contributor and learned with every script, so that eventually he would work with Jack Davies very closely." *The Square Peg* was a huge hit and did big business across the world, particularly in the Soviet Union.

After six outings, John Paddy Carstairs called time on directing Norman Wisdom films and returned to making suspense thrillers for television, coming back to the cinema to direct films for both Tommy Steele and Charlie Drake.

THE LAUGHTER MAKERS – director John Paddy Carstairs, producer Hugh Stewart and Norman Wisdom.

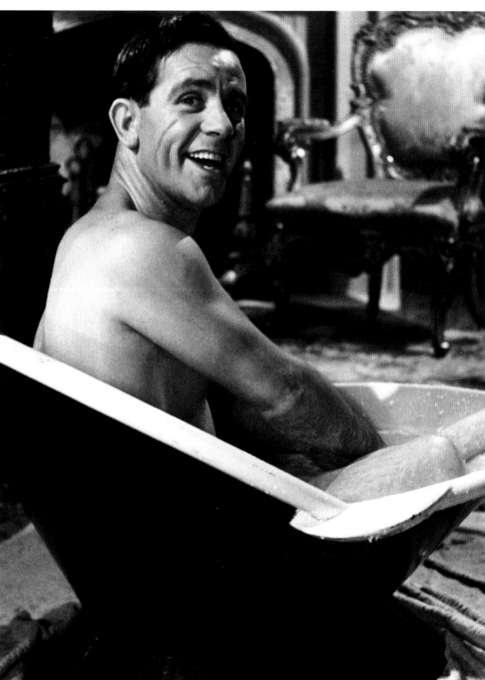

As Wisdom's seven year contract came to an end there were further comedy outings; the whimsical *Follow a Star* (1959) about a shy talented singer who lets a fading musical star use his voice, and *The Bulldog Breed* (1960), with Wisdom playing a grocer's boy who joins the navy. The slapstick adventures continued, with Wisdom still performing his own stunts in circumstances that became even more unlikely throughout each plot. However, although some critics were beginning to tire of his films, the audiences were not and though by 1960 his contract with Rank had expired, they were still keen for Wisdom to keep churning out more of the same. Wisdom always speaks highly of his relationship with the Rank Organisation: "I was quite free to do stage work, my agent would have seen to that. Once I had done a film I was free to do anything I liked. My contract was for a film a year for seven years. Once the contract was up I don't think they worried about it time-wise, and I just continued working for them from then on, film by film."

Of his 1960s films, probably the funniest was Wisdom's next production, *On the Beat*, made at Pinewood in 1962. This time around Wisdom plays a car park attendant at Scotland Yard who yearns to become a policeman. The film is busy with Wisdom, who was now in his late-40s, as fast and frenetic as ever.

Once again, he played Norman, further blurring the edges between the man and the character, which Wisdom has no regrets about: "It was just accepted from the start. I was known stage-wise as Norman and by that time I'd done television as well, so they thought they'd stick to the same name. It gave a sort of continuity to the films." *On the Beat* also allowed Wisdom a further opportunity to play a dual role, also taking on the part of Giudo Napolitani, a camp Italian hairdresser whose boutique is a "front" for some dodgy dealings. A sterling cast, including veteran actor David Lodge, and other British character actors Eric Barker, Raymond Huntley, Dilys Laye and Terence Alexander, joined in for the ride.

Wisdom returned as Norman Pitkin for *A Stitch in Time* the following year – this time as a butcher's lad who ends up in hospital and falls in love with a nurse. Once again a cast of British comedy film regulars joined Wisdom, with Edward Chapman back as Mr Grimsdale, and once again Wisdom insisted on performing even more outrageous slapstick stunts. And, even though it looked to some as if Wisdom was running out of steam and that his films were really no longer in vogue,

NORMAN WISDOM TOOK on dual roles as General Schreiber and Norman Pitkin, in the 1958 comedy on a wartime theme, *The Square Peg* (opposite).

PLAYING FOR PATHOS once again in the aptly named *The Bulldog Breed* (1960).

A Stitch in Time became his biggest money spinner, breaking records at many of the cinemas it opened at and even, for a short while, knocking *From Russia with Love* off it's number one position.

Filming *A Stitch in Time* almost knocked out Wisdom himself. There is a scene in the film where Norman is encased from head-to-toe in plaster as he plays a dummy victim for the St. John's Ambulance Brigade. In the middle of the "exercise" the ambulance men realize they're late for a football match and rush away to watch the game, leaving Norman on a stretcher. Pitkin manages to get himself off the stretcher and into a wheelchair and … well yes; it's down some stairs, through a wall, onto the top of the ambulance and so on. The gag is a long one but worth the wait as after a variety of mishaps and further trips and slips, Pitkin ends up on the floor of the ward and a doctor walks past, looks down at the plaster-clad patient and says: "Nurse, what's this man doing out of bed?".

The scene took several days to film. Bearing in mind the level of stunt work required, the director Bob Asher approached Wisdom and insisted that he allow a qualified stuntman to undertake the more difficult parts of the scene – particularly riding down a flight of stairs in a wheelchair while in plaster and for the crash through the fake wall and onto a moving ambulance. Wisdom was adamant he was doing it. Asher was adamant he was not, and filming began with a stuntman who performed the stunt perfectly – rolling down the stairs, crashing through the wall, onto the ambulance roof, but then fell of the ambulance roof, hit the ground and broke his arm, and was whisked off to a real hospital to have his injuries dealt with.

Asher was in a quandary. Cast and crew were in place but he didn't have the shot and he didn't have a stuntman to film it. He reluctantly gave permission for Wisdom to try the shot out as Norman recalls: "It worked like a dream. Every bit of that sequence you see in the film is me, even the back of my head as I go bumping down the stairs. To get the full impact, the special effects department rigged up rails so that the wheelchair would hurtle down the stairs, tilt up, and catapult me out at the right speed to meet the ambulance." Asher got his shot. Norman got through the shooting and the scene is another Wisdom classic moment.

Norman Wisdom's time at Pinewood was soon to be up. Offers of more stage work both in Britain and on Broadway, along with numerous shows on television

A TRIO OF BEHIND-THE-SCENES images from the making of Norman Wisdom's 1962 star comedy *On the Beat*, showing director Robert Asher taking the star and cast through the steps of a big chase scene.

RARE COLOUR IMAGES of the 1963 black and white Wisdom comedy, *A Stitch in Time* – with stooge Jerry Desmonde playing the upper class Sir Hector (right), about to have his pomposity pricked once again by the accident-prone but kind-hearted Norman Pitkin.

EDWARD CHAPMAN PLAYS the long-suffering Mr Grimsdale (left), a role he took on three times in the five films he made with Norman Wisdom.

ALL DRAGGED UP – Norman Wisdom poses as a nurse in *A Stitch in Time* (1963).

SHOOTING ON THE SET of Norman Wisdom's penultimate Pinewood outing, and his first colour film, *The Early Bird*, in 1965. Once again, he played the character Norman Pitkin, this time his role was that of a local milkman.

and a young family meant that something would shortly have to give. And the times – and the moods of audiences – were changing. There was a shift away from the previous popularity of the slapstick mayhem and innocence that could be found within Wisdom's films. The 1960s brought a new permissiveness and audiences grew more attuned to the nudge-nudge seaside postcard humour of the increasingly popular *Carry On* film series, which since 1958 had been clocking up at least one title a year at Pinewood.

In *The Early Bird* (1965), Wisdom plays a milkman who becomes embroiled in a delivery-round war between companies. The film has some wonderful set pieces in it, using Pinewood's gardens and car parks to great effect as Norman creates havoc and wrecks everything in his path. The film was long and the pathos was by now wearing a bit thin. Edward Chapman was back as Mr Grimsdale, but the films, now in full colour and glorious widescreen, were beginning to lose their magic. That was no reflection on Wisdom, who had just hit 50. But youthful innocence was less easy to accept in a man in middle age and now his naivety almost bordered on playing the fool – and Norman Wisdom was never a fool.

His last Pinewood film was *Press for Time*, made in 1966. Wisdom went out with a bang, playing a corner-of-the-street newspaper seller, who is possibly the illegitimate grandson of the Prime Minister and who is sent off to be a journalist in a run down seaside resort where it is hoped he can cause no harm. As well as playing the lead role, Wisdom also played many supporting cameos as members of his own family through the generations – akin to Alec Guinness's portrayal of the D'Ascoyne family in the Ealing classic *Kind Hearts and Coronets* made some 20 years earlier.

After 14 years on the payroll, a seven-year contract for Rank, 12 films and a British Academy Award, Norman Wisdom hung up his film-making boots at Pinewood. The comedian continued to make a few films both at home and abroad, appearing in *What's Good for the Goose* (1969) and *Double X* (1992) in Britain, and a highly acclaimed performance in *The Night They Raided Minsky's* (1968) in America, for which he received great reviews.

In 1995 Norman Wisdom was awarded the OBE for services to comedy, and in 1997 he returned to Pinewood to unveil a plaque in his name in the Studios'

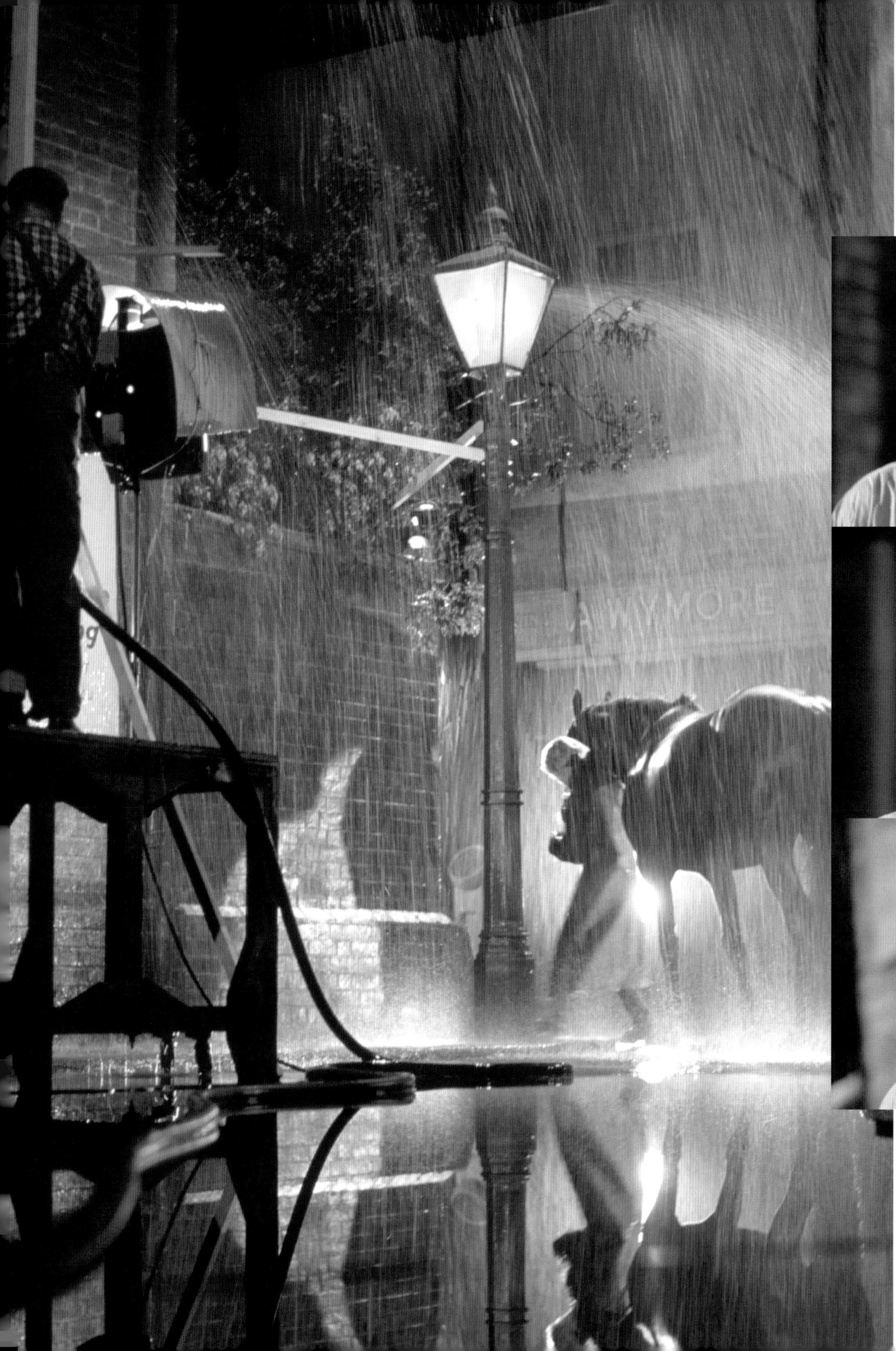

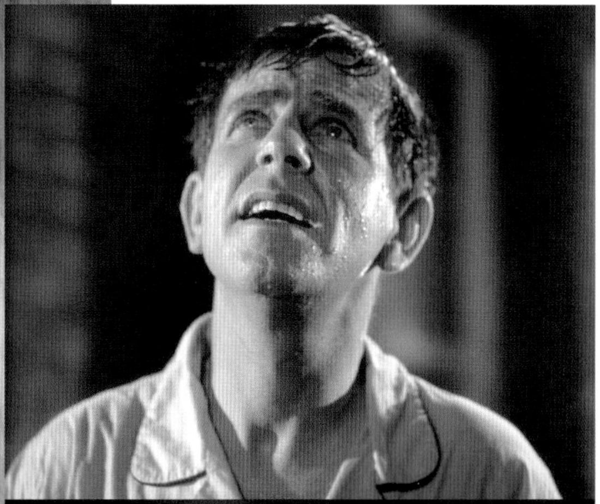

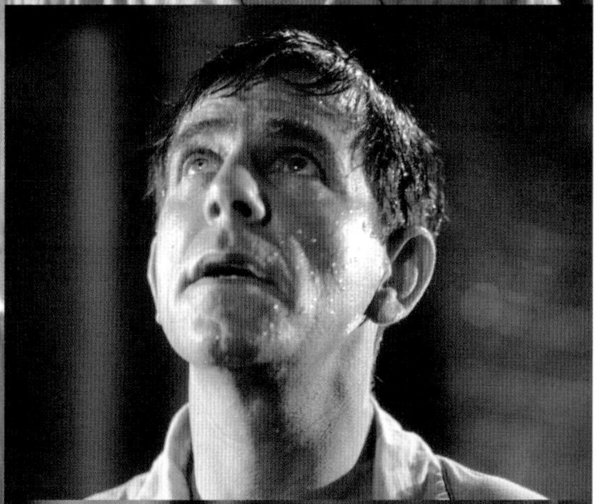

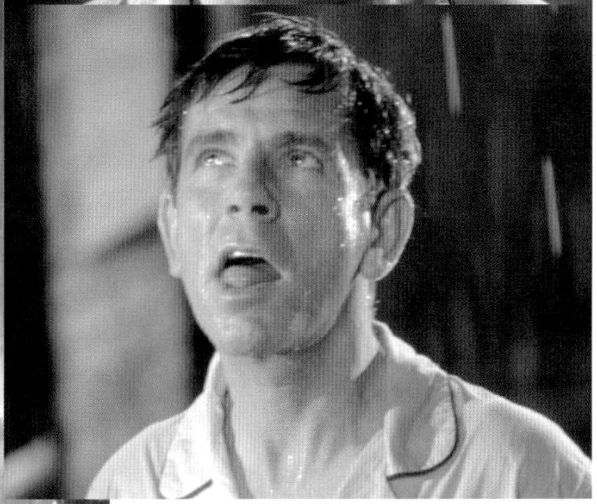

GOING UP IN THE WORLD AGAIN - as Norman Wisdom films a sequence in the last of his 12 Pinewood-based films, *Press for Time*, made at the Studios in 1966. Wisdom played no less than five different characters in the film, here being hoisted up for a slapstick fall, he is local newspaper seller, Norman Shields.

Hall of Fame, marking his 50th anniversary in showbusiness. Four years later, Norman Wisdom OBE was afforded the rare distinction for a comedian of receiving a Knighthood. The man who had started, like many of the characters in his films, as an errand boy for Liptons riding round on his bike delivering groceries, was now at Buckingham Place to receive his honour from Her Majesty the Queen. The much publicized news footage of Wisdom performing one of his trademark trips as he walked away from the kneeling stool in front of the Queen left the assembled audience laughing and the Queen smiling. If it had been anywhere less grand there is no doubt that he might also have barked out: "Mr Grimsdale!" too.

On his 90th birthday in February 2005, Sir Norman Wisdom officially retired from showbusiness. He leaves behind him a vast legacy of laughter across the mediums of television, stage, radio and – especially – film, over 50 years since he first set foot on a sound stage at Pinewood Studios, where so much of that laughter was created and is still fondly remembered.

BETWEEN TAKES of filming *Press for Time* in 1966, Norman Wisdom pictured below in drag as the lead character's mother Emily and, bottom, with director Robert Asher.

Carrying On

ON SET BETWEEN TAKES during the filming of *Carry On Spying* in 1963, (above, left to right) Barbara Windsor, Dilys Laye, Charles Hawtrey, Bernard Cribbins and Kenneth Williams. Opposite, Kenneth Connor and his cohort of incompetent recruits, watched over by a frustrated Bill Owen, in the first film of the long-running series, *Carry On Sergeant* (1958).

Something old, something new, something borrowed, and quite a bit blue. The *Carry On* film series is a record-breaking body of work, a production feat which is still unequalled in British or international cinema – some 30 films in 20 years with a 31st film made when the series was unsuccessfully revived over a decade later.

Series producer Peter Rogers started his career as a writer, becoming a local reporter for the *Kentish Express*. By night he would write plays in the hope that one day he would see his words performed on stage. Soon that was to happen but it was not a successful foray into the dramatic world. His first play ran for seven days, the second for 10. The one that lasted longer was a comedy and Peter took that as a portent that perhaps he should stick to laughter makers from now on.

Rogers returned to journalism, becoming the film editor for *World Press News*. Because of its proximity to Fleet Street, many film parties were held at the Savoy and it was there that Peter met Betty Evelyn Box. When he saw her across a crowded room he was not to know that she was already well established within the British film industry. Betty was there with her brother Sydney, who struck an instant rapport with Rogers and who asked him to work as a writer on his forthcoming film, *Holiday Camp*, a post-war comedy with dark undertones to be made at Gainsborough Studios, which the Box family ran.

As Rogers worked more for Sydney, he became closer to Betty. They moved in to a flat together in St. John's Wood and were quietly married on Christmas Eve 1948 at Marylebone Registry office, just Peter and Betty and two witnesses. The moment the wedding was over, both returned to work. Betty was involved in two productions at the time, *Marry Me!* and *Don't Ever Leave Me*. And they didn't. Peter and Betty remained together for 50 years, until her passing in January 1999.

When Gainsborough closed, Betty moved to Pinewood and picked up making films – highly successful films – where she had left off. Peter was not so fortunate

and didn't find the early 1950s as easy. He didn't make the move full time to Pinewood initially, carrying on working at Beaconsfield. It was while he was there in the mid-1950s that Peter decided that he would follow in Betty's sensible footsteps and find himself a director with whom he could team up and work on future productions. Betty had done this most successfully with Ralph Thomas. Peter noticed a young man who had been editing Betty's films. He knew that the films' popularity were due in no small part to the work of a good editor. The editor was Gerald Thomas, the brother of Ralph Thomas, who was Betty's director and who himself had started off as an editor before taking on the mantle of directing.

Gerald Thomas had originally wanted to become a doctor. The War put paid to that ambition and he returned from hostilities to a job in the cutting rooms of Two Cities Films at Denham Studios. He was the assistant editor on *Hamlet* (1948) and *The October Man* (1948) before editing the historical melodrama, *Madness of the Heart*, the next year. He edited the hit film *Doctor in the House* for Betty Box and went to Hollywood to edit Disney's *The Sword and the Rose* before returning to edit Ralph Thomas's *Above Us the Waves*. By the mid-1950s, Gerald Thomas was regarded as one of Britain's best film editors. But he was not a director and Peter Rogers had problems persuading the powers that be that he should be afforded the opportunity of directing his own production.

The pair's big break came with Peter's script of Arthur Hailey's story, *Time Lock*, in which a father accidentally locks his son inside a bank vault over a weekend. Rogers made the film for just £30,000 (less than £500,000 today). The 73-minute suspenser was a sudden and unexpected hit and allowed Rogers the leverage to bring in Thomas as his directing partner on future productions. It was to be a partnership that lasted for 35 years and many dozens of films. Thirty-one of those films were *Carry Ons*.

The original idea for *Carry on Sergeant*, the first *Carry On* film, wasn't a comedy at all. Based on a romantic drama, *The Bull Boys* by R. F. Delderfield, it told the story of two ballet dancers conscripted to the army. The rights to the story rested with Sydney Box, who had commissioned Delderfield to work on an outline back in 1955. Box tried to resurrect the idea in 1957 but couldn't find anyone interested in financing the film and so handed it over to Peter Rogers.

PROFILE

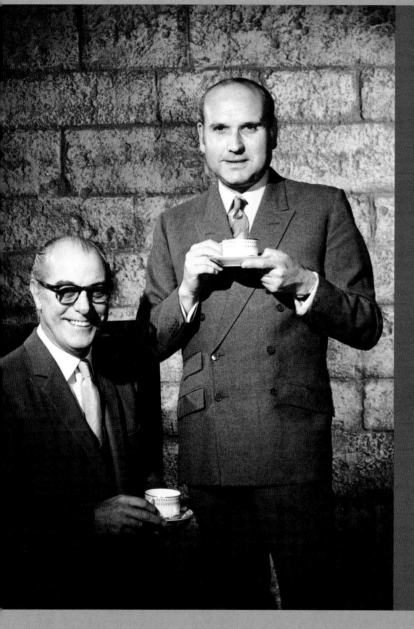

Peter Rogers & Gerald Thomas

Born one of twins on 20 February 1914, Peter Rogers began his career as a journalist, moving to the theatre and onto scriptwriting for radio and then film, for the Rank Organisation, after the Second World War. On Christmas Eve 1949, Peter married fellow film producer Betty Box.

In the 1950s Peter made films for the Children's Film Foundation, and produced some highly effective thrillers before turning his hand to comedy. His production of R. F. Delderfield's *The Bull Boys* was an instant hit under its film title *Carry On Sergeant*. Cinema history was born, as were another 30 *Carry On* films, countless television series and a long-running stage show. Hardly surprising, then, that Peter Rogers became known as Mr *Carry On*.

For most of the films that Rogers produced, he chose one director to work with him. Born on 10 December 1920, Gerald Thomas started his career as an assistant editor. The brother of director Ralph Thomas, he progressed to second unit direction before joining Rogers to direct Children's Film Foundation productions and solo features such as the masterfully tense thriller *Time Lock*, in 1957.

Along came the *Carry Ons*, which assured Gerald Thomas a place in cinema history. Actors loved him because he was never demanding and his editing expertise ensured that only what was needed in the can was ever filmed, keeping production costs and shooting schedules down to the minimum.

Gerald Thomas died on 9 November 1993.

The script by now was far too long, running to around 200 pages for a 90-minute film, twice more than would normally be expected. The script was equally as heavy in its treatment of the subject and Rogers immediately identified that the film needed a judicious edit and a deft comic touch. He visited several comedy writers – including Eric Sykes and Spike Milligan – asking if they were interested in the project. They all said no. In September 1957, screenwriter John Antrobus was commissioned to rewrite *The Bull Boys* into a filmable script. Rogers paid Antrobus £750 (more than £10,000 today) but was still unhappy with the script.

Finally, he handed the project over to Norman Hudis. Hudis, a former PR man for Rank, at Pinewood from the early 1950s, had turned his hand to script

writing in the mid-1950s and was already on Rogers' books, having successfully penned two Tommy Steele vehicles, *The Tommy Steele Story* (1957) for Anglo Amalgamated, and *The Duke Wore Jeans* (1958) for Peter Rogers' company Insignia. It was Hudis who came up with the theme that was to become central to the series' success – that of taking a well-known British institution, such as the army, police, schools and so on – place a bunch of incompetents inside, allow them to mess everything up, then come out winners at the end, proving the underdogs can come first. Add in a dash of sentimentality and love interest and that was the recipe for the perfect *Carry On*. Of course no one knew this at the time. *Carry On Sergeant* was to be just another film. There was no talk of sequels or a series. Rogers was just happy to get the film moving.

SCENES FROM *Carry On Constable*, the fourth film in the series, which went into production in late 1959, filming at both Pinewood and "on location" on the nearby streets of Ealing, west London. Among the raw police recruits were (above, left to right) Kenneth Connor, Kenneth Williams and Leslie Phillips.

EARLY *CARRY ON* TEAM STARLET and acclaimed British comedy actress Liz Fraser (left), who appeared here in *Carry On Cruising*, the sixth film in the series and the first to be produced in colour. The *Carry Ons* never went far on location and certainly never abroad. For *Carry On Cruising*, exterior shots of the cruise liner – supposedly touring the Med – were filmed, without cast, at Southampton docks (above). Interiors for the films were shot at Pinewood.

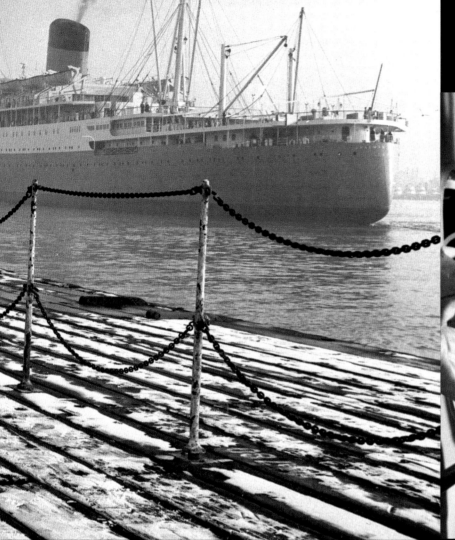

SID JAMES (above, centre) is Wellington Crowther, Captain of the *SS Happy Wanderer* in *Carry On Cruising*. Either side of him are Kenneth Williams (left) as Leonard Marjoribanks, and Kenneth Connor (right) as ship's doctor, Arthur Binn.

JUST A LITTLE PRICK! Lance Percival (right, centre) as the ship's cook, receiving treatment for seasickness! Percival replaced regular team member Charles Hawtrey after a falling out with the film's producer.

CAR PARK ONE AT PINEWOOD, doubling for the home of the taxi business central to the storyline in *Carry On Cabby*, **filmed at the studios between March and May 1963. Above right, the stars of the film, Sid James and Hattie Jacques as Charlie and Peggy Hawkins.**

Carry On Sergeant was supposed to be filmed at Beaconsfield Studios but that was full with filming for the hit TV series, *Ivanhoe*. Rogers decided to go to Pinewood instead. His distributors were horrified. Not only was Pinewood regarded as the most expensive studio in the country to film in, they argued that since Peter's film was being made for Anglo Amalgamated and was to be released through the ABC cinema circuit, he should make his film at their studios, which were at Elstree. Rogers hadn't worked at Elstree but knew Pinewood. His wife, Betty Box, was very happy at Pinewood, and he saw no reason not to join her there. Many in the industry, including some at Pinewood, were not as keen. Rogers insisted he could bring his film in at a budget of less than £80,000 at a time when even his wife's films such as *Doctor in the House* had been pared back to the bone and made for £125,000 – and that had been five years previously. Rogers ignored the snobs who said his film would look cheap and do no good for the reputation of a studio like

Pinewood, booked the space and got on with making his movie.

Filming for *Carry On Sergeant* began at the Queen's Barracks, Guildford, on 24 March 1958, with a cast that included Bob Monkhouse, Kenneth Connor, Kenneth Williams, Hattie Jacques and three of the stars from the hugely successful ITV sitcom, *The Army Game*, William Hartnell, Charles Hawtrey and Norman Rossington.

The Army Game, which revolved around the life of lazy conscripts, had already been running for 39 episodes by the time *Sergeant* was ready for release. The

TWO GLAMCAB DRIVERS, Carol Shelley and Amanda Barrie, left, and, below, Kenneth Connor in a publicity shot for *Carry On Cabby* (1963).

show had started on television in June 1957, and there were many who were concerned that a film along similar lines would lack appeal. Why pay to go to the cinema to see a film with a similar cast and a similar plot, doing similar things, when one can as easily watch it in the comfort of one's own home, for nothing, once a week? *Sergeant*'s scriptwriter Norman Hudis recognized the concern: "I recall many saying, while we were filming *Sergeant*, 'Who'll pay to see a khaki comedy with *The Army Game* free on TV?' Believe me, I'm not crowing over those who were wrong. I've been superbly wrong myself – most recently when I declared, 'No one will want to see the eighth remake of *Titanic*'."

During production on the film, Rogers sent his daily rushes up to London for viewing by Anglo Amalgamated bosses Nat Cohen and Stuart Levy. The phone rang almost immediately, with Nat Cohen demanding to know what on earth Peter thought that he was doing and why wasn't the film funny. Rogers didn't worry: "I realized they had never seen rushes before. Later I discovered that they'd never

PROFILE

Talbot Rothwell

Master of the double entendre, Talbot Rothwell, wrote 20 *Carry On* films, along with several television specials and classic comedy shows such as *Up Pompeii*, for Frankie Howerd.

Born on 12 November 1916, he held a series of different jobs from town clerk to police officer and then pilot. He started writing during WWII, while in a German POW camp after being shot down over Norway. While incarcerated, Rothwell met and befriended future comedy actor and *Carry On* stalwart, Peter Butterworth. After the war, Rothwell returned to England and was soon writing for the likes of The Crazy Gang, Arthur Askey, Ted Ray and Terry-Thomas.

In the early 1960s, *Carry On* films producer Peter Rogers, looking for a new writer following the departure of Norman Hudis, allowed Rothwell to turn a script idea, Call Me A Cab, into *Carry On Cabby*. Off Rothwell went for the next 12 years and another 19 films, before retiring from writing through poor health. Rothwell's bawdy style was well suited to the films and their casts. His scripts took the films and the series into new territory – bordering on the risqué but never the vulgar – and it is the quality of his writing that is generally perceived as one of the main reasons that the series lasted so long. As well as the *Carry On* films, Rothwell also wrote several of the shows when the series transferred to the small screen for a while during the mid-1970s.

The king of the double meaning was awarded the OBE in 1977 for his services to cinema. He died on 28 February 1981.

seen a 'fine cut' either – that is the finished film before the music or sound effects track had been added. I stopped sending them the rushes and told them to wait for the finished film. They either trusted me or they didn't. But they didn't ask me for them again."

Filming on *Carry On Sergeant* was quick. With shots in Guildford complete, the cast and crew decamped back to Pinewood for all the interior shots. Within six weeks, Rogers and Thomas had all the footage in the can. The film was edited and shown at Pinewood to the staff and management of the Studios, including many who had worked on the production. The showing was packed, standing room only, less from an interest in the film and more to see whether or not Rogers had pulled off making a "cheap" film in a "Rolls Royce" studios.

Carry On Sergeant was inexpensive. Its costs did come in at under £80,000 – just £1 million today – but Rogers was angry at suggestions that because it was inexpensive to make, the film itself was cheap. Nevertheless, he was apprehensive about what reaction to the film might be: "I didn't know what they were thinking and how they would react. For all I knew they would criticize and condemn the film just for the sheer sake of it. But, they didn't stop laughing. The whole way through the film there was laughter and that was good enough for me. I immediately sent the film to Anglo Amalgamated in London. The reaction was the same when they showed it at their offices. The film became one of the top three box-office successes of the year and no one could deny that it was a huge hit. At the Last Night of the Proms at the Royal Albert Hall that summer the conductor for the evening was Sir Malcolm Sargent and at the end someone held up a huge banner on which had been daubed Carry On Sargent!"

ALL ADRIFT IN *Carry On Jack*, **which was made at Pinewood Studios and at nearby Frensham Ponds in the autumn of 1963. Left to right, Bernard Cribbins, Juliet Mills, Charles Hawtrey and Kenneth Williams.**

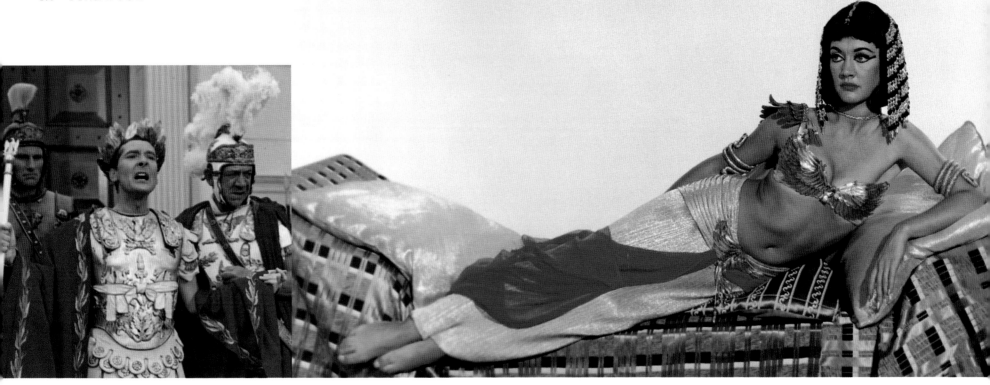

KENNETH WILLIAMS (above) as Caesar in *Carry On Cleo* **(1964), with Amanda Barrie (right) as the Egyptian Queen with the poisonous asp – a role originally intended for Barbara Windsor, who had left the series temporarily to appear on Broadway.**

"INFAMY, IMFAMY!" They've all got in for him, opposite, as Kenneth Williams' Caesar meets his end. While, below, Sid James is Brutus, in *Carry On Cleo***, filmed during the summer of 1964.**

There will always be those who would argue that the *Carry On* series actually began with the second film, *Carry On Nurse*. There had been no intention with *Sergeant* for it to be anything other than a one-off comedy. Its success prompted more of the same and it is in *Nurse* that the foundations for a regular cast of actors assembling to make films on similar themes with *Carry On* at the beginning of each title, became a reality. Certainly, Rogers could see the potential. Although less frequent, his wife Betty Box had had similar success in her *Doctor* series of films, producing three in four years. They were all on the same medical theme. Rogers knew the answer lay in gathering the same faces and putting them into similar comic situations as previously but in different environments. *Carry On Nurse* transplanted the best comedy talent from *Sergeant* to carry on all over again. That included Kenneth Williams, Kenneth Connor, Charles Hawtrey and everyone's favourite harridan matron, Hattie Jacques, who across the series would make the role her own.

It wasn't Peter Rogers' intention to go straight into *Carry On Nurse*. He approached his bosses with a drama based around life and death in a tuberculosis ward. There was humour within, as the patients' lives unfolded and Rogers was keen on the idea. The line from Anglo was: "Give us another *Carry On*, and give

BARBARA WINDSOR is secret agent Daphne Honeybutt in her first series outing, *Carry On Spying* **in 1964. She remained with the series for a further eight big-screen offerings.**

us one fast." So Norman Hudis took the idea and with the help of his wife, Rita, herself a nurse who later became a consultant on the American hit TV comedy *M*A*S*H,* set about writing the first medical *Carry On.*

Filming began at Pinewood on 3 November 1958. New to the cast was Joan Sims as an accident-prone nurse, and Leslie Phillips as Jack Bell (whose "ding-dong, you're not wrong" alongside his fruity "Hallo" inadvertently became the actor's comedy catchphrases for years to come). For most of the cast, filming *Nurse* meant spending days and weeks in bed. Leslie Phillips recalled the irony: "It was an extraordinary experience making *Carry On Nurse.* I would get up in the morning, out of bed, get dressed, leave my home in Mill Hill, go to Pinewood, take my clothes off, put my pyjamas on and get back into bed. At the end of the day's shooting, I would reverse the whole process, go home, have some dinner, and then – because we had to be back on set early – go back to bed again. This went on for five weeks. We did have great fun, though, making the film. There was a great deal of laughter around. It wasn't like a hospital at all. Kenny Williams was the funniest. He had me literally in stitches."

Stitching scenes back together after the censor had got at them was an on-going battle between Rogers and the British Board of Film Censors throughout the lifetime of the *Carry On* series. Rogers wanted the early *Carry Ons* to bear "U" certificates to make them universally available for all to see and to increase audience numbers by families attending together. After a "U" certificate in those days came the "A" certificate, which stood for "Adult" and meant that the film might contain material that was unsuitable for children. Young people were allowed entry to an "A" certificate film but had to be accompanied by an adult.

Rogers and Thomas employed clever tactics to get favoured jokes past the censor: "We would intentionally film a couple of jokes that we knew we couldn't get passed by the censor. We would visit him at his Soho office, pretend to be aggravated by the proposed cuts and then bargain with him. Most of the time he ended up taking out the gags we had intentionally put in to distract him and leave the ones we genuinely wanted left alone. It worked most of the time but not always." And with *Nurse* and all its hospital bedpan humour and life in a men's ward, it would prove much harder to escape the censor's scalpel: "There is one

CARRY ON SPYING was filmed at Pinewood during February and March 1964. Boasting one of the series' best scripts, the *Bond*-esque spoof proved a great hit. The cast and crew (right) have every reason to be smiling.

CHARLES HAWTREY, right, relishes his role as Big Heap, while below, Sid James as The Rumpo Kid, looks a little less happy, during the filming of *Carry On Cowboy* (1965).

ALL IN A LATHER is Angela Douglas as Annie Oakley, while below, Sid James leads the charge as cast and crew shoot *Carry On Cowboy* on Pinewood's back lot during the summer of 1965.

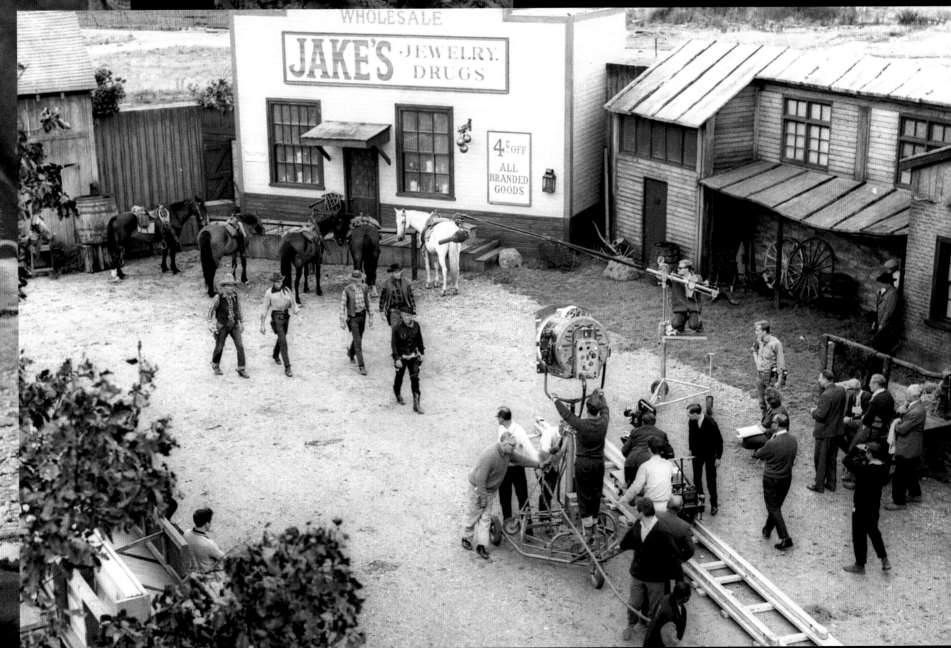

EVERYONE'S FAVOURITE VAMP, Fenella Fielding, made her only *Carry On* lead, and indeed her last appearance in the series, as Virula Watt, in the 1966 gothic entry, *Carry On Screaming!* She had appeared once before in a cameo role in *Carry On Regardless* five years previously.

scene in *Nurse* where Kenneth Connor is arguing with the nurses who want to take off the bottom half of his pyjamas for a bed bath. Eventually they manage to do it and he hops quickly back into bed covering himself over with the blankets. One of the nurses then says, 'Never known anyone make such a fuss about such a little thing!' Kenneth is supposed to smile and then catch on to what she had said, and look down, dismayed, under the covers. The censor wasn't having any of that. He said we could keep the joke so long as we didn't keep the shot of Kenneth looking under the covers. I acceded to his request. We got the best laugh. Though we could have had two." Rogers was laughing all the way to the bank. Once again he had brought in a film at the very low price of around £80,000 and this time the film was to become the highest grossing film in Britain in 1959.

By now, Anglo Amalgamated knew they were on to a good thing and they naturally demanded more of the same from Rogers. He put other projects on hold as he planned not one or two but up to six more titles in the series, to be filmed at roughly two films a year, using, where possible a regular cast of actors – a form of repertory for cinema.

Carry On Teacher was the third film in the series and took a gentle sideswipe at another famed British institution, education. With Norman Hudis still at the helm of the writing there were lots of slapstick gags as the children ran riot while the poor headmaster, Mr Wakefield (played by veteran comedian Ted Ray), tried to salvage his teaching reputation and those of the staff around him. It was to be Ray's only *Carry On* film appearance. Much as though Rogers wanted him to join the cast, legal wrangling over his contract for another film company meant Ray had to be dropped.

There was now a space in the cast for *Carry On Constable*, made at Pinewood and on the streets of Ealing, late in 1959. A newcomer to the series was already an old hand at the film game and was to prove a major player throughout the rest of the *Carry On*'s golden years. Sid James, fresh from dozens of films, replaced Ted Ray but more importantly had come hot foot from his success on *Hancock's Half Hour* on BBC radio and television. The *Carry On* audiences welcomed Sid and his lusty laugh to their collective bosom, his endearing quality over the next 15 years ensuring he would become dubbed the "father of the *Carry Ons*".

As Sid joined the team, Leslie Phillips left, concerned that he would become typecast if he stayed in the series much longer, which didn't stop one film critic giving him a mauling for his appearance in the next *Carry On*, "… and I wasn't even in it!" complains the actor. Phillips returned one last time to the *Carry Ons* more than 30 years later when the series was resurrected after a 14-year break for the 1992 reunion offering, *Carry On Columbus*.

Constable was the first *Carry On* film to show any nudity, albeit a quick flash of bum by the male police recruits as they exit a shower at great speed after it has spurted very cold water on them. According to Rogers, on this occasion, he had fewer problems from the censor than from his own cast: "The censor was all right. He just requested that we trim the shot back slightly and not show too much arse. It was Charles Hawtrey who threw up a fuss, not wanting to bare his all. He thought he looked quite pale and white – which I suppose he did – and said that his bum would flare up on screen. So we got a make-up person in to powder up the actors' bums. Some of them moaned on about it but no one more than George Blackler, the make-up man. He said that he'd made up some of the loveliest faces in showbusiness – including Margaret Lockwood and Jean Kent. He'd certainly reached the bottom now."

Carry on Regardless followed *Constable*, filming at Pinewood from late November 1960 to the middle of January 1961. The film's loose plot revolves around The Helping Hands Agency, which employs an assortment of characters to carry out a host of unlikely jobs. *Regardless* is really just a group of sketches allowing comic actors of the calibre of Kenneth Williams, Joan Sims, and Kenneth Connor et al, to do what they do best and make us laugh at the most ridiculous situations. It's by no means the best entry in the series and it was soon to become clear that the *Carry Ons* would need new material and a change of direction if they were to continue their success.

Carry On Cruising was the sixth entry in the series and the first to be shot in colour. What was to be Norman Hudis's last filmed *Carry On* screenplay revolved around a cruise liner captain who needs one final trouble-free voyage before promotion. But a bunch of new recruits aboard the *SS Happy Wanderer* look set to ruin his plans. Comedy actor Lance Percival replaced Charles Hawtrey, who had

DIRECTOR GERALD THOMAS on the set of *Carry On Don't Lose Your Head* in 1966, with Sid James and Kenneth Williams (right). Below, Charles Hawtrey as the Duc de Pommfrit, Sid James as Sir Rodney Ffing and Jim Dale as Lord Darcy de Pue.

become embroiled in an argument over cast billing with Rogers and Thomas. The problem started when a national newspaper declared that Hawtrey was the undoubted star of *Carry On Regardless*. Hawtrey demanded top billing in *Cruising*. Rogers wasn't prepared to be told what to do and replaced him: "Charlie soon came back for the next film and the argument was forgotten."

Kenneth Williams was close to walking out too, complaining that his salary had remained almost the same since the series had begun and that he, as one of the major players, should now be paid more. Rogers, whose budget for *Cruising* had been set at a new series record, £140,000, said the budget couldn't be interfered with at that late stage and promised a rise in the next film and the storm blew over.

But there was another problem that had to be faced. After a dozen films together – six of them *Carry Ons* – the time had come for Peter Rogers and Norman Hudis to part their professional ways. The matter came to a head when Hudis was unable to provide Rogers with a suitable script for *Carry On Spying*. James Bond had arrived on screens across the world and had made a huge impact with *Dr No*, with a second movie, *From Russia with Love*, just going into production. Rogers was keen to cash in on the success with a spoof of the genre and was unhappy with Hudis's take on the theme. As creative differences between the men widened, Hudis was offered work in America. He jumped at the chance, visiting the USA to work on several projects before moving there full time in 1966.

Comedy writer Talbot Rothwell, who had sent Rogers a script called *Up the Armada* on the off chance, was offered the chance to write a *Carry On* and stayed with the team for the next 20 offerings. He brought his own unique penchant for double entendres to the *Carry On* melting pot of acting and comedic talent, and ensured their continued success for the next decade. His naughty nudge-nudge, wink-wink seaside postcard style of humour also ensured that the films now moved up a certificate to an "A" for almost all of the rest of the series.

KENNETH WILLIAMS, left, enjoying his role as the big cheese, Citizen Camembert, in *Don't Lose Your Head* (1966).

FRANKIE HOWERD in a rare publicity shot, playing Francis Bigger, on the set of *Carry On Doctor* in 1967. Though often thought of as a regular cast member, Howerd starred in just two films in the series.

CARRY ON DOCTOR (opposite page) was made at Pinewood during September and October 1967, the second of four films in the series that was based on a hospital theme – producer Peter Rogers knowing from his wife, Betty Box's success with the *Doctor* films, just how popular bedpan humour was among the viewing public in the 1950s and 1960s.

For Rothwell's first film for Rogers it was back to black and white. Based on an idea by Morecambe and Wise writers Sid Green and Dick Hills, *Carry On Cabby* was originally entitled *Call Me a Cab*, but Rogers amended the title and the film became the seventh *Carry On*. Kenneth Williams didn't like the idea and refused to appear in it. His diary entry for 1 February 1963 reads: "Read the script of the Peter Rogers film, *Call Me a Cab*, and hated it. Wrote and said I didn't want to do it." Rogers didn't mind. Williams was often saying he'd had enough of the whole thing but Rogers knew he would return, which he did for the next film, *Carry On Jack* – the first of the period *Carry Ons* filmed from 2 September 1963 at Pinewood and on location at Frensham Ponds in Surrey. Set during the Napoleonic wars, Williams relished playing the role of a cowardly captain as his motley crew battled pirates on the high seas. He was reunited with Hawtrey, who had returned for *Cabby* the year before and both were joined in a small role by the ever-youthful Jim Dale, who was to play dopey love interest and dashing heroes throughout the rest of the 1960s entries.

The last *Carry On* to be made in black and white was *Carry On Spying* in 1964. It saw the series debut for British blonde bombshell Barbara Windsor and allowed Rogers his chance to spoof the by now even more popular Bond series. Rothwell had to stop short of using James Bond terminology in the film as Rogers had been threatened with legal action if he went too far. Bond became Bind, Charlie Bind, and his code number was changed from 001-and-a-half (which Bond bosses refused), to 000 – which Hawtrey delivers perfectly as "Oh. Oh. Ohhh!" The film – with its parodies on *The Third Man* and James Bond/spy overtones, nodding references to arch villains and a *From Russia with Love*-styled climax on a train of doom – became one of the most successful of the 1960s entries.

There was more legal trouble afoot during the making of *Carry On Cleo*, as Rothwell interwove Shakespeare and Shaw to bring us his take on Ancient Rome, and the story of Julius Caesar and Mark Antony falling out over the beautiful Egyptian Queen, Cleopatra. Sid James as Mark Anthony and Kenneth Williams as Caesar are an unbeatably funny duo. Amanda Barrie makes a beautiful Queen in place of Barbara Windsor, who was off on Broadway in a musical with Warren Beatty, and poor Jim Dale and Kenneth Connor, dragged up as vestal virgins, almost steal the film. Kenneth Williams' classic exclamation: "Infamy! Infamy! They've all got it in for me!" now even appears in some dictionaries, in such high comedy regard is the line remembered.

Rogers used the failure of the "straight" *Cleopatra*, which was being made at Pinewood around that time, to his own advantage. After the collapse of the multi-million pound blockbuster, with the press more interested in the on-off romance between Richard Burton and Elizabeth Taylor than Twentieth-Century Fox's epic, Rogers knew *Cleopatra* had to be his next *Carry On*: "I knew that I could make a *Carry On* version of the story in less time than it took Fox to put up their scenery. My goal was to do that in just six weeks and within budget. Which we did. My problem came when we went a step too far and spoofed the artwork for the film poster, which originally had Elizabeth Taylor reclining in a divan with Rex Harrison as Caesar and Richard Burton as Mark Antony around her. In our poster we replaced them with caricatures of Amanda Barrie, Kenneth Williams and Sid James, with Charles Hawtrey peeping out from behind the divan."

What Rogers didn't know was that Fox didn't own the copyright to that image, which had been based on an original painting by Howard Terpning. Rogers was taken to court for breach of copyright. At the High Court, with Lord Hailsham representing Rogers and his team, the canny producer agreed to

change his poster design and in the process bought himself a whole lot of useful publicity for the film.

But the legal problems didn't end there. In one scene in *Cleo*, a market trader and his stall go under the name of Markus and Spencius. High street store Marks and Spencer were less concerned by the spoofing of their name and more by the use of their trademark green and white colours. Rogers didn't even realize his art department had done anything wrong and was stupefied by the threat of being sued. He was thankful they didn't take the threat the whole way: "I am convinced that if the owners of M & S had used lawyers like Fox had we would have been in trouble. We couldn't re-cut the film at that late stage and we could have been liable for big damages. Thankfully they used in-house legal people who just asked for me to write a letter of apology to the *Daily Express*. To this day I don't know why they chose the *Express*. I sent the letter to the storeowners, which they approved but I never sent the letter to the newspaper and it was all soon forgotten about. I don't know what they were worrying about. After 40 years, the store still gets a free advertisement every time the film is shown!"

Things were calmer again for *Carry On Cowboy*, made during the summer of 1965. The back of Pinewood was convincingly turned into the Wild West as Stodge City finds itself is in the grip of the fearless Rumpo Kid, played by Sid James. In his diaries, Kenneth Williams referred to *Cowboy* as being "the first time a British Western has ever been done". And done well it was, too ,with Rogers' cast and crew

THE SAND DANCE (opposite page, left to right) Peter Butterworth, Kenneth Williams and American guest star Phil Silvers, dance a merry dance, while above left, Bernard Bresslaw as Sheikh Abdul Abulbul, and above right, the rest of the cast (and camel) are all messing about on Camber Sands during the filming of *Carry On Follow That Camel* in 1967.

of course, the British answer to all that Cowboys and Indians stuff – and had a ball making it. Naturally, we were a Western film unit without the great expanses of America's Wild West on our doorstep. Indeed, if you look closely at the film, as I stagger off at the end after having defeated Sid's Rumpo Kid, I have to take a left turn to mask the fact that behind the barn was something like the Pinewood canteen!"

The *Carry Ons* were riding high and even better was on its way with the arrival of *Carry On Screaming!* in 1966. Harry H. Corbett, who was finding huge success as one half of the rag-and-bone men duo *Steptoe and Son* on BBC TV, replaced Sid James who had suffered a heart attack. Corbett threw himself into the role of Sergeant Bung – the policeman investigating the mysterious disappearances of young ladies from a local woods – with gusto, in this spoof of everything Hammer horror. Fenella Fielding plays the vampish Virula Watt, with Kenneth Williams on sparkling form as her "undead" dead brother. The fans loved the film. The critics hated it at the time. Now it's regarded as a classic. How times change.

Times were changing then, and Anglo Amalgamated decided, after 12 *Carry Ons*, that enough was enough. Rogers parted company with them and moved across to Rank. But the Organisation didn't want to be associated with another company's franchise success and so insisted that while Rogers could make more films of the same sort – with the same scriptwriters, style of humour and cast – the films should not be called *Carry Ons*.

The two films that followed – the pastiche of the French Revolution, *Don't Lose Your Head*, and the Beau Geste parody, *Follow That Camel* did noticeably poorer box office. Even importing American comic talent Phil Silvers (aka Sergeant Bilko) to add some international appeal to *Follow That Camel* and using real sandy locations (Camber Sands in Sussex doubling up for the Sahara Desert) did little to help.

Rank soon changed their minds and the films were embraced into the *Carry On* fold and renamed when re-issued with the *Carry On* title appended.

Frankie Howerd joined the cast of *Carry On Doctor* in 1967, and Sid James was back, though still not fully recovered from his heart attack. As patient Charlie Roper, James spends most of his scenes in bed, allowing him to recuperate in real life while appearing in the film at the same time.

Two of the series' most successful entries were filmed in 1968. *Carry On … Up the Khyber* began shooting in April and saw the cast and crew decamp on location as far away as the *Carry Ons* were ever to go, to Llanberis in the Welsh mountains, which doubled for India. So convincing were the backgrounds that Rogers received letters after the film's release from war veterans who claimed to have recognised exactly where the film was shot. And as always, when the cast weren't "away" on location, Pinewood, its rooms and its surroundings, doubled up for other settings. The Governor's Residence, which is royally blown up in *Up the Khyber*, is actually the Pinewood mansion house, and the parade ground where the infantrymen lift up their kilts to the dismay of the feuding hoards is one of the Pinewood car parks. *Up the Khyber* is a series favourite and often appears in critics' lists of the Top 100 British films.

From *Up the Khyber* to up the other end of the Studios, as Rogers set an autumn shoot for *Carry On Camping* later that year. In order to meet the spring/summer release schedule for a feel good holiday film, *Camping* had to start filming in October and throughout November 1968. The conditions became progressively more atrocious as the winter weather arrived and bikini-clad Barbara Windsor and others found themselves sinking into the mud for this tale of a group of misfits finding themselves under canvas. Rogers didn't allow the bad weather to

CAST MEMBERS OF *Carry On … Up the Khyber* **(1968). Opposite page, Charles Hawtrey is Private Jimmy Widdle preparing to scare off the marauding hoards. Above, Sid James and Joan Sims and, above right, Roy Castle (on horseback) and Julian Holloway, meet up with Dick Van Dyke in the Pinewood gardens, while the American was at the Studios filming** *Chitty Chitty Bang Bang* **during the spring of 1968.**

get in the way. He had the mud and trees sprayed green to make it look like summer, the odd snow flurry was referred to as blossom. The film is most remembered by many as the one in which Barbara Windsor loses her bikini top – an exercise that looks easier on the screen than it was getting it to work during filming.

In the scene, Barbara is lined up with fellow "school girls" doing her exercises when she breathes in, stretches her arms out and off pings her bikini top. A closed set was called for, with an understandably embarrassed Windsor wanting the number of people around gawping kept to a minimum. An old and senior crew hand was given the job of holding the fishing rod at the end of which was the line and hook attached to the bikini. At the appropriate moment, Gerald

Thomas called "Action" and the man yanked the fishing rod. Unfortunately, he pulled so hard the first time that Barbara Windsor was pulled face down into the mud. She had to be washed down and dried off before attempting the shot again. This time the bikini came off without a hitch and the image has now become one of the iconic moments in British film.

Jim Dale left the *Carry Ons* with *Again Doctor* in 1969, not to return until the ill-fated *Columbus* in 1992. Dale's move was hardly surprising after some of the things he went through on set. He loved stunts and Peter Rogers was more than happy to have him perform his own stunts keeping down the costs of bringing in stuntmen to do the job. The mayhem that Dale's character causes in *Again Doctor* included a trip down the hospital stairs on a trolley. The shot took two takes as Dale, strapped to the trolley, was lowered on a pulley down a set of stairs at some speed – fast enough for the jolting metal to cut into his wrist. Dale was sent to hospital after filming and still carries the scar today. Later in the film, Dale had to

CARRY ON CAMPING was filmed at Pinewood and in its adjacent orchard during the winter of 1968 – hence some cast members looking cold and tired. Barbara Windsor is more worried than most as she – as can be seen above left – is attached to a fishing line that is being prepared to whisk away her bikini top.

JIM DALE, below, in *Carry On Again Doctor* (1969), performing another real stunt – this one leaving the adept comedy performer with stitches in his wrist. It was Dale's tenth *Carry On* outing in six years and his last until *Carry On Columbus* in 1992. Below right, Charles Hawtrey, all dragged up again, in a scene from the same film.

throw himself into a hammock, at which point all the wooden walls around would collapse on top of him. Director Gerald Thomas kindly asked if the actor would ensure he looked directly at the camera as the set gave way so that the audience could see it was really him and not a stuntman performing the jump.

After moving to America, Jim Dale won several awards on Broadway and was the first man to bring the role of Phineas T. Barnum to the stage. Dale remains a successful actor in New York and has found a new following as the voice of Harry Potter and the many characters associated with J. K. Rowling's hit series for the US audio recordings of the books.

With Dale gone, the part of the Jungle Boy in *Carry On Up the Jungle*, made the same year, was hastily recast with Terry Scott taking on the role. The film was originally to be called *Carry On Jungle Boy* but was wisely changed in the face of changing times. The film was to see Frankie Howerd's second and final *Carry On* film series appearance.

A new decade got underway, and so did the 20th film in the series. *Carry On Loving* latched on to the permissiveness that was abounding and satirized the new modern attitude towards sex. The film ends with a huge custard pie fight, filmed on the sound stages at Pinewood. It may have looked fun but filming the scene was hell according to many of the actors who appeared in the sequence. To make it look realistic, Gerald Thomas insisted on using real jelly and cream for the throw about. Actress Patsy Rowlands takes up the story: "Kenny Williams was due for a pie right in the face but try as we might, no one

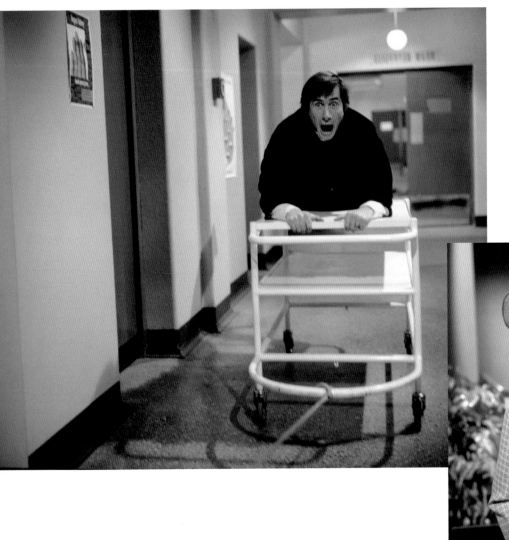

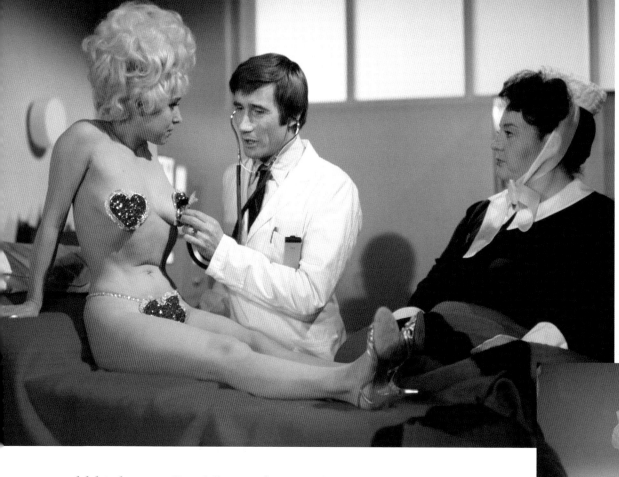

GOLDIE LOCKS, Barbara Windsor's aptly
named character, is the focal point of attention
for Jim Dale's Dr Nookey, while Hattie Jacques
as everyone's favourite harridan of a Matron,
looks on in disdain. Below, preparing for a
further scene in *Carry On Again Doctor*, filmed
at Pinewood in 1969.

could hit him to Gerald's satisfaction. So much so, that we had to
return the next morning to try again. Of course, for continuity's
sake, the set had to be left untouched. Well, with all the lights and
the heat being left out over night, you can imagine the smell that
greeted us on our return to the set. The cream had gone rancid. We
were all glad when filming was over that day, I can tell you."

From the modern to the historic and *Carry On* 21 was *Henry*.
Who else but Sid James could have played the lusty monarch, and
Rogers ensured that extra attention was given to the sets and
costumes so that the richness of the script and comedy acting
matched their surroundings. *Carry On Henry* was a big success.

Speaking on the release of the film in 1971, director Gerald
Thomas talked about working on the series: "Twenty-one *Carry
Ons* means 21 sessions of the exuberant off-set behaviour of the
artistes, which is only a hardship inasmuch as your sides ache with
laughing after a while. By the time I come to shoot a scene, I find
I'm behaving like a schoolmaster in front of an unruly class, and it

is only then, during all the *Carry Ons*, that I have to pretend to be serious. And the artistes are so professional that they believe me. People often ask me if I ever get bored making so many *Carry Ons*. Not at all. Every one has been different and a challenge. I am extremely proud to have directed all 21 *Carry Ons*." And there were still another 10 *Carry On* films to follow.

Originally entitled *Carry On Comrade* and then *Carry On Working*, the next entry, *Carry On at Your Convenience*, was made in the autumn of 1970, and angered unionists who thought its story of militancy at a toilet-making factory was taking the pee a little. Early *Carry Ons* mocked institutions. *Convenience* seemed to be having a poke at the very people who went to watch the films. Consequently, the film didn't perform as well at the box office. Peter Rogers dismisses criticism of the film: "We had no intention of offending anyone. I was just producing another film."

Rogers returned to the safer medical theme for *Carry On Matron*, the fourth of the films based at a hospital. Even though the series of *Doctor* films had come to an end two years previously there seemed to be enough mileage in the theme to squeeze out another successful *Carry On* comedy.

It was only a matter of time before the package holiday – which was booming in Britain at the time – came in for a polite ribbing from Talbot Rothwell. *Carry On Abroad* was filmed in April and May 1972. June Whitfield claims the only reason she agreed to take on the role, after a *Carry On* absence of 14 years, was because she thought the title meant they would be filming in the Mediterranean. She soon found out that the furthest they would travel "on location" would be Slough High Street for the scenes outside a travel agents; the Spanish hotel and its sandy beach were once again filmed in one of Pinewood's versatile car parks. It was to be the last of the very good films, with a strong cast and script. It was also to be the last appearance in the films for Charles Hawtrey. The actor had appeared in every film, bar *Cruising*, but regular problems with alcohol led Peter Rogers' patience to wear very thin. Rogers sadly had to let him go and the series was never the same again.

The 25th *Carry On* in 15 years was *Carry On Girls* and the plot was very much back to basics as, in the failing fictional seaside resort of Fircombe, Sidney Fiddler (Sid James) organizes a controversial beauty contest. There were lots of young ladies bouncing about in bikinis and with Hawtrey out and Williams missing, Sid James was beginning to look tired holding up the proceedings.

He may also have actually been tired, since he and other cast members were preparing for the highly successful *Carry On London!* stage play, which started its run in the autumn of 1973. The popularity of the films may have begun to ebb slightly but the cast seemed universally loved and the show was a sell out, both in Birmingham and London.

Sid James bowed out of the film series after making *Carry On Dick*, about the exploits of Dick Turpin, in 1974. It was also to be the last *Carry On* script by Talbot Rothwell – who became ill after completing the screenplay – and the last film outings for Barbara Windsor and Hattie Jacques.

A series of 13 half-hour *Carry On* shows were made for television in 1975, but it seemed that the film series' days were now numbered. TV sitcom writer Dave Freeman provided the script for *Carry On Behind* – a sort of *Carry On Camping* but with caravans instead of tents, which had become the fashion in the mid-70s. The film was shot in March and April 1975. *Behind* suffered from a lack of original

TERRY SCOTT, above, is Cecil the Jungle Boy, in *Carry On Up the Jungle* (1970).

OPPOSITE PAGE, the cast of *Carry On Up the Jungle* on set at Pinewood and Frankie Howerd discussing the script with director Gerald Thomas. Filmed during the autumn of 1969, it was released in March 1970.

team members but those who did appear, including Kenneth Williams, Joan Sims, Kenneth Connor, Bernard Bresslaw and Patsy Rowlands, as well as a guest appearance from international actress Elke Sommer, ensured the film was to be the best in the final years.

By the time *Carry On England* came to be filmed in May 1976, Sid James had just died, aged 62, following a collapse on stage on the opening night of *The Mating Game* in Sunderland. His loss cast a huge shadow over the film – it was always Rogers' hope that Sid would return for another *Carry On*, but now the father of the cast had gone.

England was a wartime comedy along the lines of *Sergeant* but with a vulgarity that was trying to keep up with the more permissive *Confessions* and *Adventures of* films that had been hitting the big screen since the early 1970s. The film contained breast nudity for the first time and received a "AA" certificate on its release, meaning it could only be seen by those over the age of 14 – the first time a *Carry On* had ever received such certification. It's not what *Carry On*

A LOVELY PAIR of scenes from *Carry On Loving*, the 20th film in the long-running series, filmed at Pinewood during the spring of 1970.

audiences went to the cinema for and the film did so badly it was pulled after its initial showings. Rogers had certain sequences recut and the film dropped a certificate, but it didn't make the film any funnier and it took some time before it made its money back.

A 1977 compilation feature, *That's Carry On*, showed the best moments from the film series, linked by pieces to camera by Kenneth Williams and Barbara Windsor, a la *That's Entertainment*. Rather than re-ignite the passion for the films, it merely served as a reminder of what had been the golden days of the *Carry Ons*, days which were not likely to be revisited. Yet Rogers still believed there was life in the old franchise yet. He had always claimed that the title was bigger than the star and he looked for new injections of life from other comedy talent. *Carry On Emmannuelle*, the 30th film in the series, parodied the hit soft sex films of the 1970s. Kenneth Williams, Joan Sims, Kenneth Connor, Peter Butterworth and Jack

A REGAL GATHERING, left to right, Sid James, Barbara Windsor, director Gerald Thomas, Joan Sims and Julian Holloway in the Pinewood gardens, during the making of *Carry On Henry* in late 1970.

CHARLES HAWTREY as the drunken Eustace Tuttle in *Carry On Abroad* (1972). Sadly, Hawtrey's off-screen antics meant this was to be his last of 23 *Carry On* film appearances.

Douglas did their best with a smutty script. Sexy newcomer Suzanne Danielle provided the eye candy, but the film, which was made in April and May 1978, lacked any feel-good factor. Once again, a *Carry On* received an "AA" certificate. This time no one bothered to recut the poorly performing film.

And that seemed to be the end of it. Thirty films in 20 years.

There was talk of more *Carry Ons*. The films and series of edited highlights continued to play to large audiences on television throughout the 1980s. The advent of sell-through video saw the titles literally fly out of the shops on their release from 1987. Talks of a 30th anniversary film were mooted for 1988 – a sequel to *Nurse*, called *Carry On Again Nurse*, penned by original series writer Norman Hudis. But the deaths of Kenneth Williams and Charles Hawtrey that very year put paid to that.

And then in early 1992, after a gap of 14 years, came the announcement that Jim Dale was to return to the *Carry Ons* with a new cinema offering celebrating the 500th anniversary of Christopher Columbus finding America. *Carry On Columbus* was written by *Behind* writer Dave Freeman. It brought together some of the original cast members, including Dale, Leslie Phillips, June Whitfield, Jon Pertwee, Bernard Cribbins and Jack Douglas, and interspersed them with the new up-and-coming comedians of the time. The exercise, while happy, was not successful. As June Whitfield aptly proclaimed: "It should have been called *Carry Off Columbus*!"

Leslie Phillips recalled: "I hadn't been with the *Carry Ons* for a long time. I didn't care a damn what it was about really. I came to join them to make a film. In the light of what happened to Gerry shortly afterwards I was never so glad to have taken on the project. Of course it could never be like it was when we were all young. There was a certain sadness hanging over it." Sadly the *Carry Ons'* director, Gerald Thomas, passed away the following year, robbing Peter Rogers of his long-term partner.

The *Carry Ons* looked finished – on the big screen at least – though their appeal both in TV schedules and with the continuing high sales of DVDs, shows they endure as much, if not more so, than ever before. And now, almost half a century after *Carry On Sergeant* started filming at an army barracks in Surrey and on a sound stage at Pinewood, there are still hopes among some that the series can be revived with a new cast and for a new generation of filmgoers. The purists' baulk at the idea, the fans are divided.

Love them or hate them, people are still talking about the *Carry Ons*. And with each of the 31 films to date made at Pinewood Studios, where else could a new production ever be made? As Peter Rogers declares: "Nowhere. Where else could we make them? This has been both my home and the home for my films for over 50 years. A *Carry On* wouldn't be a *Carry On* if it wasn't made at Pinewood. It just wouldn't be the same."

CARRY ON DICK, filmed at Pinewood in 1974, marked Sid James's last appearance in a *Carry On* and was the last of the series written by Talbot Rothwell.

Heroes and Heroines

Pinewood Studios celebrated its 21st birthday on Monday 30th September 1957. Over 500 guests sat at 67 tables in a big marquee erected in the Studios' gardens. Lord Rank (who had been elevated to the peerage that year) received a special presentation, as did Managing Director John Davis, following a host of speeches including one from Dirk Bogarde, who described himself as "the oldest living member of the contract artists". Bogarde, who was filming *A Tale of Two Cities* at the studios, attended the lunch in costume, as he was needed back on set immediately afterwards.

A host of well-known actors and actresses attended the lunch, all of them big stars, whose performances and very appearances in Rank films helped improve the chances of box-office success. Among those names were Stanley Baker, Diana Dors, Peter Finch, Anne Heywood, Glynis Johns, Margaret Lockwood, Virginia McKenna, Patrick McGoohan, Donald Sinden and, on the top table – for he had now become Rank's biggest screen star – Kenneth More.

Rank relied heavily on the star quality of its heroes and heroines. There was no "one size suits all" policy and their contract stars came in all shapes and sizes. There were the handsome "ladies' men" sorts – Stewart Granger, Michael Redgrave and Dirk Bogarde. Then there were the gritty and tough "men's men", like Peter Finch and Jack Hawkins. And there were some who just used their charm to light up the screen, like Donald Sinden and, especially, Kenneth More.

Kenneth More was born on 20th September 1914 into what was initially a wealthy family. His father had inherited a fortune from his father, but sadly he blew it all in later life. More had a good education but was a sportsman rather than a scholar and left school without qualifications. His first job

A RARE COLOUR IMAGE (the
film itself was made in black and
white) of Dirk Bogarde as Sydney
Carton and Dorothy Tutin as
Lucie Mannette, in *A Tale of Two
Cities* (1957).

LORD RANK CUTS THE CAKE,
opposite, at a special luncheon to
celebrate Pinewood's 21st
birthday at the Studios on
Monday 30 September 1957.

VIEWING THE RUSHES of Rank's *A Night to Remember,*
the 1957 depiction of the *Titanic* disaster, directed at
Pinewood by Roy Ward Baker.

TITANIC...
THE GREATEST SEA DRAMA IN LIVING MEMORY

THE RANK ORGANISATION PRESENTS WITH PRIDE

KENNETH MORE IN
A NIGHT TO REMEMBER

From the book by Walter Lord   Screenplay by Eric Ambler

Produced by William MacQuitty

Directed by Roy Baker

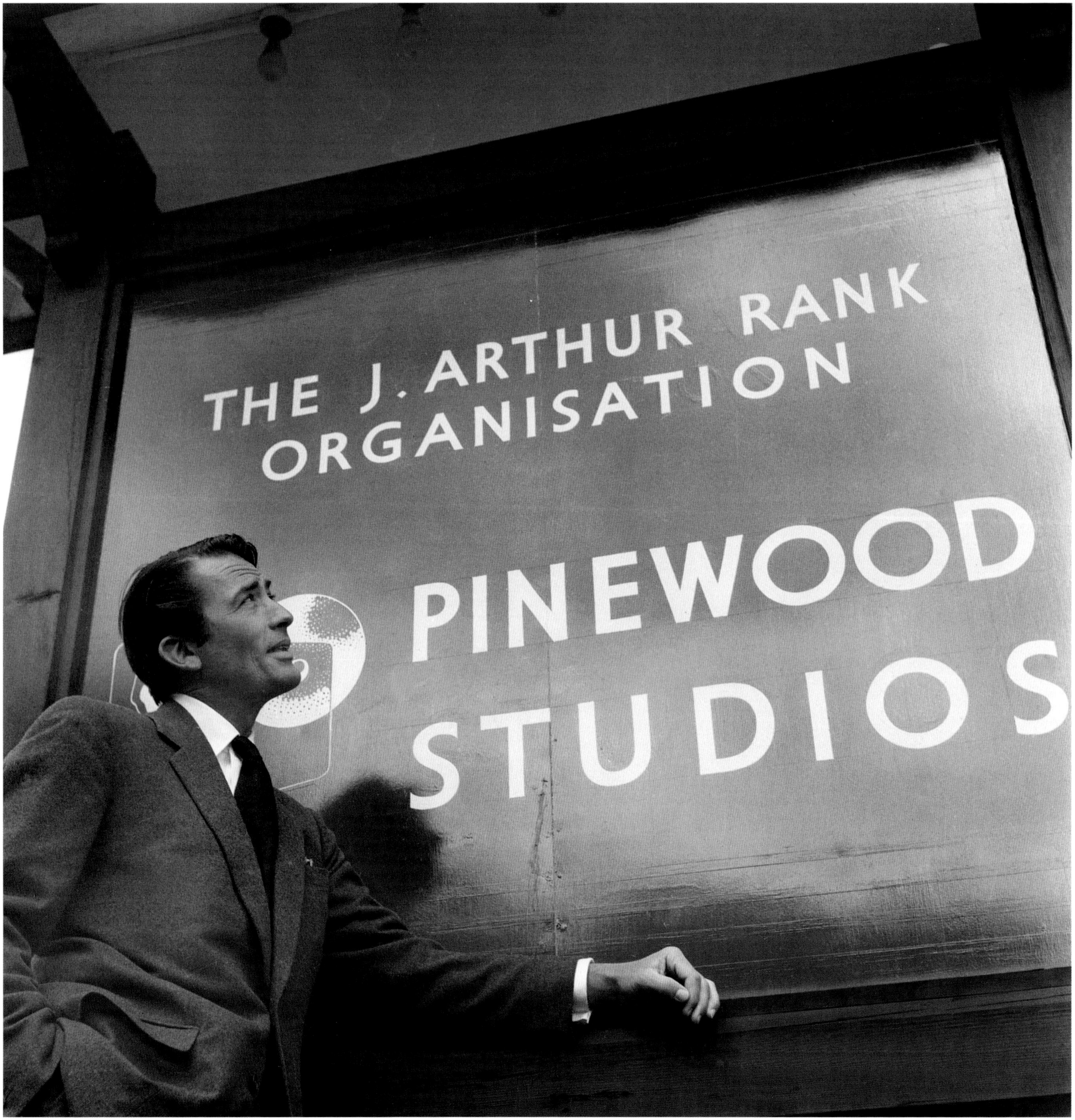
THE J. ARTHUR RANK
ORGANISATION
PINEWOOD
STUDIOS

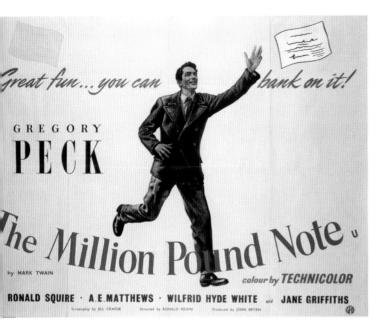

in showbusiness was as a scenery shifter at the Windmill Theatre, London, home of the world-renowned immobile nudes, as well as the starting block for up-and-coming young comedians, for whom More often acted as a "feed". He moved into rep but his acting career was interrupted by the war when he was called up to the Royal Navy, serving as a junior officer and seeing the kind of action that would be depicted later in some of his most popular movies.

After several years playing support roles in films, More, landed two co-starring roles, which, much to the chagrin of Earl St. John, who didn't reckon the actor at all, turned him into an "overnight" success … at the age of 40. The roles of Ambrose Claverhouse in *Genevieve* and medical student Richard Grimsdyke in *Doctor in the House* won him great acclaim, the latter also winning him a Bafta for Best British Actor.

Kenneth More quickly became one of the country's leading men and showed that he was equally as deft with serious drama as he was with comedy, turning in masterful performances as the courageous second officer in *A Night to Remember* (1958) the story of the sinking of the *Titanic*, and as the real-life war hero Douglas Bader, in *Reach for the Sky* (1956). Of all the roles he played, More was desperate to play Bader, the part originally earmarked for Richard Burton. More recalled: "I knew I was the only actor who could play the part properly. Most parts that can be played by one actor can equally well be played by another, but not this. Bader's philosophy was my philosophy. His whole attitude to life was mine."

More took over as Rank's number one star from Dirk Bogarde. The two often appeared together in Pinewood outings of the 1950s, though their style could not have been more different. After being demobbed from the army, Bogarde's agent newly named him Dirk and the actor immediately took up where he had left off both on stage and in film. In the late 1940s Rank signed Bogarde up after a talent

IN TOWN FOR THE MAKING OF *The Million Pound Note* **in 1953, American star Gregory Peck, talking to Pinewood's head of production, Earl St. John.**

MINGLING AT A RECEPTION at Pinewood, Bob Hope (left) who was at the Studios making *Call Me Bwana* in 1962.

scout had spotted him, and he made his first credited appearance in a film as a policeman in *Dancing with Crime* (1947). The actor recalled: "I was as scrawny as a plucked hen. The Rank Organisation did supply me with dumb-bells. All I did was put on two sweaters and then put my shirt on."

Bogarde spent the next three years beavering away in Rank films, hardly noticed. Then, playing a young thug, Tom Riley, who shoots a policeman in *The Blue Lamp* (1950), Bogarde was suddenly drawing attention. Movie stardom came in 1954 with Betty Box's *Doctor in the House*. Seventeen million people went to see the film and through the role of Dr Simon Sparrow (a role he reprised in another three *Doctor* films), Bogarde had become a heartthrob.

Bogarde continued in middling comedies and dramas throughout the rest of the 1950s, including *Simba* (1955), *The Spanish Gardener* (1957) and *A Tale of Two Cities* (1958). In 1961 he decided to break free of his matinée idol image by making *Victim*, a groundbreaking drama depicting the blackmailing of homosexuals. Playing a gay barrister, it was a huge step for Bogarde, who throughout his career had denied he was homosexual himself. He received the first of six Bafta Best Actor nominations for the film.

But his days at Pinewood would soon be over. He made his last film at the studios in 1963 – *Doctor in Distress*. He continued to make "more serious" films across the world and left Britain to live in France in 1968 with his long-term personal partner and agent, Anthony Forwood. They returned in the 1980s when Forwood was diagnosed with cancer, from which he died in 1988. Bogarde remained in Britain and turned to writing – including several highly regarded volumes of autobiography. After a series of strokes, the by then knighted Sir Dirk Bogarde died in May 1999. Of making films the much-loved actor once self-effacingly declared: "I love the camera and it loves me. Well, not very much sometimes. But we're good friends."

Growing up as a child in the very next village to Dirk Bogarde – though they never met as children – was chemist's son, Donald Sinden. Sinden had originally planned to become an architect but was spotted performing in an amateur dramatics troupe and, unable to serve in the navy because of asthma, was invited to join a company sent out to entertain the troops during the Second World War.

PROFILE

Kenneth More

Born in 1914, Kenneth More began working life as an engineer's apprentice and a fur trapper in Canada. He took an early role in Gracie Fields' *Look Up and Laugh* in 1935. A series of small roles in plays and films followed, before he joined the Royal Navy where he served during the Second World War.

After the war he attempted to break into film, but it wasn't until he hit 40 that More suddenly found himself a household name following the success of two very British comedies – *Genevieve* and *Doctor in the House*. For the latter he won the British Academy award for best actor in 1954. More went on to appear in some of Rank's biggest films of the era, most notably as hero Douglas Bader in *Reach for the Sky* (1956), the title character in *The Admirable Crichton* (1957), the first mate on the *Titanic* in *A Night to Remember* (1958) and the director of naval operations in *Sink the Bismark!* (1960).

With the arrival of the 1960s, the fashion for stiff-upper-lipped heroes that had made him such a box-office winner declined rapidly. He embraced the role of Chick Byrd in *The Comedy Man* in 1963 – which portrayed the life of a down-on-his-luck middle-age repertory actor. During the making of the film he began an affair with a young actress, Angela Douglas. A difficult and public divorce saw both shunned by the film and television industry for most of the rest of the 1960s. More returned to film in the late 1960s, with cameos in films such as *The Battle of Britain* (1969) and *Scrooge* (1970), as well as a triumphant return to television in the BBC's *The Forsyte Saga* in 1967, and the lead role in 13 episodes of *Father Brown* in 1974.

Kenneth More passed away in 1982, after a long battle with Parkinson's disease. His wife, Angela Douglas, was by his side.

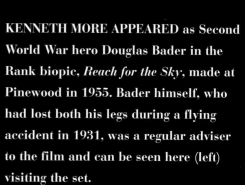

KENNETH MORE APPEARED as Second World War hero Douglas Bader in the Rank biopic, *Reach for the Sky*, made at Pinewood in 1955. Bader himself, who had lost both his legs during a flying accident in 1931, was a regular adviser to the film and can be seen here (left) visiting the set.

SCENES FROM *A TALE OF TWO CITIES*
Donald Pleasance as Barsad and Dirk Bogarde as Sydney Carton (opposite page) starred in Ralph Thomas's 1957 production.

The acting bug bit hard and, after the war, he trained at the Webber Douglas Academy of Dramatic Arts in London, quickly establishing himself in the theatre as an actor of great depth.

Sinden made his film debut in *The Cruel Sea* in 1953. He was signed up for a seven-year contract by Rank at £2,500 a year and became a favoured cast member for Betty Box. As a producer at the Studios, she could get Sinden for half the cost, and he began to appear in several of her light-hearted comedies of the 1950s, including *A Day to Remember* (1953), *Mad About Men* (1954) and as the lecherous medical student, Benskin, in *Doctor in the House* (1954). Even in scenes where he had just a few words, Benskin never failed to make his presence felt on screen by upstaging his co-stars with a little bit of theatrical movement and overplaying to the camera.

One of Sinden's favourite film stories is of working on *A Day to Remember* in which he played a young man providing the love interest

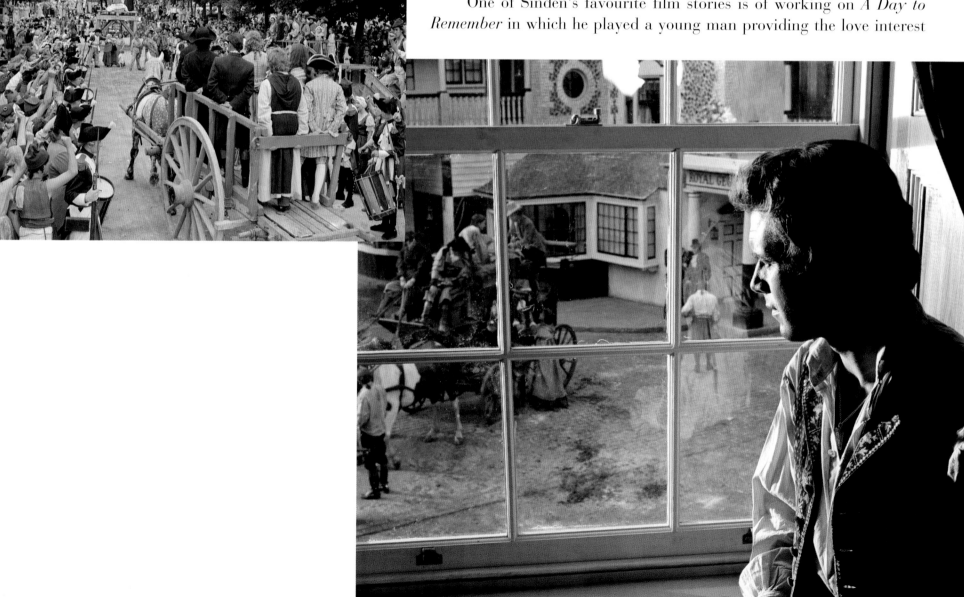

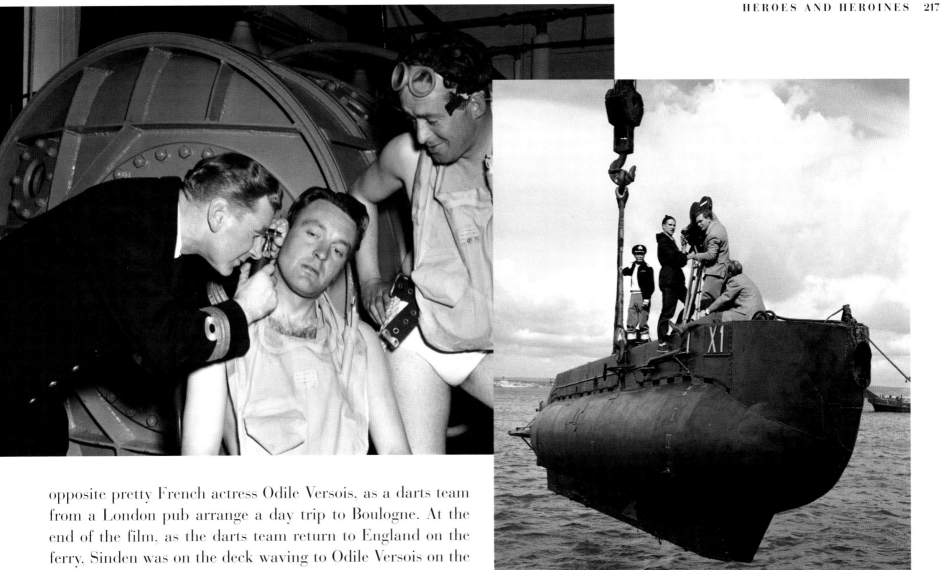

opposite pretty French actress Odile Versois, as a darts team from a London pub arrange a day trip to Boulogne. At the end of the film, as the darts team return to England on the ferry, Sinden was on the deck waving to Odile Versois on the quayside. Sinden recalled: "This touching scene was caught by two cameras, one on the quay and the other on the ship. It is always safer to do more than one take, so the Captain of the ferry was asked if he could take the ship 200 yards away from the quay and then return and do it again so we could have at least two bites of the cherry. This was met with a flat refusal. Once the ship leaves, it has to go to England. So I waved my farewells to Odile until I could no longer see her and four hours later I arrived in Dover. I telephoned the unit in Boulogne and found that Take One was useless – we must do it again.

"Back to Boulogne I went at the crack of dawn and that afternoon Odile and I bid each other a fond farewell for a second time. Will the young lovers ever meet

DONALD SINDEN AND JOHN GREGSON, above left, getting the once over by the ship's doctor in the Rank classic, *Above Us the Waves* (1954), while, above, cast and crew film on a prop submarine.

OPPOSITE: Alma Cogan, Donald Sinden and June Thorburn at a Pinewood reception.

PROFILE

Donald Sinden

Donald Sinden was born on 9 October 1923, the son of a chemist in Plymouth. Sinden hadn't planned on acting as a career, and had ambitions to become an architect. It was while performing in amateur dramatics at the Brighton Little Theatre in 1941 that he was spotted as an acting talent and, when invalided out of the Navy because of asthma, he was more than happy to join one of the companies sent out to entertain the troops.

After the War, Sinden trained at a drama school in London and quickly gained a reputation as an accomplished stage actor. He made his first big screen appearance in *The Cruel Sea* (1953), although he is always quick to admit that he could hardly swim and had to film many of his "in the water" scenes strapped to a strong swimmer beneath him. A Rank contract followed at a salary of £50 per week and with his good looks and charm, throughout the 1950s Sinden became a favourite actor in light comedies and taut low-budget thrillers, including *Eyewitness* (1956), two *Doctor* films (1954 and 1957), *Rockets Galore!* (1957) and *The Captain's Table* (1959).

Sinden extended his fame on to the small screen in a host of popular shows including sitcoms *Our Man at St. Marks* (1964–66), *Two's Company* (1975) and *Never the Twain* (1981–91). In between, the stage continued to show Sinden in his best light, with numerous harder-edge cinema roles following as the actor grew in status, including *Villain* (1971) with Richard Burton and *The Day of the Jackal* (1973) starring Edward Fox.

In recent years, Donald Sinden has made regular appearances as Sir Joseph Channing in the BBC drama series *Judge John Deed*. He received his own knighthood in 1997.

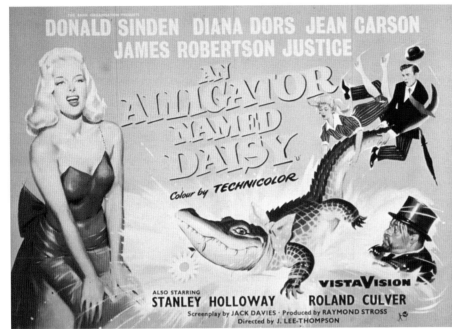
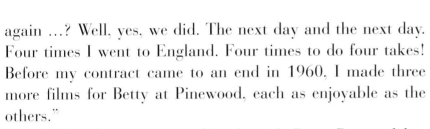

again …? Well, yes, we did. The next day and the next day. Four times I went to England. Four times to do four takes! Before my contract came to an end in 1960, I made three more films for Betty at Pinewood, each as enjoyable as the others."

Sinden became great friends with Betty Box and her husband Peter Rogers, a friendship that lasted throughout the rest of her life and saw Betty and Peter become godparents to one of Sinden's sons. Made Sir Donald Sinden in 1997, he has remained one of the most prolific and best-loved British stage, film, radio and television actors.

Peter Finch was a different type of hero altogether, whose real-life heavy drinking, hell raising and womanizing just added, in some people's eyes, to his heroic persona on screen. Finch was born in London but went with his family to live in Sydney, Australia, when he was 10. His first stage appearance was as a comedian's stooge in 1939 and it was on stage that he was spotted by Laurence Olivier who, impressed by what he saw, persuaded the actor to return to London to reprise his stage career on these shores. Finch repaid Olivier's confidence by having an affair with Olivier's wife, Vivien Leigh. Indeed, even though he married three times, Finch still found time to have several highly publicized affairs with beautiful actresses of their generation, including Kay Kendall and Mai Zetterling.

WATCH YOUR FINGERS – Donald Sinden holding a live crocodile, which starred alongside him, Diana Dors and Roland Culver in the 1955 comedy, *An Alligator Named Daisy*.

ACTRESS APRIL OLRICH, opposite, as the enchanting Dolores, captivating the troops in the 1955 Powell and Pressburger drama based on a true wartime naval expedition, *The Battle of the River Plate*, which starred many Rank leading actors including John Gregson, Christopher Lee and Peter Finch.

Finch switched to movie making after a bout of stagefright put him off live performing. His screen performances were formidable. His dashing good looks and intensity of spirit making him a hero of film in the 1950s and 1960s. At Pinewood, his most widely remembered performances were as an actor, Simon Foster, living his marriage to actress wife Laura (played by Kay Kendall) in front of the cameras – a sort of fictional, post-war silver screen version of *Big Brother*. *Simon and Laura* was a satirical look at the world of celebrity that seems just as apt now as when it was made half a century ago.

As Joe Harman in *A Town Like Alice*, Finch brought charm to the wartime drama about a group of women marched across Malaya by Japanese soldiers. His performance as a German Officer in *The Battle of the River Plate* (1957) was much admired, but probably his finest Pinewood offering was as a dissatisfied Labour MP who, overlooked for a Cabinet post by his Government, goes off the rails; his wife leaves him, he falls in with a group of militant communists and starts a passionate affair with a fashion model. Finch's convincing and charismatic performance won him the Bafta for Best British Actor in 1962.

As middle age approached, Finch continued to enthral on screen, winning a total of five Baftas and an Oscar nomination for his portrayal of a homosexual Jewish doctor in *Sunday Bloody Sunday* (1971). He won an Oscar for his role as the "mad prophet of the airwaves" in *Network* (1976). However, following a fatal heart attack, the Oscar was awarded posthumously and accepted by his third wife.

Of stardom, Finch once said: "Success is a very tough mistress. For years, while you're struggling, she wants to do nothing with you. Then, one day you find yourself in the room with her and even though the key is on the inside, you can't leave. 'You've made your choice', she says, 'I don't care how exhausted you are – you're going to stay here for the rest of your life making love to me.'"

To many filmgoers in the 1950s and 1960s, Jack Hawkins represented the archetypal screen hero. He was a rugged and strong actor whose rich, deep commanding voice and on-screen presence made him ideal for the authority roles he was to take on and make his own. Hawkins was born in 1910, the son of a master builder. Acting was in his blood and he learnt his trade under the stewardship of actor-managers Sybil Thorndike and Lewis Casson. At 21 he

THE BOARD OF ALLIED FILM MAKERS – the influential production company whose works included *The League of Gentlemen* (1960), *Whistle Down the Wind* (1961) and *Séance on a Wet Afternoon* (1964) – hold a meeting in the Pinewood boardroom, including (l to r) Basil Dearden, Bryan Forbes, Jack Hawkins, Michael Relph and Richard Attenborough.

married leading lady Jessica Tandy (a marriage that would last 10 years). He also appeared in Britain's first sound picture, Hitchcock's *The Lodger* in 1931.

The war saw Hawkins volunteering for the Royal Welsh Fusiliers and he spent most of the early 1940s arranging entertainment for the British forces in India. After the war, Alexander Korda offered him a film contract. First came the costume dramas then, following a stunning performance as the Commander of a Corvette in *The Cruel Sea* (1952), Rank signed him up and along came the roles that he will forever be associated with: sea skippers, army colonels and RAF Group captains.

As Hawkins recalled: "I played enough senior officers to stock the whole Ministry of Defence". Within two years he was a huge star: "I was voted the No.1 box-office draw of 1954. I was even credited with irresistible sex appeal, which is another quality I had not imagined I possessed." One critic of the time commented:

"Hawkins makes love better to a battleship than to a woman."

Jack Hawkins' finest Pinewood hour came with the lead role in the 1960 crime comedy *The League of Gentlemen* – the first feature from Allied Film Makers, whose founders included Bryan Forbes and Richard Attenborough, who both also appear in the film. Hawkins plays Lt Col Hyde, an embittered ex-Army officer who calls together a group of wartime veterans with the intention of perpetrating a bank robbery using the cunning and expertise they learnt within the forces. The film cost £1 million to make (around £15 million today) but the huge investment paid off and it was a great financial success.

Sadly, during filming, Hawkins developed throat problems, aggravated by three days of filming the bank raids in thick smoke. It was cancer. Faced

with a choice of death or losing his voice, Hawkins chose the latter and in the mid-1960s had his voice box removed. He continued to act, his voice dubbed on screen by actors Charles Gray and Robert Rietti. He chose as his motto in his last years some lines from Milton's *Comus* in which he had acted in his early stage career: "Yet where an equal poise of hope and fear does not arbitrate the event, my nature is that I incline to hope, rather than to fear." Jack Hawkins died in the summer of 1973, during an operation to fit an electronic voice box.

Michael Caine never had a Rank contract but he was to become a movie hero, thanks in no small part to a handful of films he made at Pinewood in the mid to

A CLASSIC CAST for a classic film, (l to r) Jack Hawkins, Roger Livesey, Bryan Forbes, Terence Alexander, Norman Bird, Kieron Moore, Richard Attenborough and Nigel Patrick, in *The League of Gentlemen*, filmed at Pinewood in 1959.

**RESPECTED BRITISH ACTOR Jack Hawkins
(left) was a firm favourite with the viewing
public and his roles in films such as *The
League of Gentlemen* (opposite page) reinforced
his box-office pulling power.**

late 1960s. Born Maurice Micklewhite on 14 March 1933, the son of a fish-market porter, Caine left school at 15, taking on whatever work he could find before serving with the British army in Korea. On his return to England, Caine became "an odd-job boy" at the J. Arthur Rank Organisation, in the hope that – with all the directors and producers who came to meet Mr Rank – he would be their next star discovery.

But Caine was not to find fame that way, as he admits, partly down to his own behaviour: "For a movie company the atmosphere in the offices seemed very quiet and austere ... the reason for this was explained to me by my boss, a woman who did not turn out to be a barrel of laughs. Mr Rank was very religious, she told me, a strict Methodist and there were certain things that he did not allow. She then began to list the things I was not allowed to do, which was just about everything, especially smoking. With my newfound wealth I had just taken this up and I soon found out I could run down to the toilet and have a quick drag whenever the craving got too much. On the second day I was sitting there having a quiet puff when there was a loud knock on the door and a male voice yelled: 'Come out, whoever you are. You're fired!' And I was."

Caine didn't give up and with a change of name, he put everything he had into becoming an actor – travelling with rep throughout the length and breadth of the country, appearing in bit parts across 100 dramas on television, and even making uncredited appearances in Rank films *Carve Her Name with Pride* (1958) and Norman Wisdom's *The Bulldog Breed* (1960), before eventually appearing in the stage hit, *The Long and the Short and the Tall*.

Caine's big cinematic break came when he played the aristocratic officer in *Zulu* in 1964. But it was his next film *The Ipcress File*, made at Pinewood, that would cement his star potential. At a time when Bond was big, Caine appeared as something of an anti-hero, as bespectacled Harry Palmer, a working-class spy with an accent to boot and few airs and graces or clever gadgets to get him through the scrapes expected of any on-screen spy hero.

MICHAEL CAINE is everyone's favourite working-class spy, Harry Palmer, here with Sue Lloyd as Jean Courtney in the 1965 Bafta award-winning thriller, *The Ipcress File*. Caine returned to the role twice more, making *Funeral in Berlin* at Pinewood in 1966 and *Billion Dollar Brain* the following year.

Caine was not the first choice to play Harry Palmer – Christopher Plummer turned it down in order to play the lead role in *The Sound of Music* (1965) opposite Julie Andrews. *The Ipcress File* was produced by Harry Saltzman, who, along with Albert "Cubby" Broccoli, was also producing Bond at Pinewood at the time. Saltzman and Caine worked hard to ensure that Palmer was to be "the antithesis of James Bond: a very ordinary bloke, someone who could mingle unnoticed in a crowd and who should have an ordinary boring name". So Caine found his character pushing a trolley around supermarkets buying his own groceries – something Bond would never have done.

"Bond … had several million dollars' worth of special effects, a great name and a number – 007 – as well as a licence to kill. And here I was, winding up with glasses, a battle with supermarket trolleys and the dullest name that anyone could think of. Even *my* massive confidence started to wane from time to time." It needn't have. *The Ipcress File* was well received and appreciated by audiences and critics alike for what it was trying to achieve – to show that being a spy was perhaps not as glamorous as we would all like it to be.

Caine's performance was lauded and the film was nominated for several awards. He went on to make two sequels, *Funeral in Berlin* (1966) and *Billion Dollar Brain* (1967). Unlike Bond, which continued to thrive from decade to decade and re-incarnation to re-incarnation, the third Palmer outing was enough and Caine, now an international star, continued his film career with many hits and a few misses both at Pinewood and at studios across the world. The much-loved British hero was knighted in November 2000.

Michael Caine may not have made it as far as being put under contract to Rank even though he worked for the Organisation for a short while. But being on their books was no guarantee of stardom either. At the end of the 1950s there were 33 artists under contract to the Rank Organisation, 15 actors and 18 actresses. The male artists were: Dirk Bogarde, Peter Finch, Philip Gilbert, David Knight, Donald Sinden, Richard Stapley, Anthony Steel, Ian Carmichael, Michael Craig, John Gregson, Jack Hawkins, Terence Longdon, Eric Portman, Norman Wisdom and Tony Wright. Several of these names are instantly recognizable, as classic actors and heroes whose films and, more importantly, performances have stood the test of time.

The female contracted artists were; Jill Adams, Julia Arnall, Susan Beaumont, Diana Dors, Eunice Gayson, Kay Kendall, Gerda Larsen, Belinda Lee, Flora Robson, Beverly Brooks, Jean Carson, Josephine Griffin, Jill Ireland, Virginia McKenna, Anne Paige, Muriel Pavlow, Maureen Swanson and June Thorburn. It seems a little harder to find names that jump out at you as stars with longevity from that list. That perhaps says more about Rank's objectives in signing female artists than a critique of the listees themselves. Rank simply wanted the men to be the heroes and the ladies to be the attractive, often sexy, starlets. The price of celebrity being what it is means that we don't remember those women as heroines as much as we do the "heroic" men. Which is perhaps unfair.

Of course there are some starlets whose names are still well remembered and who made an equally big impression on the screen as their male counterparts.

Diana Dors was one of the Rank Charm School's first signings and she was set to become Britain's first and possibly most famous sex symbol. Born Diana Fluck on 23 October 1931, both baby and mother nearly died during childbirth, and from then on Diana's mother became over protective and lavished on her anything she wanted. They went to the cinema a great deal and from the age of three Diana said she wanted to be an actress. She was educated at private school (to the annoyance of her father who thought it a waste of money). Physically, Diana matured quickly and was already showing off her blonde hair and curvaceous figure from as young as 15 in films such as *The Shop at Sly Corner* (1946). In 1948, Diana Dors, as she was then known, appeared in six films – the most outstanding being *Oliver Twist*. Throughout the 1950s, Dors was promoted as "The English Marilyn Monroe", even though her career had started earlier than her American counterpart, and some thought her acting was better too.

At age 20, Dors was the youngest registered owner of a Rolls-Royce car in Britain. Her portrayal of sexy sirens filled British cinemas, she was, in her own words: "The only sex symbol England produced since Lady Godiva". Her film career didn't have great longevity, but her performances in films such as *Value for Money* (1955) and *As Long As They're Happy* (1954) are highly regarded. Pop fans will remember that Diana Dors featured on the cover of The Beatles' album *Sgt. Pepper's Lonely Hearts Club Band*. The actress died from cancer in 1984.

A PORTRAIT OF JOAN COLLINS taken at Pinewood in the mid-1950s when the aspiring actress was in her early 20s. Joan Collins made her first film at the Studios, *Turn the Key Softly*, in 1952.

BRITAIN'S ANSWER to Marilyn Monroe, opposite, blonde bombshell Diana Dors, an early signing to the Rank charm school, who was a big hit at the cinemas in the early 1950s.

A 1950s **PUBLICITY SHOT** of actresses (l to r) **Julia Arnall, Susan Beaumont, Belinda Lee** and **Muriel Pavlow, posing in evening wear for the forthcoming Cannes film festival.**

Joan Collins was a late graduate of the Rank Charm School and though she failed to achieve the same level of British film stardom early on in her career as say Diana Dors, she went on to become one of the best known British actresses, both nationally and internationally. Born on 23 May 1933, the five-times married actress, known as much for her personal life as for her acting career, gave a memorable performance in her first Pinewood outing *Turn the Key Softly* (1952).

With a film and television career that took her round the world, Collins returned to Pinewood at the beginning of the 1970s to appear in Sidney Hayer's

adult thriller *Revenge*, and Ralph Thomas's romantic thriller, *Quest for Love*. Her most recent Pinewood filmed appearance was as Mrs Potiphar, opposite Richard Attenborough and Donny Osmond, in David Mallett's filmed-for-video version of *Joseph and His Amazing Technicolour Dreamcoat* (1999).

Some actresses will be indelibly linked with the British cinema of the 1950s. Once such starlet of her time was Muriel Pavlow. This petite actress was born on 27 June 1921 and appeared on stage from the age of 14. She made her first film appearance two years earlier in a bit part role in a Gracie Fields vehicle, *Sing As We Go*. Another early appearance was alongside Diana Dors in *The Shop at Sly Corner* (1947), and soon after that she signed up to a contract with Rank. Muriel Pavlow played the female lead in some of the classic Pinewood films of the 1950s; as officious medical student Joy, playing opposite Dirk Bogarde, Kenneth More and Donald Sinden in *Doctor in the House* (1954), as the looking-for-love television producer in *Simon and Laura* (1955), as Lucy, the prey to Donald

SIR LAURENCE OLIVIER with his second wife, Vivien Leigh (above left), at the British Academy Awards in 1956; and, above, Laurence Olivier and Marilyn Monroe in *The Prince and the Showgirl*, made at Pinewood in the same year.

Sinden's psychopath, in *Eyewitness* (1956) and most impressively as Douglas Bader's wife Thelma in *Reach for the Sky* (1956). Married to fellow actor Derek Farr, she appeared with him in films such as *Doctor at Large* (1957). Her film career waned in the 1960s and she and her husband took to the stage and more TV roles. Following his death in 1986, Muriel Pavlow continued to work on the small screen. Not always a recognizable name but always a reliably good actress.

Later remembered for her marriage to Charles Bronson, former Rank starlet Jill Ireland was a regular and very attractive face to adorn several British hit films of the 1950s and 1960s. Born on 24 April 1936, Jill Ireland was appearing in films at Pinewood from the age of 19. In May 1957 she married fellow Rank contract artist David McCallum and in their 10-year marriage she had three children as well as making more than a dozen movies. Her Pinewood highlights include playing Jill, a waitress, in the taut 1957 thriller *Hell Drivers*, as well as appearing in three Peter Rogers' comedies, *Carry On Nurse* (1959), *Raising the Wind* (1961) and *Twice Round the Daffodils* (1962). Her marriage to David McCallum over, she married Charles Bronson in 1968 (ironically both men had appeared together in *The Great Escape* five years earlier) and she worked with Bronson, appearing in many of his films until her untimely death from breast cancer in 1990.

Everyone in the business agreed that the early death of Kay Kendall at the age of 36 from leukaemia, robbed the industry of a great star. Born on 21 May 1926 into a family of showbusiness performers, she became a chorus girl at 13, went into music hall at 16 and made her first film, *Fiddler's Three* in 1944, aged 18. At Pinewood, she went down a storm, enlivening every film she appeared in, from the role of Rosalind Peters, the scatty girlfriend to Kenneth More's Ambrose Claverhouse in *Genevieve* (1953) to the lead role of a frustrated television star housewife, Laura Foster, opposite Peter Finch in *Simon and Laura* (1955). In 1953 alone, she clocked up seven film appearances.

OPPOSITE: Peter Finch as Simon Foster and Kay Kendall as his wife Laura Foster in the 1955 bittersweet comedy of marital mishaps, *Simon and Laura*.

ACTRESS KAY KENDALL with cricketing legends The Bedser Twins at the London première of the 1952 Pinewood film, *The Final Test*.

A FINE ACTOR with something of a reputation for hard drinking and womanizing, Peter Finch played a not dissimilar role as a disenchanted Member of Parliament in the much under-rated 1961 drama, *No Love for Johnnie*.

A TALENTED AND MUCH ADMIRED leading lady of the 1950s, opposite, Virginia McKenna's acting was always gritty and convincing, in films such as *A Town Like Alice* (1956) and *Carve Her Name With Pride* (1958).

Kay Kendall was equally loved in America, where she appeared as a showgirl involved with Gene Kelly in *Les Girls* (1957). She even appeared on *The Phil Silvers Show* in "Bilko presents Kay Kendall" in January 1958. After appearing in the 1954 film, *The Constant Husband*, she fell in love with its lead star, Rex Harrison. When he learned from her doctor of her leukaemia, Harrison divorced his actress wife, Lilli Palmer, and married Kendall, making a pact with the doctor never to tell her how serious her incurable illness was. She died on 6 September 1959, just before the release of her last film, *Once More, With Feeling* (1960).

One actress who left the business through choice and not by the sadness of premature death was the vivacious Maureen Swanson. Hers was to be a fairytale departure. Born on 25 November 1932, this pretty and elegant Scottish actress made her first film *Moulin Rouge* (1952) aged just 19. She fast became one of the leading ladies of 1950s cinema, as Elaine in *Knights of the Round Table* (1953), playing opposite Norman Wisdom in *Up in the World* (1956), and with Dirk Bogarde in the touching melodrama *The Spanish Gardener* (1957). She was also highly regarded for her portrayal as Ellen, with Virginia McKenna and Peter Finch, in *A Town Like Alice* (1956). Maureen Swanson gave up her filming career when she married William Ward in 1961. He later became the 4th Earl of Dudley and she became the Countess of Dudley. The pair had six children. Miss Swanson never returned to showbusiness.

If any leading lady from the 1950s and beyond could be classified as both an attractive and a persuasive actress suitable to be labelled as a heroine, as one labels Kenneth More, Jack Hawkins and so on as heroes, that actress would be Virginia McKenna. Born on 7 June 1931, Virginia came from a liberal background, daughter of an actress and cabaret pianist who was half French and half Scottish. She studied drama, went into rep and appeared on television, before her big break in film came with the role of Wren Julie in *The Cruel Sea* (1953).

A Rank contract artist, she was to appear in some of Pinewood's top productions of the decade, with her acting – in films such as *Simba* (1955), *A Town Like Alice* (1956) and *Carve Her Name With Pride* (1958) – never less than gritty and convincing. The actress recalled those happy but hard times: "It was in the mid-1950s that I first worked at Pinewood Studios. I have amazing memories of

those days as I was lucky enough to be cast opposite Peter Finch in *A Town Like Alice* and I worked with Paul Scofield and Jack Warner in *Carve Her Name With Pride*. It was during the making of the latter film that I was given a long weekend off to marry Bill Travers! The third film I made at Pinewood was *The Passionate Summer* – opposite Bill and Yvonne Mitchell. These memories are perhaps less clear as I was expecting our first child and found the heat of Jamaica, where we were on location, rather trying.

"Pinewood was a friendly place – although I found the restaurant a bit daunting – and the crew, whether on the set or in make-up and hair, were kind and sensitive and fun to work with. I must admit I felt lucky in so many ways – to work with wonderful actors and directors such as Jack Lee and Lewis Gilbert and to take part in such special films, with such important stories to tell. I'd signed a five-year contract to get the part of Jean Paget in *A Town Like Alice*, but my family started to grow and I think the powers that be got a bit tired of me announcing I was having another baby! So I made three films out of five, but the memories of those are with me still."

Virginia McKenna was married to fellow actor Bill Travers from 1957 until his death in 1994. Together they founded The Born Free Foundation and she was awarded the OBE for services to wildlife and the arts in 2004. Proving not just that Virginia McKenna was a heroine in many of her films but that she continues to be one in real life, too.

Paul Hitchcock

PRODUCER

I may well be the oldest living person still working at Pinewood.

I came to Pinewood straight from school in April 1946. The admin block hadn't quite re-opened yet for film production. I came here as a junior in the accounts department. My former music teacher recommended me for a job. That was going to be my forte, becoming an accountant. I was employed by D & P Studios (Denham and Pinewood) who had everybody on the payroll in those days – from the cameraman to the gardener. That was the great thing. All the films were crewed with Rank employees. It was a great apprenticeship.

After the war, the Studios had an eerie feeling to them – they had been closed up for a while. They used to take the new boys upstairs and intentionally lose us in the dark recesses. You'd spend ages trying to find your way out. There was a story that a cleaning lady from Iver was connected to a ghost that, it was claimed, frequented the art gallery. We were very young and impressionable in those days!

I soon moved to the budgeting department for films. We used to be given a script, we had to break it down, schedule it and give it a budget. We would be allocated to a picture and we would have to control the budget of that film. I worked mainly on Betty Box's *Doctor* films and Norman Wisdom's comedies. I worked on many other films that never saw the light of day but these films were the big money

spinners of their time. We were cost accountants and our job was to control the cost or foresee the problems in the costs and report back to Rank. We made a picture here called *Windom's Way* with Peter Finch and Mary Ure. We built a village set in the gardens at Pinewood. Every day we tried to film it rained. I've never seen rain like it for so long. So I had to anticipate where the budget was going. We went five weeks over schedule just because of the weather. It was a huge problem but was no one's fault.

I left Pinewood to undertake my national service and returned afterwards. I left Rank in 1963 and went freelancing. I did that for three years before moving to Paramount for three years and then, in 1969, I joined Warner Brothers and became their head of production outside America for 24 years. I oversaw all the Kubrick films for example. When I hit 60 I retired, but I got fed up with that and came back to Exec-produce films, which I've been doing ever since.

When I first came to Pinewood, you walked on the stages and it had this kind of smell and atmosphere. I always knew that it was a magic place to be in. It was a big family in those days. There was something wonderful about the Studios. It was exceedingly well run and there was a great spirit about the place.

The last film I made here using the Pinewood crews was *The Little Shop of Horrors*, then sadly the Studios became four-wall – you then

employed people as you needed them. You lose
something when that happens. It was the right thing to
do, but the Studios lost something.

I still love it here. It's still a thrill for me to come here. I
did try to retire but I had to come back. I enjoy making
films. Three things are important in my life – work, my
family (you have to get the work to look after the family),
and sport. Making a film is like being the captain of a
team. You have all mixtures of people. You can have a
talented cricketer who is a pain in the arse. The same
with films. But because he's so good you put up with
him. Over my long career I've had to work with some of
the most difficult people in the world. But I have no
problem with that as long as they're talented. It's working
with difficult people who are un-talented that I find
impossible. And I've worked with a few of them!

I've often referred to those people in our business that

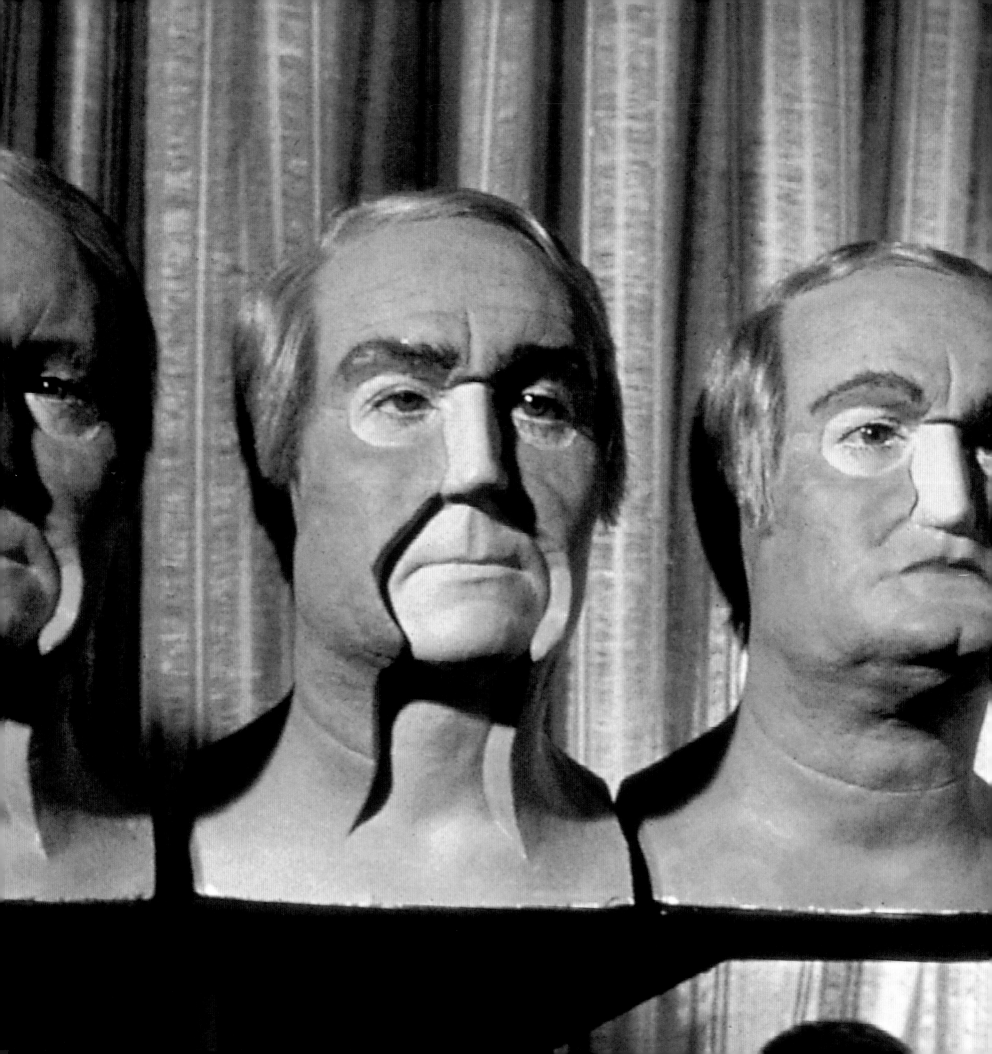

Nobody Does It Better

8

TWO EARLY PUBLICITY SHOTS of Sean Connery, from *Hell Drivers* (1957), above, and *Dr No* (1962), opposite.

James Bond was created by novelist Ian Fleming in an attempt, some claim, to take his mind of his forthcoming marriage. Bond's name was "borrowed" from that of an ornithologist who was Fleming's neighbour and his adventures and escapades were based loosely on the life of renowned British spy Sidney Reilly and double agent Dusko Popov – both of whom were accomplished womanizers. Bond made his first screen appearance in 1954 when, with Barry Nelson in the role, *Casino Royale* was adapted for American television.

When talks for Fleming's books to be turned into a series of films fell through in the late 1950s, Brian Lewis, Fleming's solicitor, introduced Fleming to another of his clients, Canadian film producer Harry Saltzman. Their meeting in 1960 proved fortuitous. Saltzman immediately bought an option on Fleming's *Bond* novels, though he couldn't get a title off the ground. Time began to run out on his option and in May 1961, screenwriter Wolf Mankowitz suggested that Saltzman meet up with another producer, Albert R. ("Cubby") Broccoli, who was known to be interested in Fleming's character.

Cubby was an experienced producer who had cut his teeth on quota quickies. One such film was the wartime flag waver *The Red Beret* (1952), directed by Terence Young and written by Richard Maibaum – both of whom would take up the same roles on Cubby's first *Bond* film. Broccoli and Saltzman were reluctant bedfellows but, realizing that time was running out on the book options, pooled their resources and formed a production company, Danjaq (derived from their wives' names, Dana Broccoli and Jacqueline Saltzman). They used Harry Saltzman's Canadian citizenship to enable them to base Danjaq in Switzerland. Eon Productions was the British arm of the operation.

Finding funding for Bond didn't prove easy. Most of the big studio backers turned the project down thinking it too British and too overtly sexual. Eventually at the end of June 1961, United Artists put up a modest $1 million, though the backing also came with the prospect of a six-film deal. Broccoli employed Richard Maibaum to work on a script for Fleming's *Thunderball*. He had finished the first draft of the screenplay before a court case surrounding the novel forced the producers to place *Thunderball* on the back burner and turn their attention to *Dr No* instead. The search was now on for an actor to play the part of 007.

In October 1961, *Kinematograph Weekly* informed film fans everywhere that production on *Dr No* would now move into 1962, while the producers concentrated on finding the right man to play James Bond. Many actors were reportedly considered for the role, including Rex Harrison, Trevor Howard and Patrick McGoohan. Broccoli was said to have been keen on Cary Grant, while Ian Fleming was thought to have favoured David Niven, Christopher Lee (Fleming's cousin), or Roger Moore – the producers ultimately considering the actor too young for the role at that time. Fleming also wanted Noel Coward to be considered for the arch-villain of the film's title, however Coward declined, sending a telegraph to the producers: "Dr No? No! No! No!"

As the search appeared to be getting nowhere, Broccoli recalled having met a young Scottish actor, Sean Connery, the previous year. The producer screened one of Connery's early films, the whimsical family fantasy *Darby O'Gill and the Little People* (1959), and was pleased with what he saw. His view that Connery could be the man was reinforced at a dinner party, when fellow producer Benjamin Fisz, who had Connery appearing in his latest film, a wartime comedy, *On the Fiddle* (1961), also suggested that Connery could be the right man for the role. Broccoli and Saltzman watched a few reels of *On the Fiddle* and promptly invited Connery to their offices for the first of a series of interviews. It was October 1961 and Sean Connery was 31.

Born in Edinburgh, the son of a lorry driver, Connery left school at 15 to join the Royal Navy. A

URSULA ANDRESS is Honey Ryder, far right, the first *Bond* girl, who played opposite Sean Connery as 007, in *Dr No* (1962).

CANADIAN-BORN ACTRESS LOIS MAXWELL played Miss Moneypenny, in 14 *Bond* films from *Dr No* in 1962, to *A View to a Kill* in 1985.

champion bodybuilder, Connery represented Scotland in the Mr Universe competition of 1950. He turned to acting and after a series of small parts in both television and film began to get noticed in movies such as *Hell Drivers* (1957) and *Tarzan's Greatest Adventure* (1959). Broccoli was sold on Connery the moment he met him, admiring his "right hint of threat behind that hard smile and faint Scottish burr". Saltzman declared that the producers "liked the way he moved. There's only one other actor who moves as well as he does and that's Albert Finney. They move like cats … for a big man to be so light on his feet is most unusual." United Artists were not so keen, but the producers stood their ground and eventually United recanted. An expectant industry read of the casting in the *Daily*

Cinema on 3 November 1961. Production on *Dr No* started two months later in Jamaica, before cast and crew returned to Britain to pick up filming at Pinewood on a 58-day studios-based shoot.

The director of *Dr No* was Terence Young with whom Broccoli had worked 10 years earlier on *The Red Beret*. Young was not the first choice. Bryan Forbes, Guy Green and future *Bond* director Guy Hamilton had all turned the project down. Yet Young proved to be a wise choice. Under his tutelage Connery grew into the role of the dapper, self-assured super spy. Young took Connery to his own Savile Row tailors, kitting him out in stylish suits and sports shirts. The two got on famously – Young having already directed Connery in one of his earliest films, *Action of the Tiger* (1957). Young ensured he was present at all of Connery's wardrobe fittings for *Dr No*. In fact, it is very much down to Terence Young that Bond's image has remained so iconic and long-lasting.

With a newfound confidence, Connery revelled in the chance to play what would soon become a world famous character: "This was like asking a boy who was crazy about cars if he'd like a Jaguar as a present. When the chance to play *Bond* came along, I hardly slept for days."

The first *Bond* girl was to make as big an impression as the first *Bond*. Ursula Andress, who played Honey Ryder, was a Swiss actress who had come to Cubby Broccoli's attention when he was sifting through hundreds of publicity stills of young, pretty actresses. The shot he came across was of her stepping out of the water – almost identical to her entrance in the finished film. Andress was advised to accept the role by her husband, photographer John Derek, whose later wife Bo Derek would also become a famous screen pin up.

Once Jamaican filming had been completed, further characters that were to become inextricably linked with the series joined the shoot at Pinewood. Canadian actress Lois Maxwell, whose husband had suffered a double coronary on her son's second birthday, had been calling around directors and producers for work, hoping someone would have some work for her to help meet the bills. Terence Young offered her Sylvia Trench – Bond's first on-screen conquest – or the ever-adoring and equally forgiving Miss Moneypenny. Maxwell was troubled about the scene where Bond find's Sylvia Trench in his room wearing just one of his shirts and

BOND NUMBER 5, PIERCE BROSNAN, is seen here on-set with Desmond Llewelyn, who played gadget-maestro, "Q", in 17 *Bond* films between 1962 and 1999.

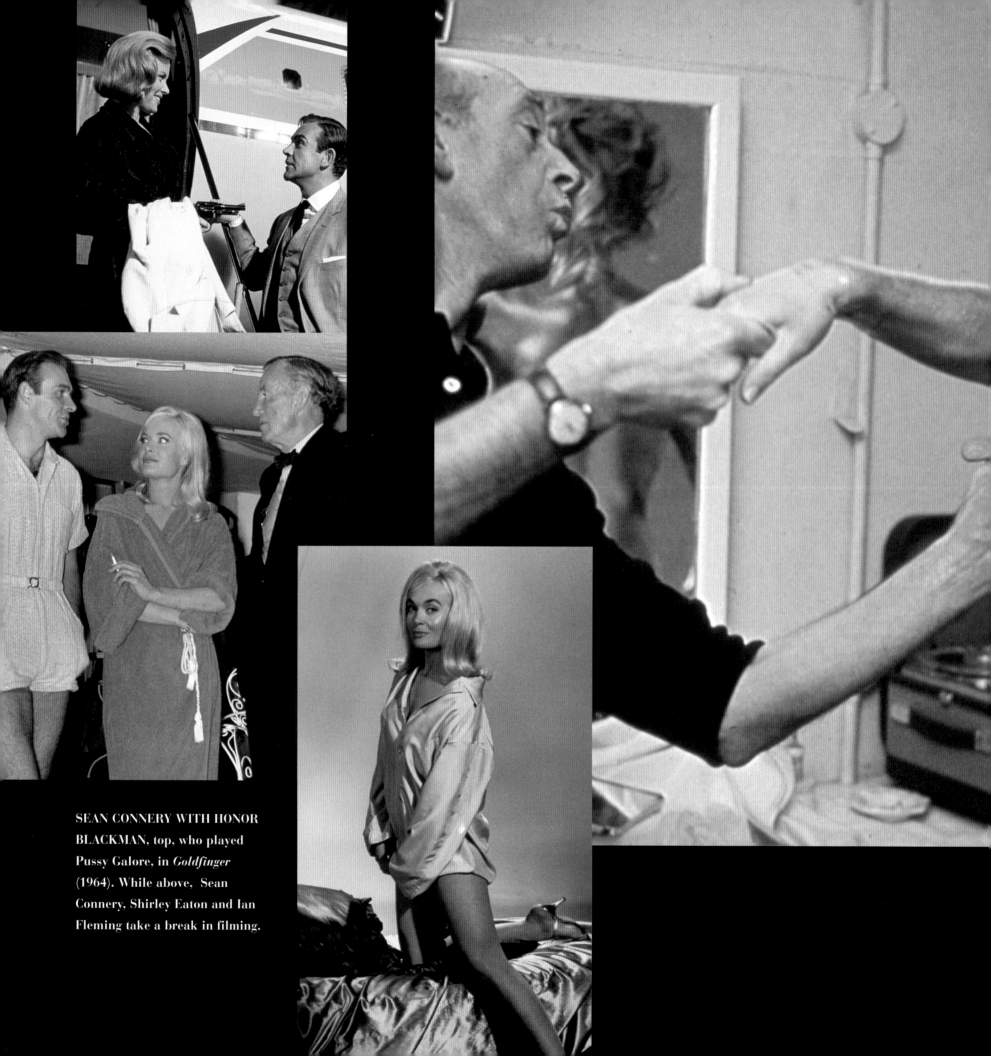

SEAN CONNERY WITH HONOR
BLACKMAN, top, who played
Pussy Galore, in *Goldfinger*
(1964). While above, Sean
Connery, Shirley Eaton and Ian
Fleming take a break in filming.

GERT FROBE, below, is the gilt-edged *Bond* baddie, Auric Goldfinger, with Sean Connery as 007.

GOLDEN GIRL – British actress Shirley Eaton, left, found international fame following her appearance as Jill Masterson in *Goldfinger*. Above, Shirley being covered from head to toe in gold paint for one of the most iconic scenes in the *Bond* canon – her short time on screen in *Goldfinger* (1964) is still one of the most remembered moments in 007 history.

A CLASSIC *BOND* ACTION SEQUENCE, above, while, above right, Donald Pleasance played the villainous Ernst Stavro Blofeld in *You Only Live Twice*, 1966.

ON THE PINEWOOD SET of *You Only Live Twice*, opposite, which had sequences filmed at the Studios during 1966.

opted for Miss Moneypenny instead. She was given two days work and £200 on the condition she supplied her own wardrobe. It soon became clear that Lois Maxwell had picked the right part.

On 25 February 1961, just a day before Pinewood filming began in earnest, Bernard Lee joined Connery and Lois Maxwell on set. Lee, an established British character actor who had started his film career in 1935, had been signed to play Bond's boss "M". Young often quipped that Lee only got the role because everyone else was away. But the choice was a good one and Lee would stay with the series until his death in 1981.

Filming for *Dr No* was completed on 30 March 1962. Editor Peter Hunt started piecing the footage together and Monty Norman was commissioned to write the soundtrack. By July, a cut had been made that Young showed at a private screening. Among the guests were Ian Fleming and his wife Anne. The screening was not a great success. In a letter to Evelyn Waugh, Anne Fleming said "it was an abominable occasion" and that she was shocked at the laughter that met the scene of a tarantula climbing up Bond's body. Fleming was not happy either and following a preview in Leicester Square dismissed *Dr No* as "simply dreadful". His attitude was to change, however, and soon he was telling readers of *The Times* that those who had never read a *Bond* novel would "find it a wonderful movie".

Dr No received its press launch at the London Pavilion on 2 October 1962, opening three days later to the public, ahead of its general release on the 8th. The film received its US première at a star-studded screening on 7 March 1963 and was a big success on both sides of the Atlantic, topping box-office charts across the

world. Bondmania had started and Connery became an international star.

Following the huge success of *Dr No*, Cubby Broccoli and Harry Saltzman set about planning a sequel. Fleming had written several *Bond* novels that could be suitable for adaptation but the producers were particularly keen on *From Russia With Love*, as United States President John F. Kennedy had just listed the title as one of his top 10 books. Sales of the paperback soared and the producers knew this was a bandwagon they had to jump on. The film's plot is tight and conjures up a wonderful atmosphere of foreign intrigue as James Bond is duped into smuggling a top secret decoding device from Turkey to the West on the Orient Express. Unlike most Cold War thrillers of its time, the baddies were not in fact Russian, but agents of SPECTRE and its evil leader, Ernst Stavros Blofeld.

From Russia With Love began shooting on 1 April 1963 at Pinewood Studios, before continuing in Turkey, Scotland and Ireland. The entire introductory sequence that plays out before the main titles was filmed in the gardens at Pinewood – the one where it appears that Bond has been killed in what turns out to be a training exercise to test the mettle of Robert Shaw's vicious character Red Grant. In an early cut of the film there was concern that the unmasked victim's face was too similar to Connery's and could cause confusion among audiences, so Terence Young reshot the scene, this time using an actor with a moustache. The Orient Express exterior shots were filmed on location in Turkey, but the infamous two-minute fistfight was shot at Pinewood, where art director Syd Cain painstakingly recreated the train's interiors. For this scene, Terence Young had two stationary cameras set up and locked off but on the advice of editor Peter Hunt brought in

THE SHORT-LIVED LOVE of Tracy Di Vicenzo (Diana Rigg) and James Bond (George Lazenby) in *On Her Majesty's Secret Service* (1969). The film was Australian actor Lazenby's first and only outing as 007.

a third roaming camera to allow more shots to be captured and to give the scene more depth and variety as Connery and Shaw (and their stunt doubles Bob Simmons and Jack Cooper) slug it out under the watchful eye of crew, director and stunt coordinator Peter Perkins.

Blofeld – even though his face is never seen on screen – was played by two actors, Anthony Dawson, who appeared previously as Professor Dent in *Dr No*, and British actor Eric Pohlman, who provided Blofeld's voice. *From Russia With Love* also saw the first appearance of "Q" (played by actor Desmond Llewelyn) and his wizard high-tech gadgetry. The love interest came in the shape of Russian diplomat Tatiana Romanova played by Daniela Bianchi, and for her steamy scene with Connery caught on SPECTRE's hidden camera, Terence Young cleared the Pinewood set save for the most essential crew needed to film the moment.

One major scene that caused the production team great difficulties was the sewer sequence where Tatiana and Kerim Bay (played by Pedro Armendariz) are chased by hundreds of rats. The use of wild rats in filming at British studios was

PROFILE

Ian Fleming

Born on 28 May 1908, Ian Fleming was educated at Eton College and the Royal Military Academy at Sandhurst. His application to join the Foreign Office was rejected and he turned to journalism, including working for the Reuters News Service in Moscow. During the Second World War, Fleming served in the Navy quickly rising through the ranks to a Commander. While in naval intelligence, he devised several plans to outwit the Germans and their allies. In 1942, Fleming pulled together a Unit of highly skilled officers trained in safe cracking, unarmed combat and intelligence gathering. The unit was known as the 30 Assault Unit and Fleming personally planned all their raids.

Fleming's intelligence work undoubtedly provided the background for many of his spy novels. His first, *Casino Royale*, which introduced the character of James Bond, was published in 1953. Initially his novels were not hugely successful but when President John F. Kennedy included *From Russia With Love* on his list of favourite books, sales jumped. Fleming wrote 14 *Bond* titles in all, their success allowing him to retire to his Jamaican estate, Goldeneye, in the late 1950s.

Fleming sold the film rights for his *Bond* titles to producer Harry Saltzman in 1961, but, sadly, Fleming did not live to witness the enduring success of the classic character he had created on the page, dying of a heart attack on August 12, 1964.

As well *Bond*, Ian Fleming's other novels included the much-loved children's story, *Chitty Chitty Bang Bang*.

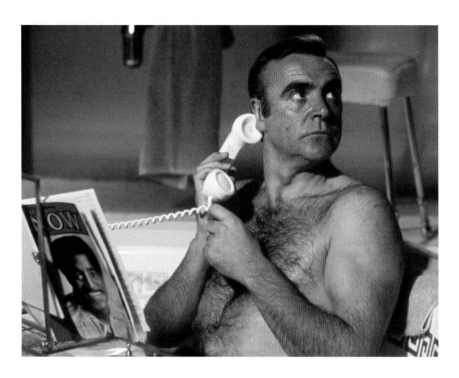

SEAN CONNERY was thought to have left the character of James Bond behind him after *You Only Live Twice* **(1967), but returned to the role in** *Diamonds Are Forever,* **four years later.**

prohibited. The props department tried coating tame white rats with cocoa dust but the rats kept licking it off themselves and each other. Eventually, Young had to take a small crew and cast members to Madrid, where the laws did not apply. Two hundred rodents were captured by a local rat catcher and the scary and now even more realistic scene was filmed. *From Russia With Love* repeated the success of *Dr No* and went further to become the top moneymaking film in Great Britain in 1963.

Buoyed with success, there was more to follow. This time an epic adventure, which with its imaginative plot, larger than life villain, high-tech gadgetry and sexy women, was to become the template not just for the establishing series but also for many other cinematic imitators. *Goldfinger* allowed Bond to fulfil Fleming's vision of the super spy able to "go wildly beyond the probable, but not beyond the possible". From henchmen with killer bowler hats to a power crazy villain with gold in his name – Auric Goldfinger (played by the late great Gert Frobe) – to a deadly laser beam and even more deadly atomic bomb planned to detonate inside Fort Knox, the scene was set for Bond's greatest hour, or two.

Filming on *Goldfinger* started on 20 January 1964 in Miami, but Connery, who was filming Alfred Hitchcock's psychological thriller *Marnie*, could not join the cast and crew until several weeks into shooting. His "Miami" hotel shots were filmed at Pinewood, with location footage rear projected to give the appearance that he was in the USA for the scenes involved.

Goldfinger saw a new director to the series, Guy Hamilton, who brought his own sense of where to take the film and the character: "I had been offered the first *Bond* film, *Dr No*, but couldn't leave Jamaica for personal reasons, so was delighted when I had a chance to direct *Goldfinger*. I'd enjoyed the previous two films, but felt there was a real danger of James Bond becoming Superman; consequently there would be no suspense in whatever predicaments were dreamt up for him. So we concentrated on the villains; Bond is only as good as his villains."

The film's most memorable image is also one of the most iconic of 20th century cinema, with Bond entering his bedroom to find Jill Masterson's gilt-covered corpse. It took two hours at a time for sexy British actress Shirley Eaton to have her body made up in gold. Shirley remembers filming the scene: "Everyone was delightful. It was hot work. My body temperature was monitored the whole time as the gold make up covered the pores on my skin. They kept an eye on my blood pressure too and a little patch of skin on my stomach was left untouched to allow my skin to breathe a bit."

While Shirley Eaton was worrying about her skin, Connery was concerned about losing his own. The scene where 007 is tied to a table with a laser beam slowly making it's deadly way towards him was filmed using a mixture of special effects added after filming and a live flame used by technicians on set during shooting. The technicians would sit out of shot under the table with an oxyacetylene torch and wait for the director's careful cues to light, blast and move it along. The climax of the film required production designer Ken Adam to construct a replica set of Fort Knox's exterior at Pinewood. Complete with a one-mile concrete driveway, the set was one of the most expensive sets built at that time. Add Honor Blackman's appearance as the deliciously named Pussy Galore

CHARLES GRAY made his first *Bond* appearance as Dikko Henderson in *You Only Live Twice*. He was "promoted" to the role of the two-faced arch villain, Ernst Stavro Blofeld in *Diamonds Are Forever* (1971), becoming the second actor to take on the role.

THE LONGEST-SERVING 007 TO DATE,
Roger Moore starred as James Bond in seven
consecutive films in the series, between 1973
and 1985.

and a rousing classic title song performed by Shirley Bassey – which made it to number eight in the charts – and the producers had all the right ingredients for a classic movie. And it worked: *Goldfinger* made it to the top moneymaking spot in Britain in 1964.

Sadly, in the summer of 1964, Bond creator Ian Fleming suffered a debilitating chest cold, which left him severely ill with pleurisy and other complications. He died on 12 August, aged 56.

Terence Young returned to direct *Thunderball*, which began filming in February 1965. This time the spy adventure had more of a comic strip feel to it, relying heavily on gadgets and hi-tech hardware, some claim, at the expense of the plot. Certainly, with much of the action sequences taking place underwater, *Thunderball* broke new ground with its innovative camera techniques and the challenges it threw up for production staff to ensure the film's excitement levels kept it afloat. Broccoli and Saltzman employed acclaimed underwater cinematographer Lamar Boren to capture the film's complicated beneath-the-surface shots. The underwater battle between Bond and SPECTRE's divers was to be one of the most elaborate underwater scenes ever filmed. Those scenes were filmed on location in the Bahamas with rehearsals taking place at a shopping centre car park in Nassau. Production designer Ken Adam played his part in making the film look visually splendid by inventing a host of sleek nautical crafts, particularly the villain Emilio Largo's versatile yacht, the *Disco Volante*. Adolfo Celi played the part of Largo with wicked relish. The final fistfight on his boat was shot at Pinewood and intercut with footage shot in the Bahamas. Although not universally loved by critics, *Thunderball* became one of the most successful Bond films, topping the box-office charts in Britain and – for the first time – in the USA, in 1966.

Sean Connery returned for a fifth successive appearance as James Bond in *You Only Live Twice*, which was released in the summer of 1967. Cubby Broccoli and Harry Saltzman decided that to keep the series fresh they should bring in new talents. So they hired famed novelist Roald Dahl to write the screenplay and brought in a new director, the acclaimed British filmmaker Lewis Gilbert who had just had a big hit with his 1966 film *Alfie*. Setting the film in Japan, both writer

ROGER MOORE MADE HIS *BOND* DEBUT IN *Live and Let Die* **in 1973, here seen under threat from Mr Big, played by Yaphet Kotto.**

and director broke the Bond mould and re-made it, creating a stunning film full of incredible action sequences and stunning sets as Bond fights SPECTRE and its evil boss, seen for the first time on screen and played with great class by Donald Pleasance – who only joined the cast at short notice when the actor pencilled in for the part was taken ill. Ken Adam's sets live up to the script and acting and the great cinematography by Freddie Young who helped bring Gilbert's imagination to cinematic reality.

The volcano set for the climatic ending was so large that there was a national scaffolding shortage that held up progress of the building of the new Hilton Hotel at Hyde Park. Indeed, the set was so large that it had to be built outdoors on a Pinewood back lot. It contained a movable helicopter platform, a fully working monorail system and a mock-up of a rocket ship that could simulate take off and rise 50 feet into the air. The set alone cost over $1 million to build – (around £5 million today) which was more than the entire budget for the whole of *Dr No* just four years earlier.

Unsurprisingly, *You Only Live Twice* also topped the British film charts. However, change was ahead. During filming in Japan, Sean Connery became increasingly frustrated by the media intrusion in his life. It is claimed that he approached the series' producers asking to become a full producing partner in the company that was to make further Bond films. Broccoli and Saltzman refused and Connery walked away from the role after production on the film was complete.

Once the shock of Connery's departure had been absorbed, there were two immediate questions to be answered: would there be more Bond films and, if so, who would be the next 007? The answer to the first question was a categorical yes: the answer to the second was trickier. Speculation was rife as to which well-known actor would take on the role. After considering a host of different actors, Broccoli and Saltzman decided that their only option was to choose, as they had with Sean Connery, a new name to the film world.

George Lazenby had been spotted by Broccoli a few years earlier, not in an acting role, but while visiting his local hair salon for a cut and trim. Lazenby, an actor more renowned at that time for his modelling work, was in the salon at the same time and the tall, handsome, well-built man left a lasting impression on the

PROFILE

Albert R. Broccoli

Albert R. Broccoli, affectionately known in the film industry as "Cubby", was born on 5 April 1909, in Long Island, New York, the oldest son of an Italian-American family. Broccoli's early career in Hollywood started as assistant director on a Howard Hughes picture, *The Outlaw*. During World War II he served for five years in the Navy and, on returning to civilian life, became a talent agent, representing many actors, including Ava Gardner and Lana Turner.

In 1952 Cubby came to England, launched Warwick Films with Irving Allen and started his film producing career with *The Red Beret*. In the next decade, Warwick Films produced many classics such as *Cockleshell Heroes*, *No Time to Die*, *Hell Below Zero* and the critically acclaimed *The Trials of Oscar Wilde*. Cubby and his wife, Dana, lived in England for many years.

When Broccoli became interested in Ian Fleming's *Bond* stories, he discovered the rights were held by Canadian producer, Harry Saltzman. Together they formed Eon Productions and, in 1962, produced the first James Bond film, *Dr No*, which set the pattern for the successive adventures of the suave British secret service agent 007. This partnership continued for the next nine *Bond* movies. During this time Broccoli also produced the hit family musical *Chitty Chitty Bang Bang* (1968). When Saltzman sold his share to United Artists in 1977, Broccoli continued as the "man behind *Bond*", producing a further seven films and thus creating the most successful film franchise ever, before handing the reins over to his stepson, Michael G. Wilson, and daughter, Barbara Broccoli.

In 1982, Cubby Broccoli accepted the prestigious Irving Thalberg award from the Academy of Motion Picture Arts and Sciences. In 1987 he received the OBE in recognition of his outstanding contribution to the British Film Industry. He died in 1996.

ROGER MOORE AND
BARBARA BACH,
below, face the biggest
baddie, Jaws, played
by Richard Kiel, in
*The Spy Who Loved
Me* (1977).

BELOW, Jane Seymour played
Bond beauty, Solitaire, in *Live
and Let Die* (1973).

ABOVE, another thrilling chase sequence from
the 1987 *Bond* outing *The Living Daylights*.

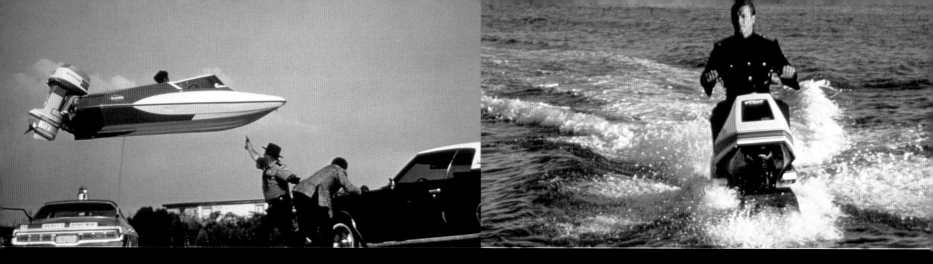

producer's mind. What Broccoli was unaware of was that the meeting was not a chance one and that Lazenby, who was trying to break into film, had orchestrated it. It may have taken a few years to pay off but when Lazenby's name was submitted for the role after Connery left, Broccoli was keen to give him a screen test. Down to just the last few names for consideration, the remaining candidates for the role had to perform a fight scene in which Bond comes up against an assassin in a hotel room. The actors were choreographed through the scene and left to rehearse it. Lazenby's performance had great panache and both the producers and the director, Peter Hunt, were convinced that Lazenby was the man. United Artists agreed.

Consideration was given within the script to explain the change in appearance and look of James Bond. A scene was discussed in which 007 would have been shown in hospital, undergoing plastic surgery. The idea was quickly abandoned and the scene not written. The only nod to the previous incumbent comes at the end of the pre-title scene, when the beautiful Tracy (Diana Rigg) manages to get away from Bond and Lazenby declares: "This never happened to the other fella!"

All the stops were pulled out for *On Her Majesty's Secret Service*. With the audience so caught up in the clever plot and hugely exciting action and fight sequences, they had little time to conside the change of face. Second-unit director John Glen supervised the action and was to be rewarded with the role of director for five consecutive *Bond* outings throughout the 1980s. The film is one of the longest in the series but there is little time to breathe as 007 fights to stop enemy Blofeld's threat of a biological warfare attack, while meeting Tracy di Vicenzo, a countess who captures his heart and becomes his wife. From Olympic-class skiers being used for the downhill chases, to the performances of Telly Savalas as Blofeld as well as Diana Rigg, the film works hard to compensate for the feeling that there was something – or someone – missing. The scene at the end of the film when Bond's new wife is killed is emotional stuff, and some were unsure about ending a Bond film on such a down note.

ROGER MOORE TAKES TO THE WATER, above, in *The Spy Who Loved Me* (1977) and, above left, a classic stunt shot from *Live and Let Die* (1973).

CHRISTOPHER LEE AS SCARAMANGA, and Roger Moore as James Bond, in *The Man with the Golden Gun* (1974).

TIMOTHY DALTON appeared twice as 007,
in *The Living Daylights* **(1987) and** *Licence*
to Kill **(1989).**

On Her Majesty's Secret Service was Lazenby's only outing as 007. Stories abound as to the reasons behind the actor's departure. Many revolve around the producers' not finding Lazenby as easy to work with as they would have wished. There was also a considerable drop in the box-office returns for the film. Whatever the reason, Lazenby wasn't coming back for *Diamonds Are Forever* and once again a new Bond had to be found.

Broccoli and Saltzman began a long and extensive audition process once again but while the film was in pre-production the president of United Artists, David Picker, flew to England to meet with Sean Connery in an attempt to entice him back to the role. Connery played hardball and a not inconsiderable deal was struck in which the Scottish actor would receive a very large salary, a percentage of the profits from the film and a commitment from United that the company would finance two further productions of Connery's choosing. The deal was so large – Connery's reported fee being $1.25 million – that it was listed in the *Guinness Book of World Records*.

Diamonds Are Forever sees 007 on the trail of high-powered jewel smugglers. The highlight of the film is a car-chase though the streets of the world's gambling capital, Las Vegas, and Bond's escape from the police as he turns his Mustang Mach 1 on its side down a narrow alley. Ford provided eight vehicles for filming the scene and though the famous Fremont Street in Las Vegas was closed for three nights for stuntmen and crew to rehearse and film the sequence, the scene had to be finished off at Pinewood for the car interior shots and close ups. However, Pinewood was used less than previously for a Bond movie. With so much filming taking place in America, Universal's studio facilities in Southern California were used instead.

The film was released on 30 December 1971 and did considerably better business than its predecessor – at $116 million in worldwide rentals, almost double the $64 million of *On Her Majesty's Secret Service*. However, this time when Connery said he'd had enough, everyone believed him and the search was on again for the third actor to play Bond in as many movies.

The producers knew they needed someone who would last in the role and gel with audiences if the massive moneyspinner that this film series had become, was

A PUBLICITY SHOT from *A View to a Kill* (1985), far left, and, left, the stars of the film, (l to r) Tanya Roberts, Roger Moore, Grace Jones and Christopher Walken.

to continue. After months of searching and countless screen tests, the producers approached an actor whom Connery himself had referred to as "an ideal Bond". Born in 1927, Roger Moore was a hugely popular and well-known face on television, having found international fame with *The Saint*. Moore would bring a whole new style to the role of 007, and, more importantly, a sense of humour which when mixed with the character's deadly traits would prove a heady cocktail for *Bond*-lovers across the world. Moore's first outing was *Live and Let Die* in which our hero becomes embroiled in the dark world of Voodoo practices after chasing a master criminal across New York, New Orleans, Jamaica and, of course, Pinewood Studios. Filming took place from late 1972 through early 1973. Much to the relief of all involved, *Live and Let Die* was a big success. Its budget was $7 million dollars – similar to *Diamonds Are Forever* – and its worldwide box-office take was around $126 million. The successful *Bond* bandwagon had not run out of steam.

Production on *The Man With the Golden Gun* started almost immediately – at the beginning of November 1973 – with location filming first in Hong Kong, then Macau, Bangkok, Phuket and on the Isle of Khow-Ping-Khan. This time round 007 is on the trail of the political assassin Scaramanga, played by Christopher Lee. Based on the last of the Fleming novels, the film was also to be the last joint Bond collaboration between the two founding producers, Cubby Broccoli and Harry Saltzman. While Cubby had been concentrating most of his energies on Bond, Saltzman had been producing successful films outside of their partnership, including the Harry Palmer workingman's spy trilogy, *The Ipcress File*

CUBBY BROCCOLI talking to Princess Diana while Prince Charles mixes with cast members including Timothy Dalton, on the set of *The Living Daylights* (1987).

THE *BOND* PRODUCERS originally considered casting Pierce Brosnan for the role of 007 in the mid-1980s but he had other filming commitments. He finally took on the role in *GoldenEye* in 1995.

A CLASSIC CHASE SEQUENCE from *GoldenEye* (1995), below, packed with the usual *Bond* style and panache.

(1965), *Funeral in Berlin* (1967) and *Billion Dollar Brain* (1967), all starring Michael Caine. Saltzman also produced *The Battle of Britain* (1969) and the fantasy musical *Tomorrow* (1972). Outside of *Bond*, the only film that the partnership had made together was the perennial children's favourite about a magical flying car, *Chitty Chitty Bang Bang* (1967), starring Dick Van Dyke and Lionel Jeffries. For their last 007 adventure the producers really did push the boat out, with an abundance of exotic locations, two beautiful female leads in the forms of Britt Ekland and Maud Adams, impressive stunts and action sequences and a convincing almost-likeable baddie.

Christopher Lee and Roger Moore had worked together some 25 years previously on a post-war Pinewood production *Trottie True* – a period comedy with Lee playing the part of Bongo and Moore uncredited as the Stage Door Johnny. Both had come a long way since then. *The Man with the Golden Gun* was a huge international hit and, as the Cold War began to thaw, it was the first *Bond* film to receive a showing at the Kremlin. Moore's position as the world's favourite spy was now assured and even with Saltzman's departure, the series was just getting better and better.

To ensure that increasing success Broccoli took his time over the next film and – after more than two years and armed with a budget almost twice as large as for the previous film – *The Spy Who Loved Me* was announced as the tenth entry in the *Bond* canon. The advertising banners declared: "It's the Biggest! It's the Best! It's *Bond* and Beyond."

The Spy Who Loved Me was the first 007 adventure not based on a story by Ian Fleming, although the title was. Writers Christopher Wood and Richard Maibaum constructed the story of Bond and a glamorous Russian spy tracking down a megalomaniac shipping magnate, while production designer Ken Adam constructed sets so large and elaborate that a new sound stage had to be

PIERCE BROSNAN as 007 and Michelle Yeoh as Wai Lin in *Tomorrow Never Dies* (1997).

DAME JUDI DENCH, who has appeared as "M" in the *Bond* series since *GoldenEye* in 1995.

built at Pinewood to accommodate it. Building of the 007 stage took seven months during the hot, dry, drought-riddled summer of 1976. The stage was officially opened on 5 December 1976, with former Prime Minister Harold Wilson in attendance, along with many leading British actors.

With *The Spy Who Loved Me*, director Lewis Gilbert created a perfect Bond adventure – a beautiful female lead (Barbara Bach as Major Anya Amasova), a callous megalomaniac (Curt Jurgens as the evil Stromberg) and the steel-mouthed giant Jaws (played by 7ft 2in tall Richard Kiel). Jaws was supposed to die when Stromberg's headquarters were blown up, but Broccoli sensed the appeal of the character and he would return once again in the next *Bond* film.

The Spy Who Loved Me was nominated for three Oscars – Best Art Direction, Best Music Score and Best Music Song, as well as two British Academy Award nominations for Best Production Design and Art Direction, and Best Film Music. The much lauded and nominated title song *Nobody Does It Better* seemed to augur well for both Cubby Broccoli and Roger Moore who were showing that, when it came to *Bond*, there really was nobody who could.

While the film was proving a great success, filmmaking in Britain was going through a difficult period and with increasingly high taxes for the wealthiest forcing talent away from the country, the announcement that Cubby Broccoli himself was upping sticks and moving out came as a blow to the industry. Consequently, there was some disappointment but no great surprise when *Moonraker* was made in France, with Pinewood being used only for special effects and post-production. This was a great shame as the sheer scale of Bond's first space outing meant huge sets had to be spread across three of France's largest studios – Boulogne, Epinay and Billancourt. With hundreds of technicians spending hundreds of thousands of hours working on producing some awe-inspiring sets, there were many who were frustrated that the film was not made at Pinewood.

Moonraker did huge business, becoming the fifth highest earning film of the series to date. Bringing in over $210 million worldwide, it set a *Bond* box-office record that would not be beaten until *GoldenEye*, 16 years later.

Bond was back at Pinewood throughout the 1980s, when the series offered up five action-packed outings. After 10 years of editing and second-unit work on

the films. John Glen became the films' director and so impressive was his work on *For Your Eyes Only* (1981), that Broccoli kept him on in that role for the next four films. Sadly, Bernard Lee passed away before his scenes could be shot and out of respect for the actor, the part was not recast for the film. His dialogue was given to "Q" and other characters.

For Your Eyes Only is a grittier, darker film than *Moonraker*, with Bond showing the more serious side to his nature and his job, reminding us all, as he traces a top secret device sunk off the Greek coast, what being a "00" is all about – a licence to kill.

Bond was back for *Octopussy* in 1983, this time finding himself in India for the 13th film in the series. Shooting began in West Berlin in August 1982 and continued throughout the rest of the year both in India and England, before wrapping up at Pinewood in January 1983. Maud Adams played the title role, becoming the first actress to have twice had a lead role in the *Bond* series.

At 20 years old, the series was still pulling in the crowds. Yet disaster was soon to strike. During the filming of Ridley Scott's fantasy *Legend*, in June 1984, a fire started on set and burnt the stage down. It was the 007 stage – the world's

PREPARING TO SHOOT – Pierce Brosnan and Robert Carlyle, above left, take their marks in *The World is Not Enough* (1999).

THE CAVIAR FACTORY SCENE, above, in *The World is Not Enough* (1999) was filmed on Pinewood's water tank and is regarded as one of the most spectacular set-pieces in *Bond* history.

largest sound stage. With *A View to a Kill* in pre-production this was not good news. Director John Glen was assured that the stage could be re-built in three months. Production designer Peter Lamont set about getting a new 007 stage up and running. He worked on and improved the original spec for the building and though there were the usual health and safety delays the stage was pre-lit ahead of Christmas and ready for the start of filming in January 1985. It was a huge feat, worthy of Bond himself. While building was underway, other stages at Pinewood were used to ensure the film came in on time and in budget. *A View to a Kill* was given its British première on 12 June 1985, in the presence of Prince Charles and Princess Diana.

A View to a Kill was to be the last Bond appearance for Lois Maxwell, who as the obedient and forever-pining Miss Moneypenny had been in every film since the series began in 1962. The film was also to see the departure of Roger Moore from the lead role after seven films and more than 12 years in the job. Moore, then in his mid-50s, decided it was the right time to leave and quit while he was ahead. Once again, as they had on Sean Connery's departure, the echoes whispered that Bond would never be the same again.

With Roger Moore out of the picture, Cubby Broccoli set about the daunting task of "trying to follow that". He selected Welsh-born Timothy Dalton who, with his experience as an acclaimed Shakespearean actor, would bring a new level of seriousness and grittiness to the role. Broccoli had considered Dalton for the role once before but had felt at that time the actor was too young. At the official announcement that Dalton was to take over as 007 for *The Living Daylights*, the actor said: "It's probably every kids dream to play James Bond. He's the ultimate fantasy figure, and I know I wanted to be 007 when I saw the Connery films. Now, I am here to get paid to live out a childhood fantasy." Dalton's playing of the role was to be more akin to Fleming's original character, darker and more dangerous.

The Living Daylights, with 007 helping the Soviets catch a defector, was released in 1987 marking the 25th anniversary of *Bond* on screen and during production the Prince and Princess of Wales came to Pinewood to visit the set. Dalton received good reviews and the film performed well. To date it is the seventh most financially successful of the series at the box office, with receipts of $191 million.

The shooting locations required for the next entry, *Licence to Kill*, along with a favourable exchange rate, meant it was more financially sound to take the film out of Britain. This was bad news for Pinewood, which, along with other studios in the country, was going through difficult times, as fewer big films came to these shores.

Licence to Kill had an all together different feel to it. Bond disobeys his bosses and resigns his commission, becomes a renegade and searches for justice his way. This harder-edged film became the first and only in the series to date to receive a "15" certificate from the British board of film censors. It did not make as much money as its predecessor – down to $156 million in 1990. Perhaps the higher classification had kept some of the potential audience away. Was this a temporary blip? The producers would have to wait to find out. A long and protracted court battle between MGM and Broccoli's company meant that no new *Bond* film would be made for six years.

Finally, in 1995, the news came that a new *Bond* film was to be made. By now a new Bond was needed and the announcement that the role was being given to Pierce Brosnan came as little surprise to those who had considered him the right person to play 007 for many years. Indeed, Brosnan had been considered for the part on Roger Moore's departure in 1986 but he was unable to take the lead in *The Living Daylights* due to filming commitments on the TV series *Remington Steele*.

Once again Pinewood would lose out on having its studios used for filming. It was unable to accommodate the production in full and the makers took their project to the old Rolls-Royce factory at Leavesden in Hertfordshire, where they built sets – indoors and out – from scratch for the film.

The years away from the big screen allowed producers Michael G. Wilson and Barbara Broccoli, under the supervision of her father Cubby, to bring *Bond* into the 21st century with *GoldenEye*. New cast, new technology, new understanding of the new world order. Audiences loved the film and Brosnan was a great success, with *GoldenEye* becoming the third most successful *Bond* to date. At over $350 million,

JAMES BOND doing what he does best, above, while, opposite, a helicopter with 17-foot razor-toothed chainsaws is lowered into position for shooting in *The World is Not Enough* (1999).

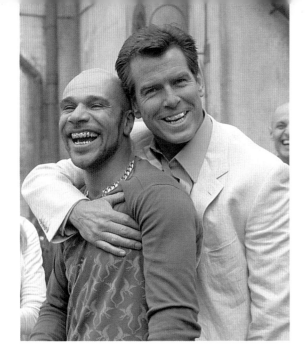

JOKING ON THE SET of *The World is Not Enough* (1999), Pierce Brosnan with musician-turned-actor, Goldie.

PIERCE BROSNAN, here filming in the water tank at Pinewood, appeared as 007 in four of the films, *GoldenEye* (1995), *Tomorrow Never Dies* (1997), *The World is Not Enough* (1999) and *Die Another Day* (2002).

it more than doubled the worldwide earnings of *Licence to Kill* six year earlier. Bond was back and then some.

Tomorrow Never Dies began production in January 1997. Leavesden was now unavailable, as filming was underway there on a new *Star Wars* film. So cast and crew decamped to a disused warehouse in Frogmore, northwest of London, which was converted and rebuilt to accommodate the film. Pinewood was used but less than previously, for scenes involving the villain's stealth ship and some interior shots and tank work. This was the first of the films to be made without the guidance and inspiration of Cubby Broccoli, who had passed away during the summer of 1996. Barbara Broccoli, alongside her stepbrother Michael G. Wilson, continued to make the films with the same thought and passion as Cubby had for over 30 years. Yet it wasn't all plain sailing – the script had to be reworked several times and there was friction among some cast members. The pressure of having the film ready for a December release added to the woes but, as if in a snub to those who would put the film down, *Tomorrow Never Dies* was released in December 1997 to a thunderous box-office reception. It had cost $90 million to make and brought in over $345 million.

Pinewood's connection with *Bond* was finally reset with the 19th film in the series and Brosnan's third appearance as Bond in *The World is Not Enough*. The producers brought a new director on board, Michael Apted, who had created several critically acclaimed films including *Coal Miner's Daughter* (1980) and *Gorillas in the Mist* (1988). Apted was not renowned for action blockbusters but as producer Michael G. Wilson explained: "We have a great team and special

effects crew who put their heads together to come up with sensational and mind-boggling gadgets, but for the character and the drama, which those aspects need to be wrapped around to shine, you need a good director. Michael Apted is one of the best performance directors around – he's renowned for it." Apted used his skills to good advantage, allowing audiences to see a Bond troubled by the death of a colleague and how those feelings affect his behaviour throughout the rest of the film as he fights to bring down a world class villain who can feel no pain.

For Pinewood, it was good to get some large-scale *Bond* sets back at the Studios, especially the caviar factory belonging to the Russian Valentin Zukovsky (played by Robbie Coltrane). This outstanding set was constructed by Peter Lamont and his team on the paddock tank at Pinewood, which had to be enlarged and extended and then surrounded by blackout coverings to give the effect of nighttime, when the explosive scenes of the factory being decimated needed to be set. *The World is Not Enough* is jam-packed full of exhilarating action pieces. The film began shooting in January 1999 and was ready for release in November. It became the second highest *Bond* earner to date, just nudging ahead of *GoldenEye*, at almost $355 million.

A new millennium saw a new *Bond* planned. *Bond XX* would be released to coincide with the series' 40th Anniversary in 2002. *Die Another Day* became the 20th entry of the most financially successful film franchise in cinema history. The producers continued in their quest to ensure a suitable mix of classic characters with an up-to-date plotline, with Bond addressing issues and concerns that are part of the time in which he and his audiences live. Ian Fleming's novels continued to form the basis for the character of Bond – and staying true to that character was paramount. For *Die Another Day* Wilson and Broccoli brought in New Zealand director Lee Tamahori, who was surprised by the offer: "I had never considered anything like that for a moment. It only took me about five minutes to say yes. I've always loved the *Bond* pictures. I have watched every single one. Movies don't get bigger or better than *Bond*. We were pushing *Bond* into a range he's never been in before. Half of the script is Bond outside MI6 operating on his own. There's betrayal and double-cross going on. Pierce and I worked on pushing the envelope and trying new things without running too far from Bond's essence. We

A WEEK AFTER FILMING HAD FINISHED on *Casino Royale* in the summer of 2006 a fire broke out and destroyed the 007 stage at Pinewood. It wasn't the first time this had happened – the *Bond* stage was also destroyed by fire in 1984 during the making of Ridley Scott's *Legend*. On that occasion Pinewood had just four months to get the set back up again in time for filming on *A View to a Kill* (1985).

wanted the series shaken up, but not at the expense of what people inherently like about the character."

Certainly Brosnan continued to shine and the actor had obviously settled into the role for which he was now universally loved: "I couldn't be happier to be around at this time of the *Bond* legacy. I am proud of *Bond* and very proud to have completed four films … The challenge now is to continually make it better than the one before. That's tough because we've set the bar so high."

That was certainly true. But, surrounded by a cast including Judi Dench returning as "M", John Cleese replacing "Q" (following Desmond Llewellyn's sad death in a car crash in December 1999), some younger, harder villains played by Toby Stephens, Rosamund Pike and Rick Yune, and one of the cleverest and most beautiful Bond girls of the series, Oscar-winning Halle Berry, the director knew he had the right cast in place to bring the script and action to life.

Once again, shooting took place across the world, from Hawaii to Spain, from the glaciers of Iceland to the Reform Club in Pall Mall. And, of course, Pinewood, at which the Ice Palace – one of the most elaborate *Bond* sets since the submarine dock in *The Spy Who Loved Me* – was built. The set was so impressive that when the director and producers saw it they decided to increase the number of scenes for which it was to be used. A new script introduced an elaborate car chase through the frozen castle, which had to be further reinforced to cope with the weight of cars and cameras. With its underwater tank, upward spiralling ramps and elaborate infrastructure the set took more than five months to build.

Die Another Day was a runaway success, smashing *Bond* box-office records and becoming, to date, the highest earning film in the series, at $393 million. After 40 years, 20 films, five lead actors and several changes in cast and crew, *Bond* proved that it was as good as it had always been.

THE 007 STAGE IS DISMANTLED following the fire that destroyed it in 2006. Its replacement – costing around £12 million – was built and ready for filming again in early 2007.

Sadly for the series, the news came that while the films were to continue, Brosnan was not. His time as James Bond had come to an end; some say through choice, others claiming that he was simply replaced. *Bond* fans and the filmmakers had been here before. As was asked after Sean Connery left, then Roger Moore and now Pierce Brosnan: who could possibly take over? The search for Brosnan's successor took in over 200 actors from across three continents. Wilson and Broccoli were aware that by the end of the 1990s, the *Bond* movies had the oldest demographic of any action-adventure series. Yet with the booming success of the video games market, and with some classic *Bond* titles doing big business in that market, the movies were now attracting a younger audience. So the producers were convinced it was time for a younger Bond. Michael G. Wilson insists the decision to drop Brosnan was not about money: "If we wanted to make a deal we would've made a deal with Pierce at some financially viable level. This was about us trying to find new inspiration for the series."

But there didn't appear to be too many nerves as British actor Daniel Craig took over as the sixth 007. Some of the press were unkind at the time of the announcement, but as Craig recalls, he tried not to let it get the better of him: "I can't deny I read it all. I didn't want to be surprised – and then I got on with it. I had already made up in my mind how I was going to do it and it spurred me on a

bit. I prepared for the role by hitting the gym. I went five times a week. There's no secret to it. I just had to work out and get into the best shape that I could."

Director Martin Campbell knew instantly that Craig was the right man for the role: "*Casino Royale* was a very different kind of *Bond*. I was fascinated to go back to the very first book, Bond on his first mission with elements of his character that you've never seen before ... It was very satisfying to be able to get elements of Bond's character to make him a more real, tougher, darker, harder, more vulnerable character than we've seen before, with a deep relationship, which then forges him into the Bond we've all come to know. Daniel Craig fits more into Fleming's concept of Bond and he has a sexiness and toughness about him that suits the 21st century Bond."

There was some disappointment that much of the filming of *Casino Royale* took place in Czechoslovakia, but several Pinewood stages were used for both pre-production, interiors and post-production and some wonderful set pieces were shot there too. The replica of Venice built on the Pinewood water tank was breathtaking, as was the "sinking" house on the 007 stage. *Casino Royale* was released at the end of 2006 to great critical and commercial acclaim. With Daniel Craig in the starring role, *Bond* was bigger and better than ever.

In the words of Sean Connery: "I don't think a single other role changes a man quite so much as Bond." And he should know, having played the part of 007 through the series' formative years. All of Connery's outings as Bond and almost every other title to date have had a base at Pinewood Studios. Indeed the words, *Bond* and Pinewood have almost become synonymous over the 40-plus years that the films have been produced. Nobody does it better than Bond and many believe that few Studios can do it better than Pinewood.

BOND IS BACK TO THE BEGINNING as Daniel Craig, opposite, brings 007 very firmly into the 21st century in a story based on Ian Fleming's first *Bond* novel, *Casino Royale*. Above, the replica set of Venice, built on the water tank at Pinewood Studios for *Casino Royale* (2006).

an interview with

Anthony Waye

EXECUTIVE PRODUCER

My career in the film industry started when I joined the Rank Organisation at Pinewood studios in July 1954 in the mailroom on a salary of £3. 8s.3p (£3.45). Discipline was tough, if we were cheeky the boss of the mailroom gave us a whack with his golf club. In those days you had to wear a jacket and tie and call everyone Sir or Madam, which was just as well as you couldn't remember their names anyway. I quickly progressed to Production Runner, then making it as a 3rd Assistant Director just before being called up to do my obligatory National Service in the Army, where I had a wonderful two years living in a tent on active service in Cyprus.

On return from military service I resumed my position as 3rd and was lucky enough to get my first foreign locations on films based at Pinewood – *North West Frontier* with Lauren Bacall and Kenneth More, *The Singer Not the Song* with John Mills and Dirk Bogarde – and both had locations in Spain. *North West* was very difficult, we shot the train sequence in an area around Gaudix, which in those days was a very remote area, to communicate with London entailed someone sitting in the local exchange for hours waiting for a connection, hard to imagine with the instant communications of mobile and internet we know today.

While still a 3rd, I was offered a film in the desert, it would mean living in a tent for several months. At that time, everyone who worked at Pinewood was permanent staff, I think we had five complete crews, camera, sound, art, editing, production, totally in house, everyone advised me to "think of my pension" and stay with Rank, so I turned the film down, the film turned out to be *Lawrence of Arabia* and the pension a mirage.

Later, on *Sink The Bismarck!*, an accounts assistant in the 20th Century Fox Accounts Dept caught my eye, a few years later Patricia was to become Mrs Waye and 40 years on she is still doing the household accounts!

My career progressed rapidly, becoming a 2nd Assistant for a short period, then up to being a 1st Assistant Director, a job I loved. I stayed in this position for over 20 years, had a wonderful time and worked on some tremendous films.

In my early days as 1st and being under contract to Pinewood I, of course, made Pinewood films, *Carry Ons*, *Doctor* films and several Norman Wisdom productions. The role of 1st in those days was considerably easier than it is now, films seemed much less complicated than they are today, when audience demands are greater. On the *Carry On*'s we would have a sweepstake to bet on the hour we would finish on the final shooting day (we never *never*, went over schedule),

I'm not saying it was fixed but surprisingly the Director, Gerry Thomas always won!

As the freelance world developed, Pinewood began to become a "4-wall studio", all permanent staff were made redundant. I left in 1964 with a golden handshake of £600 (my pension), I went straight across the road to Pinewood Garage (now a block of flats) to buy a brand new car – as a freelancer I was going to need a reliable vehicle – I drove proudly into the studios only to get a terrible dressing down by the Studio Manager, telling me I should have invested in an insurance policy (personal pensions didn't exist in those days).

Now, as a freelance technician, I had to face the outside world, I had no idea where the other studios were, MGM, Shepperton, Elstree, Bray were just names. I had no idea who to contact or how to make contact with them. Fortunately, a phone call came four days later to take over a film shooting in Greenwich, miles across London, the new car instantly came into its own. I was up and running as a freelancer and as such have continued almost non-stop since then.

To be a good 1st Assistant you need to be practical, have a degree in common sense, be extremely flexible and have a good understanding

ON THE SET of Norman Wisdom's hospital comedy A Stitch in Time, above left, at Pinewood in 1962.

HISTORY IN THE MAKING – Anthony Waye's letter of appointment from Pinewood Studios, 6 July 1954.

of how every other department works. You need to know how far you can push a crew, work closely with the Director and be able to interpret his moods, thoughts and, sometimes, tantrums. You also become the mouthpiece of the crew to the office and vice versa.

As I became more experienced I was able to handle bigger productions. My first major film was to be on the action unit of *Where*

Eagles Dare with Clint Eastwood and Richard Burton. We spent weeks on location in Austria. *When Eight Bells Toll,* based at Pinewood, followed this. Gradually I had calls to do larger productions until one day in 1976 when I had a call from a Production Manager. My diary note has one line, "call from Bruce Sharman to do a space film", that space film turned out to be *Star Wars*! Later the same year I was to do my first film with Fred Zinnemann, *Julia*, not only was it a great film to work on, the French Co 1st Assistant and I were given an award by the DGA for our work on the film.

It was on *Julia* that I met Associate Producer Tom Pevsner, I worked with him again on John Badham's *Dracula* and again in Iran on *Caravans*. It was Tom who introduced me to *Bond*, he put my name forward to be the 1st on *For you Eyes Only*. So started my long relationship with *Bond*. Two years later I was the 1st on *Octopussy*. Then, in 1983, he called me in Rome where I was working on *Ladyhawke* and asked me to become Production Manager on *A View to a Kill*. I accepted and, after over 20 years on the floor, I moved into the office, becoming Production Supervisor on *Living Daylights* then *License to Kill*.

With *GoldenEye* came a new era of filmmaking, audiences demanded much more, Visual Effects were playing a major part in films, the pressures were increasing all round. Rules and regulations were being introduced by the government, with Europe adding even more restrictions. Filmmaking was becoming more complicated, not like the old days when making a film was like being a part of a club, when we worked 8 hours a day, 5 days a week and had a great social life: now it had become 12-hour days and six-day weeks.

My title on *GoldenEye* was as Associate Producer, then I became Line Producer on *Tomorrow Never Dies* and *The World is Not Enough*, eventually becoming Executive Producer on *Die Another Day* and *Casino Royale*.

All films are tough to make and *Casino* was no exception: a very complicated production to shoot, moving two units over four countries, we had locations in the Czech Republic, the Bahamas and Italy for locations in Lake Como and Venice, then back to Pinewood to shoot an extremely difficult set on the 007 stage and a massive sequence on location. The logistics of shipping crew and gear around

was a headache for the production team, but it worked well, the weather was kind to us and the outcome was a great film.

Now, as we start the early preparation for *Bond* number 22 at Pinewood, its difficult to remember what life in the film industry was like all those years ago when the studio employees came to work by bus or bicycle and clocked in at the Timekeepers gate and I delivered mail around the studios five times a day. Like *Bond*, I have a strong affiliation with Pinewood.

BELOW, shooting in all weathers on the Island of Mull for When Eight Bells Toll *in 1969.*

ABOVE Anthony and Patricia Waye celebrate their 25th wedding anniversary at a special party hosted by Bond *producer Cubby Broccoli, in Tangier, during the making of* The Living Daylights.

Superheroes Save the Day

ON THE PINEWOOD SET OF of *Those Magnificent Men in their Flying Machines*, in 1964.

The 1960s saw a boom period for Pinewood, a huge turnaround from the financially difficult days that befell the Studios in previous decades. Although the *Doctor* films, *Norman Wisdom* comedies, the *Carry Ons* and *Bond* series were hugely important for both the film industry in general and Pinewood in particular, its sound stages played host to a raft of other big movies. Further expansion of the site also allowed for the burgeoning evolution of television and the larger scale shows and dramas needed to feed this increasingly voracious beast. It was good to have American business back in town too. With it, came big stars and big pictures, and most importantly big money, which helped contribute towards keeping the country's studios afloat and staff, at all levels, in work.

Twentieth Century-Fox's *Those Magnificent Men in Their Flying Machines* (1964) was a lavish, period, all-star comedy about a London to Paris air race at the beginning of the last century. Directed by Ken Annakin and starring Terry-Thomas, James Fox, Sarah Miles and Stuart Whitman, Pinewood chippies and props departments were kept busy constructing all the replica ancient aircraft.

Kirk Douglas and Richard Harris took the leads in the suspenseful war actioner *The Heroes of Telemark* (1965), while Bond producers Cubby Broccoli and Harry Saltzman took a short break from 007 to turn their minds to the children's fantasy *Chitty Chitty Bang Bang*. Fox began to make *Dr Dolittle* at Pinewood but an appallingly wet summer meant that the location of Castle Combe in Wiltshire looked anything but magical, so the film was relocated to Hollywood. In the middle of 1966, an interesting assortment of films was being made at Pinewood. From stage to stage, one could stumble across television's favourite comedy double act Morecambe and Wise, making one of their three, rather less than successful cinema offerings, *The Magnificent Two*, or François Truffaut shooting *Fahrenheit 451*, starring Oskar Werner and Julie Christie. Charlie Chaplin was also making his last film, *The Countess from Hong Kong*, starring Marlon Brando and Sophia Loren.

Previously associated with Shepperton and later to become the head at Elstree Studios, Bryan Forbes made three films at Pinewood during the 1960s, two with Michael Caine – the star-studded Victorian comedy of greed, *The Wrong Box* (1965) and the exciting thriller *Deadfall* (1967) – and the powerful study of old

THE STORY OF NORWEGIAN RESISTANCE attempts to stop German troops producing an atomic bomb was told dramatically in Anthony Mann's Second World War drama, *The Heroes of Telemark* (1965).

DICK VAN DYKE AND SALLY ANN HOWES, right, filming *Chitty Chitty Bang Bang* in 1967.

age, *The Whisperers* (1966), which saw veteran actress Dame Edith Evans taking the lead role.

By the end of the decade, it became abundantly clear that there was large American investment in the British film industry. Some £15 million in 1965 had risen to £20 million just a few years later. Meanwhile, Billy Wilder, whose hit films had included *Some Like It Hot* and *The Apartment*, arrived at Pinewood in 1969 to make *The Private Life of Sherlock Holmes*, an ambitious new take on the famous detective, starring Robert Stephens, Colin Blakely and Christopher Lee. Filming had to halt temporarily when Stephens was taken ill, but a great deal had been invested in the production, including an £80,000 Baker Street set on the Pinewood back lot, and Wilder waited for his star to return before resuming production.

In the 1970s, Pinewood opened its doors to more big films. Norman Jewison directed the emotional and highly regarded award-winning epic musical *Fiddler on the Roof* (1970). During Ken Russell's 18-month production schedule on *The Devils* (1970), emotions ran high, with scenes of masturbating nuns and burnings at the stake causing controversy both inside and outside the Studios. More than 30 years after having made his first film at Pinewood, Alfred Hitchcock returned to make *Frenzy*, an adult thriller about a killer rapist on the loose in London, the first

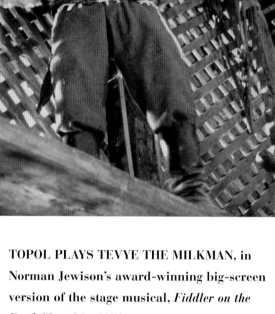

TOPOL PLAYS TEVYE THE MILKMAN, in Norman Jewison's award-winning big-screen version of the stage musical, *Fiddler on the Roof*, filmed in 1970.

of his films to receive an "X" certificate from the British film censors, who insisted it was unsuitable for audiences under the age of 18.

Sadly, at the end of March 1972, Lord Rank died, aged 83. The announcement came, by coincidence, on the day of the Rank Organisation's annual general meeting. A memorial service was held at Westminster Central Hall on 24th April attended by mourners from all walks of Rank's life, from politicians to nobility, from film stars to regular members of staff who just wanted to pay tribute to their very special boss. Rank left a large company legacy, an Organisation, which continues to thrive to this day more than half a century after it was founded, but his death coincided with a downturn for the British film industry. Throughout the 1970s, weakening exchange rates, a strike-torn Britain with its power cuts and three-day weeks, and exorbitant taxes rates for higher earners, forced investment and filmmakers away from the UK.

There were still some great films being made at Pinewood, among them *Sleuth* (1972), the Oscar® nominated film version of Anthony Shaffer's play about a policeman who pits his wits against a scheming thriller writer, starring Laurence

AVA GARDNER AND
IAN MACSHANE,
left, in Roddy
McDowall's 1969
production *The
Devil's Widow*. The
film was also known
as *Tam-Lin*.

ALFRED HITCHCOCK, right, sits in on a
music recording session for his film *Frenzy* at
Pinewood, in 1971. It was Hitchcock's first
visit to the Studios since making *Young and
Innocent* in 1937.

THE STORY OF *CINDERELLA* plays out in Bryan Forbes' lavish romantic
musical, *The Slipper and the Rose* (1976).

Olivier and Michael Caine. Jack Clayton directed Francis Ford Coppola's version of *The Great Gatsby* (1973), starring Robert Redford, Mia Farrow and Sam Waterston. And Alan Parker's musical gangster spoof starring children, *Bugsy Malone*, was shot at Pinewood in 1975. As *The Illustrated London News* declared: "I only wish the British could make adult movies as intelligent as this one." Unfortunately, the number of British movies of any kind was diminishing fast. The year *Bugsy Malone* was made, there were just eight films produced at Pinewood and only one, Bryan Forbes's *The Slipper and the Rose*, had anything like a big budget.

So the industry was in the doldrums and studios across Britain were getting nervous. Then a light appeared at the end of the tunnel. As it got closer it became obvious it wasn't a light, it wasn't even a bird, or a plane: it was *Superman*. And just as the comic book hero had, since the character's creation in 1938, saved the world on countless occasions through cartoons, television shows and Saturday morning movie serials, *Superman* would do more of the same on the big screen; hopefully, at the same time, also lifting the ailing fortunes of Pinewood Studios.

THE GREAT GATSBY, starring Robert Redford and Mia Farrow, was filmed at Pinewood in 1973. The film won two Oscars® and three British Academy Awards.

ALAN PARKER, right, directs the all-children gangster-style musical *Bugsy Malone* in 1975. The film went on to win five British Academy Awards for its cast and crew, including one for Parker for Best Screenplay.

The character of Superman was a native of the planet Kryptonite, brought up in Smallville, USA, and a resident of Metropolis, the brainchild of writer Jerry Siegel and cartoonist Joe Shuster. *Superman The Movie* was the brainchild of father-and-son production team, Alexander and Ilya Salkind and their friend Pierre Spengler, who between them had come up with the idea for the film while drinking coffee on the sidewalks of Paris. Like so many good ideas, thinking of them is the easy part, turning them into reality is much harder. There were copyright issues to overcome, and the sheer scale of an all-or-nothing production if the film was to convince and prove a success. This did not seem to faze the producers, however, who were still celebrating the success of their recent box-office hit, *The Three Musketeers*. To add weight to their proposal, highly respected former Bond director Guy Hamilton was announced as the man who would direct *Superman The Movie*, but his tenure was short-lived.

The production had originally been pencilled in to shoot in Rome, but financial and logistical reasons forced it to the UK, in the process forcing Hamilton out – as a tax exile trying to escape the punitive British laws, he was only allowed to work in the country for 30 days a year. The Salkinds turned their minds to other directors. A young fresh-faced Steve Spielberg, in the process of finishing off *Jaws* (1975), was offered the position but allegedly asked too high a salary; although that film's success on its release soon proved that Spielberg was worth every penny he demanded. So it was in the summer of 1976, with *The Omen* climbing towards the $100 million mark in worldwide box office earnings, that the supernatural thriller's director Richard Donner, received a call from Alexander Salkind inviting him to take on the film. Donner demanded assurances that he would have complete control over the script and then began two years of solid and exhausting commitment to the project.

Donner was born and brought up in New York City. Other than an uncle who had produced musicals during the Second World War, he was the first of his family to enter show business. He'd wanted to be an actor, but after a series of bit parts off-Broadway found himself on a television production of Somerset Maugham's *Of*

JODIE FOSTER was just 13 when she played the role of Tallulah in *Bugsy Malone*, for which she won two British Academy Awards – Best Supporting Actress and Best Newcomer.

Human Bondage. The show's director, Martin Ritt, told him there was good news and bad news for Donner. The bad was that he couldn't act. The good was that Ritt thought he could direct. Donner moved to California and started directing, at first commercials, then documentaries. Then came the popular *Wanted: Dead or Alive* with Steve McQueen, and a succession of TV weeklies such as *Kojak* and *Bronk*. His special, *Portrait of a Teenage Alcoholic*, received critical acclaim, and from then on Donner was in constant demand.

It was producer Harvey Bernhard who asked Donner to direct *The Omen*, which was made at Shepperton in 1976. Working on *Superman* was harder than anything he had ever done before: "After working seven days a week, 15 hours a day, I'd sometimes go home at night and dream about doing a two-character love story, set in one room. The challenges were enormous – they had to be – and many of them were of our own making. That's what you thrive on in this business. If there were two ways to film a scene – an easy way that would look easy on the screen – and a way that we all agreed was impossible, the answer was never in doubt. We'd shoot for the impossible."

Casting the film was proving equally impossible. Patrick Wayne was offered the role of Superman but dropped out so that he could look after his father, John Wayne, who was suffering from cancer. Other actors considered for the lead role included Paul Newman, Robert Redford, Kris Kristofferson, Nick Nolte, Steve McQueen and even Ilya Salkind's dentist, who undertook a screen test for the part. Eventually, the Salkinds decided to opt for a complete newcomer, the 24-year-old actor Christopher Reeve, who had just one film and a soap opera role to his credit. To begin with, Donner was unsure; Reeve was young and puny. But

Star Wars' Darth Vader actor and muscleman Dave Prowse, came to the rescue, and devised the "Superman Exercise Routine" to beef Reeve up. Weeks of exercise seemed to do the trick and Donner came to realize that Reeve, who could switch between playing the dashing hero and the bumbling accident-prone Clark Kent, was exactly the man for the part. The director declared: "I didn't find him. God gave him to me! He looks more like Superman than Superman, and more like Clark Kent then Clark Kent does."

Superman The Movie began filming at Shepperton Studios on 28th March 1977, but it soon became apparent that the space the production had booked could not accommodate the increasingly grand plans for the film.

Within two months the production had begun to fall behind schedule. There had been delays from the outset. Marlon Brando, who was reportedly paid a staggeringly high fee to appear for a relatively short time in the film, was laid low with the flu. The crew kept active in between takes by sitting and playing games, working out how much Brando's salary equated too – around $245,000 per shooting day, or $27,000 an hour, some $450 a minute or $8 a second. As production assistant Michael Green calculated, Brando could have ordered a brand new Rolls-Royce from Jack Barclay's in London and almost had it entirely paid for by the time the driver got to Shepperton! Rumours over star salaries continue to circulate to this day but few people realize that some of the actors, including Brando were booked to appear in *Superman II* and were paid for a two-picture deal accordingly, even though a change of direction later meant Brando and others did not appear in the sequel.

Filming scenes to include in an intended sequel while making the first movie further derailed the schedule. The Salkinds had filmed a sequel to *The Three Musketeers* back-to-back, though at the time the actors involved in the production were unaware of this, believing they were making one much longer film about the exploits of D'Artagnan and his lusty friends. Warned of the Salkind's practice on *The Three Musketeers*, the actors were more wary for *Superman The Movie* and ensured that if sequel filming was taking place, contracts and salaries were adjusted accordingly. Even so, the production was under pressure and more space needed to be found.

CHRISTOPHER REEVE in the lead role of Superman, which moved filming to Pinewood when the production ran out of shooting space at Shepperton in 1977.

CHRISTOPHER REEVE AND MARGOT KIDDER,
inset, at lunch at Pinewood while making
Superman The Movie (1977) and, left, in character.

With Pinewood very quiet – not even a *Bond* occupying the sound stages in 1976 – the film moved Studios. Ironically Pinewood has been the preferred choice when initial pre-production discussions were taking place but at that time, a year or so earlier, Pinewood hadn't enough space to accommodate the production. Now the Studios welcomed *Superman* with open arms.

Construction work on the offices of the *Daily Planet* got underway on "E"stage. Donner worked to wrap up shooting at Shepperton as quickly as possible but the "flying unit" continued there for work on the interior of the Fortress scenes. Reeve remained focused on making the film a success wherever he was shooting. He stayed in most evenings, venturing out from time to time, with a beautiful woman on his arm, to important parties where positive PR for the film was guaranteed. As Reeve said at the time: "I'm not here to win a popularity contest. I'm not here to have fun. I'm here to put something on the screen that's going to entertain people later. I mean, you go to a party on Friday and by Monday no one remembers you were there. But they'll always remember what you put on the screen – good or bad. And I have a responsibility to see that it's good. That's why I'm willing to make the sacrifices that I do ... that's why I'm anti-social to the extent that I am. I come home every day from work. Sometimes in agony because I feel that a scene wasn't one hundred percent ... so that's why when I'm walking round the set, I can't take visitors, I can't take screwing around, I can't take lateness. I go nuts, because I'm so rigidly focused into the work." As the schedules for filming drew longer, Reeve had to summon up extra strength to get himself through the long and tiring days.

There were further delays when, with the *Daily Planet* set built, Quincy-star Jack Klugman pulled out just a few days before shooting was due to start on his scene and the role of the editor Perry White became vacant. The back-up actor for the role, Eddie Albert, also pulled out, leaving veteran Hollywood actor Keenan Wynn to take over at very short notice. Wynn was suddenly taken ill with a suspected heart attack, which then turned out to be exhaustion. But the Pinewood costume department were equally exhausted with new measurements for different actors being sent through almost daily, for clothes that they were told needed to be ready for the next day's shoot. Finally, with just hours to prepare, Jackie Cooper

(the former child star) took over the role of Perry White and filming for the scenes got underway.

Filming on the "E" set proved difficult. The *Daily Planet* offices comprised small glass cubicles, so Donner had little space for his crew whilst trying to ensure that their and the cameras' reflections didn't show on screen. Then, a few days into shooting at Pinewood, the huge demands placed on the Studios' generators, which provided light for the set, caused a blowout of the main power line in nearby Iver. This set the production back another two days and "tens of thousands of dollars". Insurance wouldn't cover this problem, and Pinewood gave the production an extra day's free usage of the sound stage.

Filming resumed but the producers were concerned. The schedule was way off, and rumours circulated that Donner would be replaced. Tensions were exacerbated by the difficulties experienced by the special effects team, whose job

ONE OF THE MANY SPLENDID SETS constructed at Pinewood for the shooting of Richard Donner's *Superman The Movie* in 1977. The film received a Bafta nomination for John Barry, for Best Production Design and Art Direction.

THE GROUNDBREAKING SPECIAL EFFECTS on *Superman The Movie* helped audiences to believe that Christopher Reeve's character really could fly.

it was to get Superman to fly, convincingly. Musketeer's director Richard Lester was brought in by the Salkinds to act as an intermediary producer and the situation began to calm. Shooting on both *Superman The Movie* and *Superman II* continued. Further stages and spaces at Pinewood were converted into stunning sets for the films – "D" stage becoming Lex Luthor's Lair, the back lot turned into the Golden Gate Bridge, "F" stage housing a large miniature of the planet Krypton, and the paddock tank converted into the Boulder Dam, to be burst in one of the thrilling action scenes in the film. And the 007 stage accommodated the Fortress of Solitude, a remarkable set by production designer John Barry, comprising glaciers and ice peaks, artificial snow and dry ice, forming an unparalleled cold and eerie North Pole setting.

The hardest part of all in shooting *Superman* was making it believable that a man could fly. Well before the advent of convincing computer-generated imagery, special effects had to work overtime to make it look as if Christopher Reeve was up among the clouds. Director Richard Donner knew that the film would succeed or fail on his ability to deliver a man who could fly: "I knew what I wanted. I didn't know how to get it. There are some really amazing feats in that film. And 99 per cent of them, for me, involve, the believability of Superman. We were handicapped with the liability of having a man who had to fly. No lights came out of his ass, and there was no noise to dazzle the audiences' senses – just a guy flying. And boy, it was difficult. It was months – six or eight months – before I accepted the first flying shots. Usually we'd try things and then modify them. We used a number of systems, but our main one was a very mobile, new form of front projection that enabled us to zoom both camera and projector and float them both, too. This was very unusual because the old front projectors weighed a ton. Ours weighed only 35 pounds."

By "floating" the projector and camera, Donner meant that he had his crew hang both from a hook, known as a sky hook, and move them around. It was down to the camera to give the impression of flight. After many months of work on the problem, Donner settled on suspending Reeve before front projection and blue screens by wires, or sometimes cables hung from overhead rigs, or stage cranes, and hydraulic arms that came out of the screen at zero degrees from the lens. He was happy.

Then, just when the flying was sorted, suddenly the crew realized there were problems with Superman's cape. It just didn't move right. For Donner it was a nightmare: "That cape was a bitch. We had to build all kinds of gimmicks and little things to go under the cape. We tried electronic movements, bottled air, everything.

ROBERT POWELL is Richard Hannay in the third British film version of the conspiracy thriller, *The Thirty Nine Steps* (1978). The film had already been made by Alfred Hitchcock at Lime Grove Studios in 1935 and then again by Rank at Pinewood in the late 1950s with Kenneth More in the lead role.

And finally, Les Bowie came up with the idea of wiring the cape inside like an umbrella, which we could control with little gears to give a feeling of flight."

All the effort would later prove worth it when audiences and critics were thrilled by the effect, and the assorted film academies across the world came to recognize the outstanding contribution made to cinema by *Superman's* visual effect creators. Not only did Les Bowie, Colin Chilvers, Denys Coop, Roy Field, Zoran Perisic and Derek Meddings receive a Special Achievement Oscar® from the

American Academy in 1979, *Superman* also received Oscar® nominations for Best Editing, Best Music and Best Sound. Christopher Reeve won the British Academy Award for Best Newcomer and there were further Bafta nominations for Cinematography, Production Design, Sound, and a Best Supporting Actor nomination for Gene Hackman.

  After 18 months of filming, the shoot finally finished in October 1978, and was released in time for Christmas. *Superman* was estimated to cost $55 million to

LAURENCE OLIVIER as Zeus leads an all-star cast of acting greats, including Claire Bloom and Ursula Andress, here on set at Pinewood, for the shooting of *Clash of the Titans* in 1979.

CLIMBING THE WALLS – an action sequence from the 1982 thriller *Who Dares Wins*, below, in which the Pinewood mansion house doubled as an embassy under siege by terrorists.

PINEWOOD'S WATER TANK, left, plays host to another impressive set, this time during the making of the 1983 television mini-series, *The Last Days of Pompeii*.

make. It grossed $300 million worldwide and became the sixth most popular film of the 1970s, just behind the *The Exorcist* at number five. It wasn't all good news for Donner, however. He was taken off *Superman II* even though, by his calculations, around 80 per cent of it had already been filmed under his directorship during production of the first movie. The film's cinematographer Geoffrey Unsworth also died just before *Superman* was released. Donner was the first to admit that the film would not have been possible without the creative talent of Unsworth who developed the new more realistic photography process; it was dedicated "with love and respect" to his memory.

Pinewood was again chosen for *Superman II*, its huge set including a Manhattan street built on the Studios' back lot. When it came to making the third film in the series in 1982, Pinewood was happy to welcome back Reeve and fellow cast and crew; *Superman II* was considered by many to be as good if not better than the original yet *Superman III* did not fare so well.

In 1983, Alexander Salkind brought *Supergirl* to Pinewood, with Helen Slater playing the lead role as Superman's niece. It was a cute angle on a well-trodden theme and the effects just kept getting better and better as technology advanced, but the film was not a huge success. That said, the financial investment that came with the film, including a back lot set costing almost $500,000, ensured a sustained and regular income at a difficult time for British film studios.

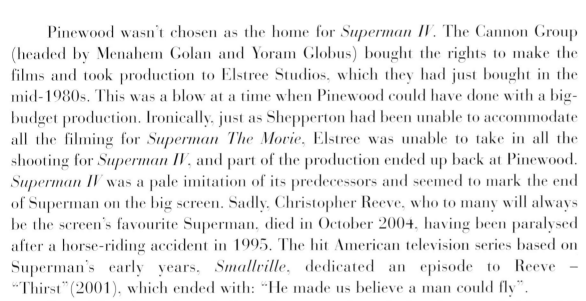

SCIENCE FICTION FANTASY ADVENTURE
KRULL, directed by Peter Yates, was shot at
Pinewood in 1982.

Pinewood wasn't chosen as the home for *Superman IV*. The Cannon Group (headed by Menahem Golan and Yoram Globus) bought the rights to make the films and took production to Elstree Studios, which they had just bought in the mid-1980s. This was a blow at a time when Pinewood could have done with a big-budget production. Ironically, just as Shepperton had been unable to accommodate all the filming for *Superman The Movie*, Elstree was unable to take in all the shooting for *Superman IV*, and part of the production ended up back at Pinewood. *Superman IV* was a pale imitation of its predecessors and seemed to mark the end of Superman on the big screen. Sadly, Christopher Reeve, who to many will always be the screen's favourite Superman, died in October 2004, having been paralysed after a horse-riding accident in 1995. The hit American television series based on Superman's early years, *Smallville*, dedicated an episode to Reeve – "Thirst"(2001), which ended with: "He made us believe a man could fly".

Peter Hyam's made us believe there were drug dealers in space in his sci-fi thriller *Outland*, which was made at Pinewood in 1980. Sean Connery was back, not as Bond but as Marshall W. T. O'Neil, scouring one of the moons of Jupiter, searching for those responsible for the death of mining colony workers. Dubbed by some as *"High Noon* in Space" (not entirely pleasing *High Noon's* director Fred Zinneman), most of the film was shot at Pinewood including the model of Jupiter's moon, Io, which was almost 20 feet long and comprised four miles of fibre optic cables. The giant greenhouse and exterior sets depicting the mine camp were also magically created at the Studios.

Other fantasy films made at Pinewood in the 1980s included the patchy sci-fi comedy, *Morons from Outer Space* (1986) starring Jimmy Nail, Griff Rhys Jones and Mel Smith and directed by Mike Hodges, who agreed to make the film if Thorn

SIGOURNEY WEAVER is
Ellen Ripley and Carrie Henn
is Rebecca Jorden in James
Cameron's, *Aliens*, filmed at
Pinewood in 1985.

EMI financed the making of his script for *Mid-Atlantic*, which never actually got off the ground. Then there was *Santa Claus: The Movie* (1985) featuring

THE TENSION BUILDS in *Aliens*. The sci-fi horror sequel deservedly won two Oscars®, for Best Sound Effects and Best Visual Effects.

Dudley Moore, Burgess Meredith and John Lithgow, and Ridley Scott's *Legend* (1984), starring Tom Cruise in his first visit to Pinewood, a film remembered less for its dark and beautiful story of fairytales and sorcery and more as the production that burnt down the 007 stage. Frank Oz's *Little Shop of Horrors*, a musical version of the 1959 film by Roger Corman, starring James Belushi, Rick Moranis, Steve Martin and John Candy, was shot at Pinewood in 1986.

In September 1986, Pinewood celebrated its golden anniversary. Fifty years after opening its doors to filmmakers, the Studios were very much in business, even though business was not quite as good as it could have been. Frustratingly, the situation worsened, and 1987 saw one of the poorest years in Pinewood's long and glorious history, with less than a handful of films produced there. In the autumn of 1987, managing director Cyril Howard came to the conclusion that the site could no longer survive as fully serviced Studios. It would have to go the way others had gone and become "four-wall" – a facility whereby Pinewood would hire out the sound stage space and filmmakers would bring in their own teams to work on their

ABOVE AND OPPOSITE: The crew of the salvage ship fight for their survival in *Aliens* – shot on the sound stages of Pinewood some seven years after filming on the original film, *Alien*, took place at Shepperton.

LEFT AND RIGHT: Sigourney Weaver returns for a third time to the role of Ellen Ripley, the sole survivor of an attack on the mining ship Nostromo in *Alien* (1979), this time in *Alien3*, filmed at Pinewood in 1991.

RICK MORANIS, top left, as Seymour Krelborn and Steve Martin, above and above right, as Orin Scrivello DDS, in the green-fingered cult comedy of giant man-eating plants, *The Little Shop of Horrors* (1986), directed by Frank Oz.

TIM BURTON made his British directorial debut with *Batman* (1989). The stunning sets were rewarded with more than just critical acclaim, winning an Oscar® for Best Art Direction and set decoration for Anton Furst and Peter Young.

own productions. Pinewood was the last of the British studios to go four-wall. It had little choice if it was to survive. The payroll was slashed almost overnight from around 500 staff to 150. Although fortunes wouldn't change instantly, the Studios had a chance again. Having shied away from commercials and pop videos in the past, Pinewood was now happy to hire out space to companies who wanted to use the facilities to make these projects. The result was a lot less film and a lot more television. And while commercials alone couldn't keep the Studios afloat, they helped Pinewood through the dark days of the 1980s.

Then another superhero came to Pinewood's rescue, this time in the form of caped crusader Batman. The first draft of a modern-day movie version of *Batman*, which recounted the story of the origins of Batman and Robin had been written in 1980, by *Superman* co-writer Tom Mankiewicz. Planned villains for the film included the Joker and the Penguin. The film went into pre-production and was scheduled for filming and release in 1985, with a budget of around $20 million. But the production stalled and had to be shelved.

In 1985, after the surprise success of Tim Burton's *Pee-wee's Big Adventure*, Burton was offered the job of reinvigorating the *Batman* project. Dissatisfied with the script, Burton and his then girlfriend Julie Hickson provided their own 30-page treatment for the film, which was approved by the producers and Warner Brothers. Shortly after, Burton met Sam Hamm, who had just started a two-year contract with Warners, and gave him the job of writing the screenplay. The writing stretched on, and a writer's strike in America prevented him from finishing the

HOLLYWOOD MEETS PINEWOOD, with American street sets built on the Buckinghamshire Studios' back lot for *Superman The Movie* (1977).

MICHAEL KEATON is the caped crusader, and Kim Basinger plays Vicki Vale, opposite, in Tim Burton's award-winning fantasy thriller, *Batman*, filmed at Pinewood in 1988.

SPECIAL EFFECTS WERE THE ORDER OF THE DAY for the epic cinematic treatment of a tale from Greek mythology, *Clash of the Titans* (1981).

script. Burton hired *Beetlejuice* co-writer Warren Skaaren to take over. By now it had taken nigh on three years for Burton to get *Batman* written and green-lit, yet when it finally began filming in October 1988 at Pinewood, it took just 12 weeks to shoot.

Pinewood was delighted to have the film at its site. Britain's unfavourable exchange rate and the rising costs of UK production had frightened many productions away, and it was good to have a blockbuster back in town. With plenty of space available, *Batman* had an almost free rein over the site. Gotham City was built on the back lot, the biggest outdoor film set at the Studios since *Cleopatra* in 1960. A construction team of 200 worked under production designer Anton Furst and his 14-strong department, toiling at breakneck speed for five months to have the sets ready for shooting. Main Street was a quarter of a mile long, which meant a lot of buildings, scaffolding, plywood, fibreglass and paint. Furst deliberately mixed and clashed the architectural styles of the buildings to make Gotham City appear ugly and bleak. His cathedral set built for the show down between the caped crusader and the Joker (played with style and wicked panache by Jack Nicholson) was impressive, with full-sized stretches being created for the top and bottom of the cathedral and sets of a smaller scale used for stretches of the building in between giving the overall effect of a full-scale building. It was complicated but effective stuff, so effective that Furst's designs for Gotham City were to be incorporated into the *Batman* comic books during the 1990s.

While the sets were going up, Tim Burton and *Batman* star Michael Keaton re-wrote parts of the script. Keaton also spent two of those months working out and learning kickboxing for the role. He needed the extra strength as Batman's costume weighed 70 pounds. Once the film was finished, and in the light of negative rumours about the production, Burton had a trailer edited together that was sent around cinemas in the USA. The 90-second teaser was given its first showing at a theatre in Westwood, California, and received a standing ovation. This augured well for the film and *Batman* went on to become a huge success across the world. It became the seventh highest grossing film of the 1980s, sandwiched between *Raiders of the Lost Ark* at number six and *Back to the Future* at number eight. The film won an Oscar® for Best Art Direction.

Production designer Terry Ackland-Snow recalls working on the blockbuster success: "We are in the art of illusion. We pretend things are what they are not. Probably the biggest film I've worked on in 40 years in this business was *Batman*. We all spent a year at Pinewood on that film. The Batmobile was made at Pinewood and we all worked together on the street set that was a quarter of a mile long. Anton had the original designs for the Batmobile. I had to supervise the making of it with John Evans – it was very exciting. The car was a completely new invention, made in clay then modelled in polystyrene and finally plastered over.

"There were so many things we didn't think of. Tim Burton came in one day to see how it was coming along and suddenly he asked: 'Terry, how do they get into it?' We'd forgotten about doors. But I'd been in a harrier jump jet so I soon worked out how we could do it. Once that was sorted, we started on the lights for the back. They needed to be big and round. I'd already worked on the exhaust pipe, the design of which I copied from a jet engine. Then, by coincidence, I was in a traffic jam behind a Ferrari. I thought those lights will do nicely. My wife's Honda provided me with the lights for the front – these are the ideas you get.

"As it was an American film, the Batmobile also had to be a left-hand drive. I remember shooting on the back lot one evening and Michael Keaton was in the car, ready for filming. It was raining outside. Then we realized we hadn't got any demisters built in either. You just don't think of those sorts of things. It was quite a laugh – there really was a great atmosphere worknig on *Batman*."

Hoping that the success of *Batman* would lead to a sequel and the need once again to film in Gotham City, the sets were kept in place at Pinewood for some time after production finished. But it didn't happen. The franchise returned, but not to Pinewood.

Behind the scenes there were those in the industry who had become convinced that Rank was losing interest in Pinewood. As well as the Studios, Rank ran a distribution business, maintained control over its film library, owned a duplication company and a chain of cinemas. However, there was growing evidence that Rank was moving away from its core businesses and focussing more on the higher, quicker returns to be made in gambling and nightclubs. Former controller of BBC1 and then Chief Executive of Channel 4, Michael Grade, was convinced that the

PROFILE

Tim Burton

Timothy William Burton, born in August 1958, has become renowned as a director with an offbeat style. Brought up in Burbank, California, Burton described his childhood as quirky, self-absorbed and highly imaginative. He would escape the humdrumness of everyday life by visiting the cinema to watch low-budget horror films. He was inspired by the likes of Vincent Price and moviemaker Ray Harryhausen.

Burton won a Disney scholarship to the California Institute of Arts and studied animation for three years. In 1982 Burton made his first film short, *Vincent*, about a young boy who fantasises that he is Vincent Price. Price narrated the film. The success of *Pee-Wee's Big Adventure* (1985) led to increased offers of directing work. The supernatural comedy *Beetlejuice* (1988) was also a financial hit at the box office and he was offered *Batman*. Beset with problems before it had even started, Burton pulled filming away from America and into a quiet Pinewood. *Batman* went on to become the seventh highest-grossing film of the 1980s and Burton has tried, whenever possible, to return to Pinewood for filming further projects.

Through the 1990s, Burton had successes with *Edward Scissorhands* (1990), *Batman Returns* (1992) and *Sleepy Hollow* (1999), among others. His version of *Planet of the Apes* (2001) was a commercial if not critical success. He went on to break all manner of box-office records with *Charlie and the Chocolate Factory* made at Pinewood in 2004 and the Studios has recently welcomed him back once again for the filming of *Sweeney Todd*.

time was right for a takeover. He had a great affection for Pinewood, something which he felt Rank no longer held for the famed production site: "I first came to Pinewood Studios in the mid 1960s. I had just started as a talent agent with The Grade Organisation, which was later to become London Management. My partner and mentor was Billy Marsh who was the agent for Norman Wisdom and Morecambe and Wise. We used to pay regular visits to Pinewood to meet the producer of Norman's films, Hugh Stewart. Hugh also produced the three Morecambe and Wise pictures made at Pinewood. I had never been to a film studio before. I thought Pinewood was magic. It was busy, busy, busy. I returned several times to Pinewood over the years with my various broadcasting hats on.

"In the late 1980s I could see that the Rank Group clearly wanted out of the film business. I met with some banks and put to them the idea of creating a Hollywood-style studios – where you'd own the studios, the film library, a film distribution business, a chain of cinemas to play the films in, and, if necessary, a duplicating and processing arm. I got a consortium together and we reckoned we could make a go of it as an integrated business. On the fateful day I went to see Rank's chief executive with our takeover plans. He kicked me out and that was the end of that. Which was a shame because I think we could have kept the whole vertically integrated structure together. Everyone says the problem with the British film industry is that there is no one, big, sustainable critical entity; we could have created that, everyone working off and with each other."

Down but not out, Grade's plans to take over the Studios were all but put away and forgotten about. It would be more than 10 years before the offer to take over Pinewood would cross his desk once again. For now though, Rank was holding on, in the hope that things would begin to pick up and that half a century after shooting had begun at the Studios, Pinewood would regain its reputation as a world-class venue for film production.

an interview with

Graham Hartstone

FORMER HEAD OF POST-PRODUCTION

I joined the Sound Department at Pinewood Studios in the August of 1961.

On the Studio lot was the spectacular but decaying *Cleopatra* set. I was awestruck operating a second mic on a pole for some retakes with Elizabeth Taylor and Richard Burton – they were not nice to each other – the language!! In the middle of a particularly volatile row, I was trying not to be noticed as I crouched behind a rostrum. The rest of the unit seemed to have disappeared. In mid-profanity, Richard spotted me – "Who is this boy?" he boomed. Fortunately the mixer emerged from the shadows to explain the necessity for my presence.

During my time as Sound Camera Operator on production I was isolated from the unit in my recording room and boredom drove me to spend as much time on the set as possible.

In the summer of 1966 two films from Pinewood had locations in Berlin at the same time. *Funeral in Berlin* and *The Quiller Memorandum*. I was on the *Quiller* crew, and after a week or so our German driver/interpreter set me up on a blind date with his landlady's

daughter, Gina, a budding actress who had a small part in *Funeral in Berlin*. The rest, as they say, two children and two grandchildren later, is history.

In the early 1970s the industry went through one of its quieter periods. Production was low and Pinewood decided to shed its production sound crews and concentrate on post- production. I moved to the Dubbing Theatre. My first experiences were in Theatre 1 with Ken Barker and Otto Snel – mixing a variety of titles, including Children's films, horror films, *Carry On* films, two *Bond* films and other major features like *Sleuth* and *The Great Gatsby*.

The mixing of *Superman The Movie* in 1977 produced personal and technical firsts. It was my first screen credit, and we were nominated for an Oscar with Gordon McCallum. We didn't win but it was a fantastic trip to Hollywood.

The adrenaline was pumping again for *Pink Floyd The Wall* in 1981. We were supporting the Floyd's mixing engineer James Guthrie, trying to contain ear-splitting levels within the confines of a 70mm

Dolby film sound format. The soundtrack won us a
Bafta in 1982, to go with a nomination we also received
for *Blade Runner*.

In 1988 I was promoted to Head of Post-Production for
Pinewood. The demands of administration meant less
time for mixing, but I kept my hand in premixing the
dialogue tracks for *Tomorrow Never Dies* and *Die
Another Day*.

As I turned 60 my thoughts were turning to retirement
and spending more time with my grandchildren.

I am privileged to have spent a rewarding career at a
major film studio in an interesting, demanding and
fascinating industry. A film set, a location shoot or a
dubbing theatre throws together unique and cohesive
teams of people. For the majority, what binds them is a
passion for cinema, usually that is enough to make the
long working days pleasurable.

I have gained a great deal of job satisfaction blending sound
elements into final soundtracks, particularly for the more
sound conscious of the directors, editors and sound editors
with whom I have had the opportunity to collaborate.

Big Films, Bright Future

10

The 1990s began much as the 1980s had finished. Pinewood was quiet, and few were optimistic about the difficulties in which studios across the country found themselves. Financially, it was still proving more cost effective to make films abroad. After the USA and its allies went to war with Iraq in 1992, the world's finances, stock markets and oil industries were thrown into disarray. Just as worryingly for filmmakers, some big name actors refused to fly out of the States, which certainly didn't help in casting big movies.

Aliens3, the third film in what turned out to be a quadrilogy, landed at Pinewood in 1991, and saw the return of Sigourney Weaver as Ellen Ripley. This time, David Fincher, rather than Ridley Scott, directed the sci-fi blockbuster. In the same year, Harrison Ford starred as a CIA analyst who finds himself the target of a renegade IRA faction in Tom Clancy's *Patriot Games*, directed by Phillip Noyce. But the big films were few and far between and the slide in Pinewood's fortunes continued. In October 1992, cameras were about to start rolling on *Shakespeare in Love* when the project was shelved. Julia Roberts was due to star opposite Daniel Day-Lewis as the Bard, but when he turned down the role, she walked away. It was just one of several problems the film would encounter, including financial difficulties, before it was finally made at Shepperton Studios six years later. Then it would become an Oscar®-winning success. But in the early 1990s, with two hundred crew on board and several months of stage space booked at Pinewood, a halt in production added to the sting.

At the beginning of November 1992, a new managing director arrived at the Studios. Cyril Howard had retired and Steve Jaggs joined for a two-month handover period before taking the reins on his own at the beginning of January 1993. Jaggs had left school at 16, not interested in staying on for his "A"-levels but going out to work instead as a sales trainee in an

PORTRAYING THE STORY of the first American bomber crew to complete a full tour of 25 missions during the air battles of Europe during the Second World War, *Memphis Belle* (1990), was a powerful film about courage in wartime.

RICHARD GERE, left, as Lancelot and, below, Sean Connery as King Arthur in Jerry Zucker's tale of the legendary Knights of the Round Table, *First Knight* shot at Pinewood in 1994.

FILMED MAINLY ON LOCATION in Argentina and Hungary, Pinewood played host to the recording of the songs for Alan Parker's Oscar®-winning *Evita* (1996), starring Madonna as Evita Duarte.

engineering firm. He loathed the work, but loved golf; and it was on a golfcourse that he met the managing director of Colour Film Services who offered him a job as a trainee in customer liaison dealing with clients and the rushes from their previous day's filming. Jaggs worked there for seven years and then spent another seven at Universal Film labs. He left Universal when he was approached by AGFA to work as a sales rep in their motion picture division. After 17 years he was headhunted for the MD's job at Pinewood.

Steve Jaggs remembers his first day at the Studios: "The day I joined, on 2nd November 1992, two things happened – there was only one feature film here at the time, which was *Love Actually*, building on three stages and it got pulled. And, in the papers that morning, the headlines proclaimed that Rank were to sell Pinewood. What a great start. Thankfully they weren't. Rank supported my plan to upgrade the Studios over the next eight years. I took over as MD of Pinewood on 1 January 1993. The early 1990s were not good for the British film industry in general but it was all there to build on. The Americans would come back in time and they started to in 1993 and 1994. There had been a lack of capital expenditure in Pinewood and I put a project together to enhance the Studios."

Jaggs was soon to gain a reputation as a hard but fair man. His honest, down-to-earth approach was appealing to those who were nervous about what would happen next at the Pinewood site. For Jaggs, the good of the Studios always came first. He liked films – his heroes being Humphrey Bogart and Steve McQueen – but you couldn't have films without good facilities in which to make them. When, in 1996, I asked him how he wanted to celebrate Pinewood's 60th anniversary, he was adamant: "It would cost around £30,000 to put on a good party here, but for the same money I can put new roofs on two of the sound stages at the back of the Studios that are in urgent need of repair." And that's what he did. The Studios came first and would do throughout his 13-year tenure. Jaggs set about bringing Pinewood into the 21st century.

In 1993, no films at all were produced at the Studios. While many worried, Jaggs and his team got on with the job of reshaping, rebuilding and refurbishing. Then they started on working to attract big productions back. The first big film to book in to Pinewood was Neil Jordan's *Interview With The Vampire: The Vampire Chronicles* in 1994. An all-star cast including Tom Cruise, Brad Pitt and Antonio Banderas, recounted the story of a vampire looking back at the past two centuries and his relationships with other vampires he meets and creates along the way. Richard Gere and Sean Connery starred in Jerry Zucker's medieval tale of love and betrayal, *First Knight*, also based at Pinewood in 1994. The back lot was the home for the film's magnificent Camelot Castle set, complete with blue roofs, turrets and flags. The drawbridge and ensuing water chase sequences were filmed on the

GETTING HIS TEETH INTO THE ROLE, Tom Cruise is Lestat de Lioncourt in Neil Jordan's *Interview With The Vampire: The Vampire Chronicles* (1994).

TOM CRUISE IS ETHAN HUNT, right and below, in the big screen action thriller adaptation based on the 1960s hit television series, *Mission Impossible*.

ON SET AT PINEWOOD STUDIOS, right, filming Brian De Palma's *Mission Impossible* in 1995.

BRITISH PICTURES

MISSION I

A130A

DIRECTOR B DE PALM
CAMERAMAN S BURUM

26 JUNE 95   NIGHT

EXPECTING THE IMPOSSIBLE, as Tom Cruise prepares for another daring stunt during the filming of *Mission Impossible*. The film has, to date, spawned two sequels.

MILLA JOVOVICH, left, is Leeloo, Ian Holm, above, is Father Vito Cornelius and Bruce Willis, top, is Korben Dallas in Luc Besson's sci-fi thriller, *The Fifth Element*, filmed at Pinewood in 1996.

paddock tank and inter-cut with shots from a location in North Wales. Bob Anderson, who had worked many years before with Errol Flynn trained Gere in swordsmanship. *First Knight* wasn't the success many had predicted, costing some $60 million to make and bringing in just $37 million at the US box office.

While more television productions were welcomed to Pinewood in the mid-1990s, star names also continued to return for big budget films. Tom Cruise returned as a producer as well as a star for the blockbuster movie *Mission Impossible*, armed with a cast including Vanessa Redgrave, Kristin Scott Thomas and Jon Voigt, director Brain de Palma and a $64 million budget. It became almost impossible to get Cruise to listen to the advice of the director and stuntmen, and the actor insisted on performing many of his own, often-difficult manoeuvres. After one explosion, which sent him flying across a sound stage, he recalled to *Film Review* magazine: "I was flying across the James Bond stage at Pinewood Studios and I hit a train. It really hurt and I didn't have to act at all." *Mission Impossible* became one of the smash hit films of the 1990s, grossing more than $452 million across the world. Yet again, Pinewood had played its part, and more big films and big names were attracted back.

Alan Parker brought Madonna to Pinewood to record the songs for the soundtrack of *Evita*, which had been filmed on location in Argentina, Hungary and Spain. Bruce Willis arrived in 1996 to make two big-budget movies. The first, the sci-fi extravaganza *The Fifth Element* by Luc Besson, cost around $89 million and became France's most expensive picture to date. Pinewood's futuristic sets were visually stunning and millions flocked to see a 23rd-century world in which a taxi driver, a monk and a "supreme being" save the planet from destruction. Launching the 50th Cannes Film Festival, the film went on to take $63 million in the US and

VETERAN AMERICAN ACTOR Sidney Poitier as FBI Deputy Director Carter Preston, and Richard Gere as Declan Mulqueen, left, filming *The Jackal* (1997).

BRUCE WILLIS, above, plays the lead role of the faceless assassin in Michael Caton-Jones' *The Jackal* (1997).

a further $200 million internationally. Bruce Willis was back for a remake of the 1972 classic political assassination thriller *The Day of the Jackal*, directed by Michael Caton-Jones and co-starring Richard Gere and Sidney Poitier. Full of fast-moving action and thrilling chase scenes, it wasn't quite the homage many had hoped for, and the author of the source novel, Frederick Forsyth, asked for his name not to be used in the titles. Val Kilmer starred in an update of the 1960s hit TV series, *The Saint*, which was made at Pinewood in 1996. A good deal of time and effort went in to building some stunning interior sets – including a two-and-a-half storey high mansion bedecked in marble and gold with a domed roof and impressive chandelier – but the film was not received well by the public.

The late 1990s continued to see a slow but steady resurgence of large-scale films arriving back at Pinewood. The management's plans to increase the number of sound stages and facilities available were also underway, and by 1997, the Studios were very busy. Big budget outer-space horror thriller *Event Horizon* began filming. This starred Laurence Fishburne, Sam Neill and Joely Richardson, and was a creepy, bloody tale of a 21st-century spaceship crew who go to the rescue of another seemingly empty vessel and experience terrible hallucinations. The film was shot entirely at Pinewood with the biggest of the spaceships sets occupying the 007 stage.

Stanley Kubrick, who had shot some of his film *Full Metal Jacket* at Pinewood in 1986, returned just over a decade later to make *Eyes Wide Shut* with Tom Cruise and Nicole Kidman. Pinewood blocked off stage space for a six-month shoot, with Cruise and Kidman so keen to work on the project they signed open-ended contracts. Ultimately, filming on the movie lasted some 400 days, with changes of cast and crew needed mid-shoot. Kubrick's fear of flying kept him in England, and sets of New York were erected on the Pinewood back lot. Cruise and Kidman returned home to LA in February 1998, after nearly a year-and-a-half on the film but were called back less than two months later because Kubrick was unhappy with scenes involving Jennifer Jason Leigh. Leigh had other filming commitments and had to be recast and more months of filming followed. Finally, on 2nd March 1999, a private screening of the film was arranged for the stars and studio executives in Los Angeles. Just days later, Kubrick died in his sleep. The

VAL KILMER is Simon Templar in a modern day updating of a favourite 1960s television action hero, *The Saint* (1997).

ROWAN ATKINSON, above, brings his accident-prone comic creation Mr Bean to the big screen, while Sir John Mills, above right, as "the Chairman" looks on in disdain, in Mel Smith's *Bean* (1997).

70-year-old director passed away before he had time to see his film of sexual fantasy make it on to the big screen. *Eyes Wide Shut* was estimated to have cost $65 million and took $31 million in its first week in the US alone. Audiences fell away sharply, however, and its final take was below industry expectations.

Expectations continued to run high at Pinewood. *The Avengers* was back for a big screen outing, and with Ralph Fiennes, Uma Thurman and Sean Connery all booked for a 1990s makeover of the 1960s television classic, what could go wrong? Even Patrick MacNee, who appeared as the original Steed on television, had a cameo role as Invisible Jones – we heard him but never saw his face on screen. Pinewood's stages were used for the magical, over-the-top sets, and when the production couldn't get permission to film on London's Trafalgar Square, they found themselves having to depend more on sets, using CGI and special effects. Pinewood's gardens were covered in artificial snow in the middle of a very warm June in 1997. Tenants would drive into a hot car park two, while just yards away snow was falling heavily and wind machines were blowing blizzards across the lawns. It was an odd experience, and sadly so was the film. *The Avengers* took 18 months to make and ran to less than 90 minutes. It flopped badly.

The situation wasn't helped by a fire in the roof of sound stage "E" which blazed on the same weekend that a host of familiar names and faces from the industry were coming together at Pinewood to pay tribute to Norman Wisdom and celebrate his 50 years in showbusiness. Extra security was laid on to ensure that

ANOTHER REWORKING OF A
FAVOURITE 1960s television
series, was *The Avengers*, starring
Ralph Fiennes as John Steed and
Uma Thurman as Emma Peel.
The film was shot at Pinewood
during 1997.

A DISTURBING MYSTERY unfolds on a
stranded spacecraft in the 1997 sci-fi horror
thriller, *Event Horizon*.

ANOTHER BREATHTAKING Pinewood set created for the out-of-this-world horror thriller, *Event Horizon* (1997).

TOM CRUISE AND STANLEY KUBRICK
during the making of *Eyes Wide Shut* **(1999),**
which also starred Nicole Kidman. The film
was two years in production and Kubrick died
a few days after showing his final cut to
Warner Brothers executives.

no press photographers got anywhere near stage "E" to catch an exclusive of the smouldering *Avengers* sets. While Wisdom basked in the sun having his picture taken, smoke rose slowly from the roof of "E" at the other end of the Studio.

As the 1990s drew to a close, there were many changes at Pinewood. Gone was the old "gong man" as Rank focused on a new brand name, Deluxe, the leading film processing laboratory, which it had acquired a few years previously. Two new sound stages were completed, and an adjoining office block, named The Stanley Kubrick Building and dedicated by the Studios in his honour, was opened by his widow, Christiana. "R" and "S" stages were important for Pinewood's success. Until that time, the Studios had three large stages and the 007 stage, which could accommodate a big picture that came to Pinewood, but not two pictures that needed large facilities at the same time. The two new stages put paid to that problem. The building of the new stages was overseen by property development consultant, Michael Brown, who was not a new face to the Studios: "My father had been involved with Denham Studios and the Kordas – together they put a couple of stages up at Shepperton. I came to Pinewood as a young man at the beginning of the 1970s and was involved in the design of "J" and "K" stages

and then "L" and "M" stages. I've been in and out of the Studios ever since. I've now designed and overseen the building of 13 stages at Pinewood. "R" and "S" were the last two I did at the end of 2000 – they were at the cutting edge of film stage facilities. I believe they still are."

As the new millennium dawned, it became clear that Pinewood was about to enter a new era. In February 2000, the news broke that a consortium of investors, led by Ivan Dunleavy and Michael Grade, had bought Pinewood for £62 million. Rank sold its cinema chain, Odeon, for £280 million around the same time. Dunleavy, who was to become chief executive, had his eye on Pinewood for some time: "The first occasion I visited Pinewood was when it was owned by Rank. I was running a video publishing business, which was distributing much of the Rank catalogue of films, and my main reason to visit the Studios at that time was I was just dying to see it. The association between our companies grew and developed. By 2000 Rank had disposed of all its interests in the film industry bar Pinewood, the Odeon cinema chain and Deluxe, and it was clear that the Rank group wanted to do other things and that Pinewood was no longer core to its activities. I immediately took the idea of buying Pinewood to Michael Grade and the city to get the necessary financial backing."

TOM CRUISE AND NICOLE KIDMAN, above left, play William and Alice Harford in Stanley Kubrick's portrayal of sexual jealousy between a New York City doctor and his art curator wife, *Eyes Wide Shut* (1999). It is estimated that the film took some 400 days to shoot.

TOM CRUISE AND STANLEY KUBRICK, above, on a New York set built at Pinewood for *Eyes Wide Shut* (1999).

SEAN CONNERY plays art thief Robert
MacDougal and Catherine Zeta-Jones is
insurance agent Virginia Baker, out to snare
him in Jon Amiel's romantic crime thriller,
Entrapment (1999).

This time round when they visited Rank's offices with
an offer to buy Pinewood, the reaction could not have been
more different to Grade's reception a decade previously. Says
Michael Grade: "This time when I sat down at Rank, we did
the deal. Steve Jaggs had run the Studios exceedingly well for
Rank. They'd made the transition from being a captive studio
to four-wall. They'd invested in and looked after the Studios.
But it wasn't on their radar at Rank. It wasn't loved there. We
thought we could make a better go of it."

Fears that Pinewood would be turned into a film-styled
theme park were quickly allayed by Grade who became
Chairman of the Board: "At no time did we ever believe that we
wanted to be in the theme park business, that it was possible to
do it at Pinewood or that you could ever make money doing it.
It was never part of our plans but it made for a story in the newspapers."

Existing MD Steve Jaggs was invited to stay on in the role. Together, he and
the new owners sought to assure a nervous industry that further positive plans for
the Studios' future were afoot. Exactly one year later, the announcement came that
Pinewood was to merge with one of its former rivals, Shepperton Studios. Jaggs
knew the move was a good thing: "We had always had a friendly rivalry with the
Shepperton management. The size of productions that came into the UK could fit
into both Studios – so we were both after the same films, the bigger the film the
more we both wanted it. We wouldn't get into any price wars but we had to ensure
we had the quality of facilities and management cooperation to give the client
value for money. Pinewood was the bigger site and we have an exterior lot, good
stages of varying sizes, the gardens, the paddock tank, a tank in the 007 stage and
five other tanks – not that they were in very good order then. Shepperton had no
exterior tank, few other facilities for water shoots and no back lot at that time. The
relationship between us was always good. We shared the same clients. We rarely
shared the films though. But that has all changed now.

"Our whole philosophy is that if we had Shepperton, then by managing the
estate properly we could take in at least one extra film over a period, than the two

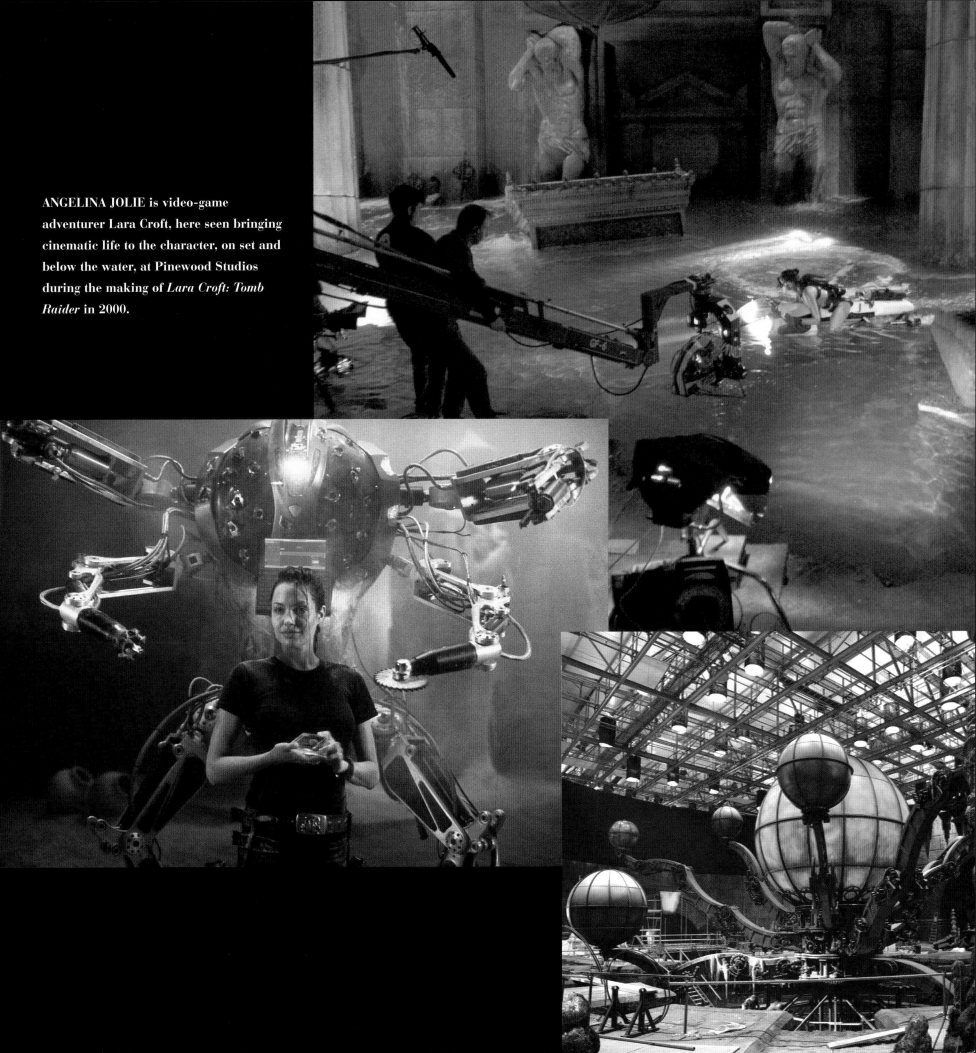

ANGELINA JOLIE is video-game adventurer Lara Croft, here seen bringing cinematic life to the character, on set and below the water, at Pinewood Studios during the making of *Lara Croft: Tomb Raider* in 2000.

could separately. For example, a production wants five stages but there are only three empty at Pinewood and three empty at Shepperton. Neither of the Studios could take it. However with good scheduling and with the two Studios joined together, we can get that feature in. It took sometime to merge the two businesses. Some people will always want to go to one Studio or another. But you know you've made it when a client comes in and asks, 'Which Studios are we in this time?'"

The merger of Pinewood and Shepperton created a firm valued at £100 million and meant that the enlarged business would have the same number of stages as its Hollywood counterparts. For some, like Michael Grade, the move was inevitable: "We knew that Shepperton was owned by venture capitalists and we hoped that they would be sellers rather than holders. It wasn't a difficult deal to make in the end. Of course, there were cultural differences between the two Studios but we had a business model that was working well at Pinewood and we needed it in place at Shepperton to make a return on our investment. Change doesn't come easy in this country. The Studios were like Oxford and Cambridge; you spend so many years fighting each other and then when you join together you have to figure out how to work together. But we got there. We have secured the long-term future of these studios for the British film industry. We are a dedicated film and television studio business. That's what we do. We are not a small division of a larger company. We come to work each day to sell those stages and get the place busy and get people here to make their films and televisions shows."

These words are a boost for the British film industry regularly rocked by concerns over new and emerging facilities opening up in competition for the same clientele. With studios across Europe such as Barrandov in Prague, UFA Studios in Germany and Fox Studios in Australia all vying for the same trade now, competition for studios in Britain, such as Pinewood and Shepperton, has never been stiffer. No longer taking each other on, but joining together to take others on and win the business for Britain, was a rational way forward.

Chief executive, Ivan Dunleavy, insists that merging the two Studios, while not always an easy exercise, now means the Studios are set to be stronger than ever they were as two separate sites: "As far as the business of the Studios is concerned, what was clear then – as it is now – is that there is a global marketplace in which

JUDI DENCH, opposite, is Iris Murdoch in the true story of the lifelong romance between the famous novelist and her husband, John Bayley, from their college days through to her battle with Alzheimer's disease, in the award-winning *Iris* (2001).

to make films and that you need to have a large scale studio provider in the UK. By putting Pinewood and Shepperton together there were all sorts of efficiencies we could extract while at the same time respecting the wonderful heritage and reputation for making films that both Pinewood and Shepperton possess. Pinewood and Shepperton had been rivals for the best part of 70 years and though their business was technically the same, they had a different culture in the way they approached the business.

"From my point of view what was interesting was the ability, in a neutral way, to try and pick the best from both. That's where we have ended up now. We've taken the best of each and made one and one equal three – adding something extra special to the equation."

So far, it appears to have been a successful way forward. Pre-merger, in the year 2000 for example, filming of Stephen Sommers' hit sequel *The Mummy Returns* was divided between Pinewood and Shepperton. Post-merger, it has been easier to accommodate entire productions in one or other of the studios, a move which the majority of producers seem to be pleased about. As Sir Alan Parker says: "I get a great feeling when I drive through the gates of either Pinewood or Shepperton. For a filmmaker there's an incredible sense of security that everything is going to be great and the sets are going to be built beautifully. Both Studios are incredibly well run and very friendly." The merging of the Studios now means that Pinewood Shepperton covers over 200 acres and more than 60 acres of back lot for film sets. Pinewood continues to have its formal gardens, woodlands and magnificent mansion house.

Pinewood Shepperton plc bought Teddington Television Studios in 2005, allowing the group to diversify even further

OPPOSITE PAGE: The Phantom of the Opera, in Joel Schumacher's 1994
big screen adaptation of Andrew Lloyd Webber's hit stage musical,
starring Emmy Rossum as Christine and Gerard Butler as the disfigured
musical genius.

EDWARD SPEELERS, above, plays the title role
opposite a CGI dragon in the action-packed
adventure film, *Eragon* (2006).

across the spectrum from blockbuster filmmaking to light entertainment small-screen fare. There are now more than 280 companies based at the Studio company sites – from legal advisors and accountants to special effects houses and prosthetics makers. Kenneth Branagh insists that having everything under one roof is essential for bringing in films on budget and on time: "The infrastructure means that if a camera breaks or a light explodes, everything's there, it doesn't cost you time in your shooting day."

Pinewood's water tank had always been the envy of studios across the globe. Now, further investment into the site and its facilities saw the Studio's underwater stage opening in 2005. Technological advancement means that the underwater stage has a state-of-the-art ultraviolet filtration system, which provides crystal clear water while eliminating "red-eye". Janine Modder, the production supervisor for *Basic Instinct 2: Risk Addiction*, filmed at Pinewood in 2005, appreciates the new facilities: "Underwater sequences are traditionally difficult, but Pinewood have successfully overcome this with their world-class underwater stage and excellent management team." It is this added value that Pinewood now has which makes the Studios easier to sell, at a time when there is stiff competition among studios across the world.

Nick Smith, sales and marketing director for Pinewood Shepperton plc, admits that Pinewood can no longer just sell itself off the back of its historic reputation. He and his team work hard to respect the past while striving to keep Pinewood successful for the future: "I joined Pinewood at the end of April 2002, as sales and marketing director, the first time Pinewood had such a role. In the past it was a different market place. We had a special relationship with the States and more often than not if a film was being made out of the States they'd come to the UK and talk to Pinewood. But the global market place has changed that – Prague, Eastern Europe and Australia, all coming online and talking to the American market, all pitching for a slice of the cake – and it became harder to attract work into the Studios and so we needed to be more proactive.

"There are such wide ranges of people we attract into the Studios now. The icing on the cake is always going to be a blockbuster film that will be here for six months to a year. But there are also the smaller independent films, television

5 ... 4 ... 3 ... 2 ... 1 ... **THUNDERBIRDS ARE GO!, in Jonathan Frakes' movie take on the 1960s small screen fantasy adventure series, filmed at Pinewood in 2003, and substituting the puppets with "real" actors.**

SOME OF THE STUNNING SETS built on the 007 sound stage at Pinewood for Tim Burton's *Charlie and the Chocolate Factory*, filmed at the Studios in 2004.

JOHNNY DEPP plays the eccentric Willy Wonka in *Charlie and the Chocolate Factory*. The film was the third highest grossing film in the year of its release, 2005.

dramas, light entertainment, commercials, pop promos, band rehearsals and now corporate events to attract in. Our team specialize in different areas to target the broadcasters to get the next series of a well-known drama into the Studios and so on. We generate an awareness of what we are. Particularly for television drama. Television companies often think of us as being film studios, so they may not talk to us in the first instance. We need to change the mindset. Bring people here to show them what we've got and the facilities that are available to everybody and not just big blockbuster films."

DAVID MORRISSEY is psychiatrist Michael Glass, pitting his wits against novelist Catherine Tramell, played by Sharon Stone, in *Basic Instinct 2* (2006).

TOM HANKS is Dr Robert Langdon and Audrey Tatou is Agent Sophie Neveu, opposite, in Ron Howard's adaptation of Dan Brown's novel, *The Da Vinci Code*, filmed at Pinewood during 2005.

Blockbusters are still more than welcome though. *Thunderbirds* was made at Pinewood in 2003, and director Jonathan Frakes immediately saw the benefit of Pinewood's new investment and merger ethos: "It has been a delight working at Pinewood ... I'm very impressed with the whole set-up. Casting a crew is just as important as casting the cast, the team here are wonderful, they take the work seriously but not themselves – I've never seen such collaboration without screaming. *Thunderbirds* has benefited tremendously from their dedication and I would return in a heartbeat."

This is just the sort of news Pinewood wants to hear – expressions of satisfaction from those in the film industry who will hopefully return to the Studios because of the level of service. While much of Bond XXI – *Casino Royale* (2006) – was not filmed at Pinewood, opting instead to shoot at studios in the Czech Republic, all or some of *Charlie and the Chocolate Factory* (2004), *Harry Potter and the Goblet of Fire* (2004), *Finding Neverland* (2002) and *The Da Vinci Code* (2006) were.

So the plaudits really do count for a great deal. Michael Grade insists that cheapest is not always the best: "In the end you have to calculate what is value for money. Pinewood is not the cheapest Studio in the world, but are we the best, the most secure, the most reliable? The *Da Vinci Code* came to Pinewood. Why? Because of the facilities we have, because of what they knew they could achieve here with the huge pool of talent this country possesses in its actors, technicians, special effects people and so on. Everything you want is here or only a cab ride away. You get a very secure feeling when you come to Pinewood that whatever you've been promised, will be delivered and that you'll finish your film on time regardless of how big or small your picture is." For fans of film, most can claim that Pinewood's legacy has played a very important part in their collective hearts as the Studios where so many of their celluloid dreams were brought to life, and so many treasured moments were created. For them too, for the audiences across the world, it's good to know that with 70 years past, Pinewood is still going strong and looking to the future.

Now, all film fans can log on to the company's website (www.pinewoodgroup.com) and study plans for future developments, which include large-scale building programmes that will increase capacity of stage and office accommodation across the sites. Pinewood, Shepperton and Teddington evidently aren't going anywhere. Pinewood seems set for the future, notwithstanding the ups and downs of filmmaking.

More than 30 years after he first designed and oversaw the building of a sound stage at Pinewood, Michael Brown is back working on Pinewood's master plan for the years ahead: "I'm working on the advancement of developing various parts of the Studios for the future. There is a masterplan in place. We are looking to enhance the Studios and the facilities. Some years ago I undertook a large scheme proposal in the Bahamas and one in Bermuda, I did one in Paris and one in Syria. It helps to see how it works elsewhere and to pick up ideas. One of the things I've learnt is that you can go to a hundred different art directors and producers and they'll all come back with different ideas. There have been some very learned people to listen to including Peter Lamont, Ken Adams, Barbara Broccoli and Michael Wilson, Paul Hitchcock and Iain Smith. It's important to

listen to what they say and absorb their requirements. Basic concepts have always been the same – don't cut corners. We've never done that here. Pinewood is now a premier studio. All of the new studios coming along have their basic faults. At Pinewood there are certain home comforts that cannot be replicated. There's still a lot to do, but people listen here. There are lots of new stages to go in, better facilities for housing stars and the staff. I see no reason why Pinewood won't go from strength to strength."

After 13 years at the helm, Steve Jaggs retired as Pinewood's managing director. Always a film fan, he remains passionate about the industry and he is quick to remember all those who have helped keep Pinewood alive: "We have put stability and continuity into Pinewood. The client can see what we're doing, where we're going with both Studios. More facilities at both. I believe that is a comfort to the industry. We are now a Studio group with many stages. And Pinewood's future is more secure than it ever has been. The industry has changed; it's more of a business now than it was even 20 years ago. The films and outlets for them now

CLIVE OWEN plays Theo Faron and Julianne Moore plays Julian Taylor in Alfonso Cuaròn's award-winning futuristic drama, *Children of Men* (2006).

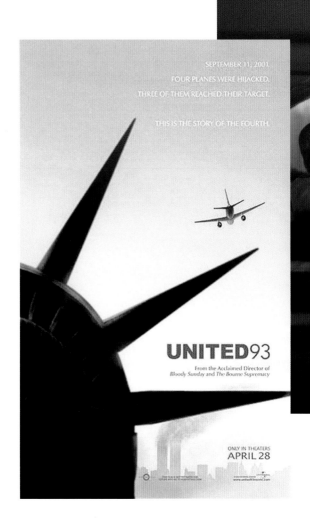

POSTER ARTWORK for *United 93.* **Written and directed by Paul Greengrass (top right) this critically acclaimed real time account of the events on United Flight 93 on 11 September 2001, was filmed at Pinewood during 2005.**

are so different. The machine needs to be fed. But what a great history and track record of films Pinewood has had. Yes, the future is equally as important as the past. This industry will still be going in the decades ahead. I hope that people will still want to be entertained with the moving image in the generations to come. And so, for Pinewood, the next 70 years are as important as the 70 that have gone. Pinewood will forever continue to be linked with the very best of British and international cinema and television production."

That is certainly the plan. Chief executive Ivan Dunleavy and the team that has been put into place at Pinewood, Shepperton and Teddington intend to do just that: "We build on the heritage we have inherited but we don't stand still. We have to change to cope with what is happening in the media world. We want Pinewood to be the focal point for the producers of content. Film is important to us. We're not taking our eye off that ball but we want to add to it with all the other kinds of media out there in a world where the distinctions between film, television, mobile content and so on, are far more blurred than 10 years ago."

Michael Grade believes they will be well into the future: "Why shouldn't they be? The demand for content is insatiable and is getting greater and it's got to be made somewhere. So why not make it at Pinewood? We offer the best facilities, we look after the place, people enjoy coming here, and they get their work done. The Studios is run in a professional manner and customers and visitors have the security of knowing that everything is here, where and when they need it, and that there is the whole infrastructure of the British film industry and talent to support it."

As a wise observer on the film industry once stated, there are no such things as bad

films; there are well-made films and badly made films. After 70 years, most people in the industry will tell you that Pinewood helps people to make well-made films. It is a proud Studio with a proud heritage and a seemingly positive future. Across the world filmmakers, studios, peers and customers continue to hold Pinewood in high regard. The special mystique that has built up at this favoured Buckinghamshire site continues to grow. Some seven decades after Pinewood first opened its doors to filming, the Studios are still very much open for business.

RISING FROM THE ASHES – The brand new 007 stage opened for business in the spring of 2007.

Awards & Filmography

PINEWOOD Award Winners

1938
Academy Awards
Best Adapted Screenplay: Ian Dalrymple,
Cecil Lewis, W. P. Lipscomb, George Bernard
Shaw (*Pygmalion*)

1943
Academy Awards
Best Documentary Feature: Ministry of
Information (*Desert Victory*)

1945
Academy Awards
Best Documentary Feature: Government
of Great Britain, Government of USA (*The
True Glory*)

1947
Academy Awards
Cinematography – Black and White:
Guy Green (*Great Expectations*)
Cinematography – Colour: Jack Cardiff
(*Black Narcissus*)
Art Direction – Black and White: John Bryan
(*Great Expectations*)
Art Direction – Colour: Alfred Junge
(*Black Narcissus*)

1948
Academy Awards
Art Direction – Colour: Hein Heckroth
(*The Red Shoes*)
Music: Brian Easdale (*The Red Shoes*)

1953
British Film Academy Awards
Best British Film: Genevieve
Most Promising Newcomer to Film:
Norman Wisdom (*Trouble in Store*)

1954
British Film Academy Awards
Best British Actor: Kenneth More
(*Doctor in the House*)

1956
British Film Academy Awards
Best British Film: Reach for the Sky
Best British Actor: Peter Finch (*A Town
Like Alice*)
Best British Actress: Virginia McKenna
(*A Town Like Alice*)

1959
British Film Academy Awards
Best British Film: Sapphire

1960
Academy Awards
Cinematography – Black and White:
Jack Cardiff (*Sons and Lovers*)

1961
British Film Academy Awards
Best British Actor: Peter Finch
(*No Love for Johnnie*)

1963
British Film Academy Awards
Best British Cinematography - Colour:
Ted Moore (*From Russia With Love*)

1964
Academy Awards
Sound Effects: Norman Wanstall (*Goldfinger*)

British Film Academy Awards
Best British Actor: Richard Attenborough
(*Guns at Batasi*)

1965
Academy Awards
Special Visual Effects: John Stears
(*Thunderball*)

British Film Academy Awards
Best British Film: The Ipcress File
Best British Cinematography – Colour:
Otto Heller (*The Ipcress File*)
Best Art Direction – Colour:
Ken Adam (*The Ipcress File*)
British Costume Design – Colour:
Osbert Lancaster/Dinah Greet (*Those
Magnificent Men in Their Flying Machines*)

1966
British Film Academy Awards
British Costume Design – Colour:
Julie Harris (*The Wrong Box*)

1967
British Film Academy Awards
Best British Actress: Edith Evans
(*The Whisperers*)
*Best British Cinematography – Black and
White:* Gerry Turpin (*The Whisperers*)

1968
British Film Academy Awards
Best Supporting Actress: Billie Whitelaw
(*Charlie Bubbles*)

1971
Academy Awards
Cinematography: Oswald Morris (*Fiddler on
the Roof*)
*Music – Best Adaptation and Original Song
Score:* John Williams (*Fiddler on the Roof*)
Sound: Gordon K. McCallum and David
Hildyard (*Fiddler on the Roof*)

1973
British Film Academy Awards
Film Editing: Ralph Kemplen
(*The Day of the Jackal*)

1974
Academy Awards
*Music – Best Adaptation and Original Song
Score:* Nelson Riddle (*The Great Gatsby*)
Costume Design: Theoni V. Aldredge
(*The Great Gatsby*)

British Film Academy Awards
Cinematography: Douglas Slocombe
(*The Great Gatsby*)
Art Direction: John Box (*The Great Gatsby*)
Costume Design: Theoni V. Aldredge
(*The Great Gatsby*)

1975
British Film Academy Awards
Art Direction: John Box (*Rollerball*)

1976
**British Academy of Film and
Television Arts Awards**
Best Supporting Actress: Jodie Foster
(*Bugsy Malone*)
Most Promising Newcomer to Leading Film
Roles: Jodie Foster (*Bugsy Malone*)
Screenplay: Alan Parker (*Bugsy Malone*)
Production Design: Geoffrey Kirkland
(*Bugsy Malone*)
Soundtrack: Les Wiggins, Clive Winter and
Ken Barker (*Bugsy Malone*)

1978
Academy Awards
Special Achievement Award – Visual Effects:
Les Bowie, Colin Chilvers, Denys Coop, Roy
Field, Derek Meddings and Zoran Perisic
(*Superman*)

**British Academy of Film and
Television Arts Awards**
*Most Promising Newcomer to Leading Film
Roles:* Christopher Reeve (*Superman*)

1981
Academy Awards
Irving G. Thalberg Memorial Award:
Albert R. "Cubby" Broccoli

1982
Academy Awards
Music – Best Original Score: Henry Mancini
and Leslie Bricusse (*Victor/Victoria*)

**British Academy of Film and
Television Arts Awards**
Original Song: Another Brick in the Wall by
Roger Waters (*Pink Floyd The Wall*)
Sound: James Guthrie, Eddy Joseph, Clive
Winter, Graham Hartstone and Nicholas Le
Mesurier (*Pink Floyd The Wall*)

1986
Academy Awards
Sound Effects – Editing: Don Sharpe (*Aliens*)
Visual Effects: Suzanne Benson, Robert
Skotak, Brian Johnson, John Richardson, Stan
Winston (*Aliens*)

**British Academy of Film and
Television Arts Awards**
Special Visual Effects: Suzanne Benson,
Robert Skotak, Brian Johnson, John
Richardson, Stan Winston (*Aliens*)

1989
Academy Awards
Art Direction: Anton Furst and Peter Young
(*Batman*)

1994
**British Academy of Film and
Television Arts Awards**
Cinematography: Philippe Rousselot
(*Interview With the Vampire*)
Production Design: Dante Ferretti
(*Interview With the Vampire*)

1996
Academy Awards
Best Score: Rachel Portman (*Emma*)

1997
**British Academy of Film and
Television Arts Awards**
Achievement in Special Visual Effects:
Mark Stetson, Karen E. Goulekas, Nick
Allder, Neil Corbould, Nick Dudman (*The
Fifth Element*)

2001
Academy Awards
Supporting Actor: Jim Broadbent (*Iris*)

British Academy Film Awards
Best Actress: Judi Dench (*Iris*)

2002
Academy Awards
Actress: Nicole Kidman (*The Hours*)
*The Anthony Asquith Award for
Achievement in Film Music:* Philip Glass
(*The Hours*)
British Academy Film Awards
Best Actress: Nicole Kidman (*The Hours*)

2004
Academy Awards
Best Score: Jan Kaczmarek
(*Finding Neverland*)

2005
British Academy Film Awards
Production Design: Stuart Craig
(*Harry Potter and the Goblet of Fire*)

2006
British Academy Film Awards
*The David Lean Award for Achievement in
Direction:* Paul Greengrass (*United 93*)
Cinematography: Emmanuel Lubezki
(*Children of Men*)
Editing: Clare Douglas, Christopher Rouse
and Richard Pearson (*United 93*)
Production Design: Jim Clay, Geoffrey
Kirkland and Jennifer Williams
(*Children of Men*)
Sound: Chris Munro, Eddy Joseph, Mike
Prestwood Smith, Martin Cantwell and Mark
Taylor (*Casino Royale*)

Using the best available sources for reference, the following filmography attempts to list details of every film made at Pinewood Studios since the start of production in 1936. A film's title – alphabetically listed within its year – along with director and actor's credits are included for each production. Where a film may have had one or more alternative titles, that is, for American or international release, the most widely recognized film name is listed.

Drawing up such a list is not without its potential pitfalls. For example, deciding just how much of a film needs to have been produced at Pinewood for it to be included within the filmography, has led to an interesting debate. The author and publishers have concluded that if Pinewood played any significant part in the production of a film, it should rightfully be included in the filmography.

With the increasing popularity of the Studios' use for television production, it seems only right and fitting to at least include a list of titles made for that medium. Pinewood has played host to the filming of many television productions across the years. A list of the most well-known titles appears at the end of the filmography. Additionally, all television shows and programme titles from the year 2000 produced at the Studios have also been appended. Where made-for-television films and mini-series have been produced at Pinewood, they are listed within the body of the filmography.

Should readers feel that there are any omissions or inaccuracies, the author and publishers would be happy to receive such details, for consideration and possible inclusion in any future updated editions of this book.

1936

Cross My Heart
Director: Bernard Mainwaring
Starring: Kathleen Gibson, Tully Comber,
             Sylvia Coleridge, Robert Field

The Gang Show
Director: Alfred J. Goulding
Starring: Ralph Reader, Gino Malo,
             Stuart Robertson, Richard Ainley

London Melody
Director: Herbert Wilcox
Starring: Anna Neagle, Tullio Carminati,
             Robert Douglas, Horace Hodges

Our Fighting Navy
Director: Norman Walker
Starring: Robert Douglas, H.B. Warner, Noah
             Beery, Richard Cromwell, Hazel Terry

The Scarab Murder Mystery
Director: Michael Hankinson
Starring: Wilfred Hyde White, Kathleen Kelly,
             Wally Patch, Graham Cheswright

The Street Singer
Director: Jean de Marguenat
Starring: Arthur Tracy, Margaret Lockwood,
             Arthur Riscoe, Hugh Wakefield

Splinters in the Air
Director: Alfred J. Goulding
Starring: Sydney Howard, Richard Hearne,
             Ralph Reader, Nelson Keys

Talk of the Devil
Director: Carol Reed
Starring: Ricardo Cortez, Sally Eilers,
             Basil Sydney, Randle Ayrton

1937

Break the News
Director: Rene Clair
Starring: Jack Buchanan, Maurice Chevalier,
             June Knight, Garry Marsh

Cavalier of the Streets
Director: Harold French
Starring: Margaret Vyner, Patrick Barr,
             Carl Harbord, James Craven

Command Performance
Director: Sinclair Hill
Starring: Arthur Tracy, Lilli Palmer, Mark Daly,
             Rae Collett

The Fatal Hour
Director: George Pearson
Starring: Edward Rigby, Moira Read,
             Dick Hunter, Moore Marriot

Follow Your Star
Director: Sinclair Hill
Starring: Arthur Tracy, Belle Chrystall,
             Mark Daly, Horace Hodges,

The Frog
Director: Jack Raymond
Starring: Gordon Harker, Carol Goodner,
             Noah Beery, Jack Hawkins

Gangway
Director: Sonnie Hale
Starring: Jessie Matthews, Barry Mackay,
             Nat Pendleton, Alastair Sim

Holidays End
Director: John Paddy Carstairs
Starring: Leslie Brady, Rosalyn Boulter,
             Elliott Seabrook, Wally Patch

Incident in Shanghai
Director: John Paddy Carstairs
Starring: Patrick Barr, Margaret Vyner,
             Derek Gorst, Ralph Roberts

Jericho
Director: Thornton Freeland
Starring: Paul Robeson, Henry Wilcoxon,
             Wallace Ford, John Laurie

Kicking the Moon Around
Director: Walter Forde
Starring: Ambrose and his Orchestra,
             Evelyn Dall, Hal Thompson,
             Florence Desmond

Lancashire Luck
Director: Henry Cass
Starring: Wendy Hiller, George Carney,
             Muriel George, Nigel Stock

The Last Curtain
Director: David MacDonald
Starring: Campbell Gullen, John Wickham,
             Keene Duncan, Greta Gynt

Midnight Menace
Director: Sinclair Hill
Starring: Charles Farrell, Fritz Kortner,
             Margaret Vyner, Evan John

Mr Smith Carries On
Director: Lister Laurance
Starring: Edward Rigby, Dorothy Oldfield,
             Julien Mitchell, H. F. Maltby

Museum Mystery
Director: Clifford Gulliver
Starring: Jock McKay, Gerald Case,
             Elizabeth Inglis, Tom Wylde

Night Ride
Director: John Paddy Carstairs
Starring: Julian Vedey, Wally Patch,
             Jimmy Hanley, Joan Ponsford

Sailing Along
Director: Sonnie Hale
Starring: Jessie Matthews, Roland Young,
             Barry Mackay, Jack Whiting

The Sky's the Limit
Directors: Lee Garmes and Jack Buchanan
Starring: Jack Buchanan, Mara Loseff,
             William Kendall, David Hutcheson

Smash and Grab
Director: Tim Whelan
Starring: Jack Buchanan, Elsie Randolph,
             Arthur Margetson, Antony Holles

Strange Boarders
Director: Herbert Mason
Starring: Tom Walls, Renée Saint-Cyr,
             Googie Withers, Ronald Adam

Sunset in Vienna
Director: Norman Walker
Starring: *Lilli Palmer, Tullio Carminati,*
            John Garrick, Geraldine Hislop

Sweet Devil
Director: René Guissart
Starring: *Jean Gille, Bobbie Howes,*
            William Kendall, Syd Walker

Young and Innocent
Director: Alfred Hitchcock
Starring: *Derrick de Marney, Nova Pilbeam,*
            Percy Marmount, Edward Rigby

1938

Beyond Our Horizon
Produced by: Religious Films Ltd
Director: Norman Walker
Starring: *Milton Rosmer, Josephine Wilson*

Climbing High
Director: Carol Reed
Starring: *Jessie Matthews, Michael Redgrave,*
            Noel Madison, Alastair Sim

Crackerjack
Director: Albert de Courville
Starring: *Tom Walls, Lilli Palmer, Noel Madison,*
            Leon M. Lion

The Greatest of These
Produced by: Religious Films Ltd
Director: Norman Walker
Starring: *Neal Arden*

Inspector Hornleigh
Director: Eugene Forde
Starring: *Gordon Harker, Alastair Sim,*
            Miki Hood, Hugh Williams

Keep Smiling
Director: Herbert I. Leeds
Starring: *Jane Withers, Gloria Stuart,*
            Henry Wilcoxon, Helen Westley

The Lambeth Walk
Director: Albert de Courville
Starring: *Lupino Lane, Sally Gray,*
            Seymour Hicks, Wilfrid Hyde White

Lightning Conductor
Director: Maurice Elvey
Starring: *Gordon Harker, John Lodge,*
            Sally Gray, Ernest Thesiger

The Mikado
Director: Victor Schertzinger
Starring: *Kenny Baker, Martyn Green,*
            Sydney Granville, Jean Collin

Pygmalion
Director: Anthony Asquith
Starring: *Leslie Howard, Wendy Hiller,*
            Wilfrid Lawson, Scott Sunderland

St Paul
Produced by: Religious Films Ltd
Director: Norman Walker
Starring: *Neal Arden*

So This is London
Director: Thornton Freeland
Starring: *Robertson Hare, Alfred Drayton,*
            George Sanders, Fay Compton

Spot of Bother
Director: David MacDonald
Starring: *Robertson Hare, Alfred Drayton,*
            Kathleen Joyce, Sandra Storme

A Stolen Life
Director: Paul Czinner
Starring: *Elisabeth Bergner, Michael Redgrave,*
            Wilfrid Lawson, Richard Ainley

This Man is News
Director: David MacDonald
Starring: *Barry K. Barnes, Valerie Hobson,*
            Alastair Sim, John Warwick

1941

Listen to Britain
Produced by: Crown Film Unit
Directors: Humphrey Jennings,
            Stewart McAllister
Starring: *Bud Flanagan, Chesney Allen,*
            Leonard Brockington, Myra Hess

1942

The Coastal Command
Produced by: Crown Film Unit
Director: J.B. Holmes

Beyond the Line of Duty
Director: Lewis Seiler
Starring: *Ronald Reagan (narrator),*
            Hewitt T. Wheless, Hubert R. Harmon,
            Franklin Delano Roosevelt (voice)

Malta GC
Directors: Eugeniusz Cekalski,
            Derrick De Marney
Starring: *Laurence Olivier (narrator)*

The Silent Village
Director: Humphrey Jennings

1943

Close Quarters
Produced by: Crown Film Unit
Director: Jack Lee

Desert Victory
Produced by: Royal Air Force Film Unit
Directors: Roy Boulting, David Macdonald
            (both uncredited)
Starring: *Harold Alexander, Winston Churchill,*
            General Montgomery, Adolf Hitler (all
            appearing in archive footage)

Fires Were Started
Produced by: Crown Film Unit
Director: Humphrey Jennings
Starring: *Philip Dickson, George Gravett,*
            Fred Griffiths, Johnny Houghton
            (all uncredited)

1944

A Harbour Goes to France
Produced by: Crown Film Unit

Tunisian Victory
Produced by: United States Army Signal Corps, British Army Film and Photographic Unit
Directors: Frank Capra, John Huston, Hugh Stewart
Starring: *Leo Genn (narrator), and archive footage appearances including Harold Alexander, Kenneth Anderson, Winston Churchill*

Western Approaches
Produced by: Crown Film Unit
Director: Pat Jackson
Starring: *Eric Fullerton, Captain Duncan Mackenzie, Captain W. Kerr, Eric Baskeyfield*

1945

Burma Victory
Produced by: British Army Film Unit
Director: Roy Boulting

Diary for Timothy
Produced by: Crown Film Unit
Director: Humphrey Jennings
Starring: *Michael Redgrave (narrator), Myra Hess, John Gielgud, George Woodbridge (uncredited)*

Instruments of the Orchestra
Produced by: Crown Film Unit
Director: Muir Mathieson
Starring: *The London Symphony Orchestra, Malcolm Sargent*

Journey Together
Director: John Boulting
Starring: *Richard Attenborough, Jack Watling, Rex Harrison, George Cole*

The True Glory
Produced by: United States Office of War Information, UK Ministry of Information
Directors: Garson Kanin, Carol Reed (uncredited)
Starring: *Dwight D. Eisenhower, Peter Ustinov, Robert Harris (narrator)*

1946

Black Narcissus
Director: Michael Powell
Starring: *Deborah Kerr, David Farrar, Sabu, Jean Simmons*

Captain Boycott
Director: Frank Launder
Starring: *Stewart Granger, Kathleen Ryan, Alastair Sim, Robert Donat*

Great Expectations
Director: David Lean
Starring: *John Mills, Martita Hunt, Valerie Hobson, Alec Guinness*

Green for Danger
Director: Sidney Gilliat
Starring: *Alastair Sim, Sally Gray, Rosamund John, Trevor Howard*

Take My Life
Director: Ronald Neame
Starring: *Hugh Williams, Greta Gynt, Marius Goring, Francis L. Sullivan*

1947

Blanche Fury
Director: Marc Allegret
Starring: *Valerie Hobson, Stewart Granger, Michael Gough, Walter Fitzgerald*

End of the River
Director: Derek Twist
Starring: *Sabu, Esmond Knight, Bibi Ferreira, Robert Douglas*

Esther Waters
Director: Ian Dalrymple
Starring: *Kathleen Ryan, Dirk Bogarde, Cyril Cusack, Ivor Barnard*

London Belongs to Me
Director: Sidney Gilliat
Starring: *Alastair Sim, Stephen Murray, Richard Attenborough, Fay Compton*

Oliver Twist
Director: David Lean
Starring: *Alec Guinness, Robert Newton, Francis L. Sullivan, John Howard Davies*

The Red Shoes
Director: Michael Powell
Starring: *Anton Walbrook, Moira Shearer, Marius Goring, Robert Helpmann*

Woman in the Hall
Director: Jack Lee
Starring: *Ursula Jeans, Jean Simmons, Cecil Parker, Joan Miller*

1948

All Over Town
Director: Derek N. Twist
Starring: *Norman Wooland, Sarah Churchill, Cyril Cusack*

The Blue Lagoon
Director: Frank Launder
Starring: *Jean Simmons, Donald Houston, Susan Stranks, Peter Jones*

Dear Mr Prohack
Director: Thornton Freeland
Starring: *Cecil Parker, Hermione Baddeley, Dirk Bogarde, Sheila Sim*

Floodtide
Director: Frederick Wilson
Starring: *Gordon Jackson, Rona Anderson, John Laurie, Jimmy Logan*

Fools Rush In
Director: John Paddy Carstairs
Starring: *Sally Ann Howes, Guy Rolfe, Nora Swinburne, Thora Hird*

Kind Hearts and Coronets (filmed at Ealing Studios and at Pinewood)
Director: Robert Hamer
Starring: *Dennis Price, Alec Guinness, Valerie Hobson, Joan Greenwood*

Obsession
Director: Edward Dmytryk
Starring: *Robert Newton, Sally Gray, Phil Brown, Naunton Wayne*

Once a Jolly Swagman
Director: Jack Lee
Starring: *Dirk Bogarde, Renée Asherson, Bonar Colleano, Sidney James*

Once Upon a Dream
Director: Ralph Thomas
Starring: *Cecil Bevan, Dora Bryan, Wilfred Caithness, Hubert Gregg*

The Passionate Friends
Director: David Lean
Starring: *Ann Todd, Trevor Howard, Claude Rains, Isabel Dean*

Warning to Wantons
Director: Donald B. Wilson
Starring: *Harold Warrender, Anne Vernon, David Tomlinson, Sonia Holm*

1949

The Astonished Heart
Director: Terence Fisher
Starring: *Noel Coward, Margaret Leighton, Celia Johnson, Graham Payn*

Boys in Brown
Director: Montgomery Tully
Starring: *Jack Warner, Dirk Bogarde, Michael Medwin, Jimmy Hanley*

Golden Salamander
Director: Ronald Neame
Starring: *Trevor Howard, Anouk Aimée, Herbert Lom, Walter Rilla*

Madeleine
Director: David Lean
Starring: *Ann Todd, Leslie Banks, Elizabeth Sellars, Ivor Barnard*

Poet's Pub
Director: Frederick Wilson
Starring: *Derek Bond, Rona Anderson, James Robertson Justice, Barbara Murray*

Prelude to Fame
Director: Fergus McDonell
Starring: *Jeremy Spenser, Guy Rolfe, Kathleen Ryan, Kathleen Byron*

So Long at the Fair
Directors: Antony Darnborough, Terence Fisher
Starring: *Jean Simmons, Dirk Bogarde, David Tomlinson, Marcel Poncin*

The Spider and the Fly
Director: Robert Hamer
Starring: *Eric Portman, Guy Rolfe, Nadia Gray, George Cole*

Stop Press Girl
Director: Michael Barry
Starring: *Sally Ann Howes, Gordon Jackson, Basil Radford, Naunton Wayne*

1950

The Adventurers
Director: David MacDonald
Starring: *Dennis Price, Jack Hawkins,*
Dennis Price, Siobhan McKenna

Blackmailed
Director: Marc Allegret
Starring: *Dirk Bogarde, Mai Zetterling,*
Fay Compton, Michael Gough

The Browning Version
Director: Anthony Asquith
Starring: *Michael Redgrave, Jean Kent,*
Nigel Patrick, Wilfrid Hyde White

The Clouded Yellow
Director: Ralph Thomas
Starring: *Trevor Howard, Jean Simmons,*
Barry Jones, Sonia Dresdel

Highly Dangerous
Director: Roy Baker
Starring: *Margaret Lockwood, Dane Clark,*
Marius Goring, Naunton Wayne

Night Without Stars
Director: Anthony Pelissier
Starring: *David Farrar, Nadia Gray,*
Maurice Teynac, Gilles Queant

Tony Draws a Horse
Director: John Paddy Carstairs
Starring: *Cecil Parker, Anne Crawford,*
Derek Bond, Barbara Murray

Trio
Directors: Ken Annakin, Harold French
Starring: *James Hayter, Kathleen Harrison,*
Nigel Patrick, Jean Simmons

Waterfront
Director: Michael Anderson
Starring: *Robert Newton, Kathleen Harrison,*
Susan Shaw, Richard Burton

White Corridors
Director: Pat Jackson
Starring: *James Donald, Googie Withers,*
Petula Clark, Jack Watling

The Woman in Question
Director: Anthony Asquith
Starring: *Jean Kent, Dirk Bogarde, Susan Shaw,*
Hermione Baddeley

1951

Appointment with Venus
Director: Ralph Thomas
Starring: *David Niven, Glynis Johns,*
George Coulouris, Kenneth More

The Card
Director: Ronald Neame
Starring: *Alec Guinness, Glynis Johns,*
Petula Clark, Valerie Hobson

Encore
Directors: Harold French, Pat Jackson,
Anthony Pelissier
Starring: *Nigel Patrick, Roland Culver,*
Kay Walsh, Glynis Johns

High Treason
Director: Roy Boulting
Starring: *Liam Redmond, André Morell,*
Anthony Bushell, Kenneth Griffith

Hotel Sahara
Director: Ken Annakin
Starring: *Peter Ustinov, Yvonne De Carlo,*
David Tomlinson, Roland Culver

Hunted
Director: Charles Crichton
Starring: *Dirk Bogarde, Kay Walsh,*
Elizabeth Sellars, Frederick Piper

The Importance of Being Earnest
Director: Anthony Asquith
Starring: *Michael Redgrave, Michael Dennison,*
Edith Evans, Margaret Rutherford

Valley of Eagles
Director: Terence Young
Starring: *Jack Warner, John McCallum,*
Nadia Gray, Anthony Dawson

1952

Desperate Moment
Director: Compton Bennett
Starring: *Dirk Bogarde, Mai Zetterling,*
Philip Friend, Albert Lieven

The Final Test
Director: Anthony Asquith
Starring: *Jack Warner, Robert Morley,*
Brenda Bruce, George Relph,

Genevieve
Director: Henry Cornelius
Starring: *Dinah Sheridan, John Gregson,*
Kay Kendall, Kenneth More

It Started in Paradise
Director: Compton Bennett
Starring: *Jane Hylton, Ian Hunter,*
Terence Morgan, Muriel Pavlow

The Long Memory
Director: Robert Hamer
Starring: *John Mills, John McCallum,*
Elizabeth Sellars, Geoffrey Keen

Made in Heaven
Director: John Paddy Carstairs
Starring: *David Tomlinson, Petula Clark,*
Sonja Ziemann, A. E. Matthews

The Malta Story
Director: Brian Desmond Hurst
Starring: *Alec Guinness, Anthony Steel,*
Muriel Pavlow, Jack Hawkins,
Flora Robson

Meet Me Tonight
Director: Anthony Pelissier
Starring: *Ted Ray, Kay Walsh,*
Stanley Holloway, Betty Ann Davies

The Net
Director: Anthony Asquith
Starring: *Phyllis Calvert, Noel Willman,*
Herbert Lom, James Donald

Penny Princess
Director: Val Guest
Starring: *Dirk Bogarde, Yolande Donlan,*
A. E. Matthews, Anthony Oliver

The Planter's Wife
Director: Ken Annakin
Starring: *Claudette Colbert, Jack Hawkins,*
Ram Gopal, Jeremy Spenser

Something Money Can't Buy
Director: Pat Jackson
Starring: *Patricia Roc, Anthony Steel,*
A. E. Matthews, Moira Lister

The Sword and the Rose
Director: Ken Annakin
Starring: *Richard Todd, Glynis Johns, James Robertson Justice, Michael Gough*

Top of the Form
Director: John Paddy Carstairs
Starring: *Ronald Shiner, Anthony Newley, Harry Fowler, Alfie Bass*

Turn the Key Softly
Director: Jack Lee
Starring: *Yvonne Mitchell, Terence Morgan, Joan Collins, Kathleen Harrison*

Venetian Bird
Director: Ralph Thomas
Starring: *Richard Todd, Eva Bartok, John Gregson, George Coulouris*

1953

Always a Bride
Director: Ralph Smart
Starring: *Peggy Cummins, Terence Morgan, Ronald Squire, James Hayter*

The Beachcomber
Director: Muriel Box
Starring: *Robert Newton, Glynis Johns, Donald Sinden, Donald Pleasence*

The Black Knight
Director: Tay Garnett
Starring: *Alan Ladd, Peter Cushing, Patricia Medina, Harry Andrews*

A Day to Remember
Director: Ralph Thomas
Starring: *Stanley Holloway, Donald Sinden, Joan Rice, Odile Versois*

Doctor in the House
Director: Ralph Thomas
Starring: *Dirk Bogarde, Kenneth More, Donald Sinden, Donald Houston*

Fast and Loose
Director: Gordon Parry
Starring: *Brian Reece, Stanley Holloway, Kay Kendall, Reginald Beckwith*

Forbidden Cargo
Director: Harold French
Starring: *Nigel Patrick, Elizabeth Sellars, Terence Morgan, Jack Warner*

Hell Below Zero
Director: Mark Robson
Starring: *Alan Ladd, Joan Tetzel, Basil Sydney, Stanley Baker*

The Kidnappers
Director: Philip Leacock
Starring: *Duncan Macrae, Vincent Winter, Jon Whitely, Theodore Bikel*

The Million Pound Note
Director: Ronald Neame
Starring: *Gregory Peck, Jane Griffiths, Ronald Squire, Joyce Grenfell*

Personal Affair
Director: Anthony Pelissier
Starring: *Gene Tierney, Glynis Johns, Leo Genn, Walter Fitzgerald*

The Seekers
Director: Ken Annakin
Starring: *Jack Hawkins, Glynis Johns, Noel Purcell, Kenneth Williams*

Trouble in Store
Director: John Paddy Carstairs
Starring: *Norman Wisdom, Jerry Desmonde, Margaret Rutherford, Moira Lister*

You Know What Sailors Are
Director: Ken Annakin
Starring: *Akim Tamiroff, Donald Sinden, Sarah Lawson, Bill Kerr*

1954

Above Us the Waves
Director: Ralph Thomas
Starring: *John Mills, John Gregson. Donald Sinden, James Robertson Justice*

As Long As They're Happy
Director: J. Lee Thompson
Starring: *Jack Buchanan, Janette Scott, Brenda de Banzie, Diana Dors*

Mad About Men
Director: Ralph Thomas
Starring: *Glynis Johns, Donald Sinden, Margaret Rutherford, Dora Bryan*

One Good Turn
Director: John Paddy Carstairs
Starring: *Norman Wisdom, Joan Rice, Shirley Abicair, Thora Hird*

Passage Home
Director: Roy Baker
Starring: *Peter Finch, Anthony Steel, Diane Cilento, Geoffrey Keen*

The Prisoner
Director: Peter Glenville
Starring: *Alec Guinness, Jack Hawkins, Wilfrid Lawson, Kenneth Griffith*

The Purple Plain
Director: Robert Parrish
Starring: *Gregory Peck, Maurice Denham, Win Min Than, Lyndon Brook*

Simba
Director: Brian Desmond Hurst
Starring: *Dirk Bogarde, Donald Sinden, Virginia McKenna, Basil Sydney*

To Paris With Love
Director: Robert Hamer
Starring: *Alec Guinness, Vernon Gray, Odile Versois, Jaques Francois*

Up To His Neck
Director: John Paddy Carstairs
Starring: *Ronald Shiner, Harry Fowler, Laya Raki*

The Young Lovers
Director: Anthony Asquith
Starring: *Odile Versois, David Knight, David Kossoff, Joseph Tomelty*

1955

All For Mary
Director: Wendy Toye
Starring: *Kathleen Harrison, Nigel Patrick, David Tomlinson, Jill Day*

An Alligator Named Daisy
Director: J. Lee Thompson
Starring: *Donald Sinden, Diana Dors, Jean Carson, James Robertson Justice*

The Battle of the River Plate
Director: Michael Powell
Starring: *John Gregson, Anthony Quayle, Peter Finch, Bernard Lee*

The Black Tent
Director: Brian Desmond Hurst
Starring: *Anthony Steel, Donald Sinden, André Morell, Anna Maria Sandri*

Doctor at Sea
Director: Ralph Thomas
Starring: *Dirk Bogarde, Brigitte Bardot, James Robertson Justice, Brenda De Banzie*

Jumping For Joy
Director: John Paddy Carstairs
Starring: *Frankie Howerd, Stanley Holloway, A. E. Mathews, Tony Wright*

Lost
Director: Guy Green
Starring: *David Farrar, David Knight, Julia Arnall, Anthony Oliver*

Man of the Moment
Director: John Paddy Carstairs
Starring: *Norman Wisdom, Lana Morris, Belinda Lee, Jerry Desmonde*

Reach For the Sky
Director: Lewis Gilbert
Starring: *Kenneth More, Muriel Pavlow, Lyndon Brook, Lee Patterson*

Simon and Laura
Director: Muriel Box
Starring: *Peter Finch, Kay Kendall, Ian Carmichael, Maurice Denham*

A Town Like Alice
Director: Jack Lee
Starring: *Virginia McKenna, Peter Finch, Kenji Takagi, Maureen Swanson*

Value for Money
Director: Ken Annakin
Starring: *John Gregson, Diana Dors, Susan Stephen, Derek Farr*

The Woman for Joe
Director: George More O'Ferrall
Starring: *Diane Cilento, George Baker, Jimmy Karoubi, David Kossoff*

1956

The Big Money
Director: John Paddy Carstairs
Starring: *Ian Carmichael, Belinda Lee, Kathleen Harrison, Robert Helpmann*

Checkpoint
Director: Ralph Thomas
Starring: *Anthony Steel, Stanley Baker, James Robertson Justice, Odile Versois*

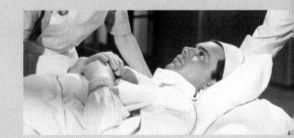

Doctor at Large
Director: Ralph Thomas
Starring: Dirk Bogarde, Donald Sinden, Muriel Pavlow, James Robertson Justice

Eyewitness
Director: Muriel Box
Starring: Donald Sinden, Muriel Pavlow, Michael Craig, Belinda Lee

High Tide at Noon
Director: Philip Leacock
Starring: Betta St John, Michael Craig, Patrick McGoohan, William Sylvester

House of Secrets
Director: Guy Green
Starring: Michael Craig, Julia Arnall, Brenda de Banzie, David Kossoff

Ill Met By Moonlight
Director: Michael Powell
Starring: Dirk Bogarde, Marius Goring, David Oxley, Cyril Cusack

The Iron Petticoat
Director: Ralph Thomas
Starring: Bob Hope, Katherine Hepburn, James Robertson Justice, Robert Helpmann

Jacqueline
Director: Roy Baker
Starring: John Gregson, Kathleen Ryan, Jacqueline Ryan, Noel Purcell

The Prince and the Showgirl
Director: Laurence Olivier
Starring: Laurence Olivier, Marilyn Monroe, Sybil Thorndike, Richard Wattis

The Secret Place
Director: Clive Donner
Starring: Belinda Lee, Ronald Lewis, Michael Brooke, David McCallum

The Spanish Gardener
Director: Philip Leacock
Starring: Dirk Bogarde, Michael Hordern, Jon Whitely, Cyril Cusack

Tiger in the Smoke
Director: Roy Baker
Starring: Tony Wright, Muriel Pavlow, Donald Sinden, Bernard Miles

True as a Turtle
Director: Wendy Toye
Starring: John Gregson, June Thorburn, Cecil Parker, Elvi Hale

Up in the World
Director: John Paddy Carstairs
Starring: Norman Wisdom, Martin Caridia, Jerry Desmonde, Maureen Swanson

1957

The Abominable Snowman
Director: Val Guest
Starring: Peter Cushing, Forrest Tucker, Maureen Connell, Richard Wattis

Across the Bridge
Director: Ken Annakin
Starring: Rod Steiger, David Knight, Marla Landi, Bernard Lee

Campbell's Kingdom
Director: Ralph Thomas
Starring: Dirk Bogarde, Michael Craig, Stanley Baker, Barbara Murray

Carve Her Name With Pride
Director: Lewis Gilbert
Starring: Virginia McKenna, Paul Scofield, Jack Warner, Sidney Tafler

Dangerous Exile
Director: Brian Desmond Hurst
Starring: Louis Jourdan, Belinda Lee, Keith Michell, Richard O'Sullivan

The Gypsy and the Gentleman
Director: Joseph Losey
Starring: Melina Mercouri, Keith Michell, Patrick McGoohan, June Laverick

The Heart of a Child
Director: Clive Donner
Starring: Jean Anderson, Donald Pleasence, Richard Williams, Maureen Pryor

Hell Drivers
Director: C. Raker Endfield
Starring: Stanley Baker, Patrick McGoohan, Herbert Lom, Peggy Cummins

Innocent Sinners
Director: Philip Leacock
Starring: Flora Robson, Catherine Lacey, David Kossoff, Barbara Mullen

Just My Luck
Director: John Paddy Carstairs
Starring: Norman Wisdom, Jill Dixon, Leslie Phillips, Margaret Rutherford

Miracle in Soho
Director: Julian Aymes
Starring: John Gregson, Belinda Lee, Cyril Cusack, Peter Illing

The Naked Truth
Director: Mario Zampi
Starring: Peter Sellers, Terry-Thomas, Peggy Mount, Dennis Price

A Night to Remember
Director: Roy Baker
Starring: Kenneth More, Laurence Naismith, David McCallum, Honor Blackman

The One That Got Away
Director: Roy Baker
Starring: Hardy Kruger, Michael Goodliffe, Colin Gordon, Alec McCowen

Robbery Under Arms
Director: Jack Lee
Starring: Peter Finch, David McCallum, Ronald Lewis, Maureen Swanson

Rooney
Director: George Pollock
Starring: John Gregson, Barry Fitzgerald, Muriel Pavlow, June Thorburn

Seven Thunders
Director: Hugo Fregonese
Starring: James Robertson Justice, Stephen Boyd, Kathleen Harrison, Tony Wright

A Tale of Two Cities
Director: Ralph Thomas
Starring: Dirk Bogarde, Dorothy Tutin, Christopher Lee, Athene Seyler

Violent Playground
Director: Basil Dearden
Starring: Stanley Baker, Anne Heywood, David McCallum, Peter Cushing

The Wind Cannot Read
Director: Ralph Thomas
Starring: Dirk Bogarde, Yoko Tani, Ronald Lewis, John Fraser

Windom's Way
Director: Ronald Neame
Starring: Peter Finch, Mary Ure, Natasha Parry, Robert Flemyng

1958

The Captain's Table
Director: Jack Lee
Starring: John Gregson, Peggy Cummins, Donald Sinden, Reginald Beckwith

Carry On Nurse
Director: Gerald Thomas
Starring: Kenneth Connor, Kenneth Williams, Hattie Jacques, Leslie Phillips

Carry On Sergeant
Director: Gerald Thomas
Starring: William Hartnell, Bob Monkhouse, Shirley Eaton, Kenneth Connor

Ferry to Hong Kong
Director: Lewis Gilbert
Starring: Curt Jurgens, Sylvia Syms, Orson Welles, Jeremy Spenser

Floods of Fear
Director: Charles Crichton
Starring: Howard Keel, Anne Heywood, Harry H. Corbett, Cyril Cusack

Nor the Moon by Night
Director: Ken Annakin
Starring: Joan Brickhill, Michael Craig, Patrick McGoohan, Anna Gaylor

Operation Amsterdam
Director: Michael McCarthy
Starring: Peter Finch, Tony Britton, Eva Bartok, Alexander Knox

Passionate Summer
Director: Rudolph Cartier
Starring: Virginia McKenna, Bill Travers, Yvonne Mitchell, Alexander Knox

Rockets Galore
Director: Michael Relph
Starring: Jeannie Carson, Donald Sinden, Roland Culver, Noel Purcell

Sapphire
Director: Basil Dearden
Starring: Nigel Patrick, Michael Craig, Yvonne Mitchell, Paul Massie

Sea Fury
Director: Cy Endfield
Starring: Stanley Baker, Rupert Davies, Grégoire Aslan, Francis De Wolff

1958–1961

Sea of Sand
Director: Guy Green
Starring: Richard Attenborough, John Gregson, Vincent Ball, Michael Craig

The Sheriff of Fractured Jaw
Director: Raoul Walsh
Starring: Kenneth More, Jayne Mansfield, Robert Morley, Ronald Squire

The Square Peg
Director: John Paddy Carstairs
Starring: Norman Wisdom, Honor Blackman, Edward Chapman, Hattie Jacques

The 39 Steps
Director: Ralph Thomas
Starring: Kenneth More, Taina Elg, Brenda de Banzie, Barry Jones

Too Many Crooks
Director: Mario Zampi
Starring: Terry-Thomas, George Cole, Brenda de Banzie, Sidney James

Whirlpool
Director: Lewis Allen
Starring: Juliette Greco, O. W. Fischer, William Sylvester, Muriel Pavlow

1959

Carry On Constable
Director: Gerald Thomas
Starring: Sidney James, Kenneth Connor, Charles Hawtrey, Kenneth Williams

Carry On Teacher
Director: Gerald Thomas
Starring: Ted Ray, Leslie Phillips, Kenneth Williams, Joan Sims

Conspiracy of Hearts
Director: Ralph Thomas
Starring: Lilli Palmer, Sylvia Syms, Yvonne Mitchell, Albert Lieven

Dentist in the Chair
Director: Don Chaffey
Starring: Bob Monkhouse, Peggy Cummins, Kenneth Connor, Ronnie Stevens

Follow a Star
Director: Robert Asher
Starring: Norman Wisdom, Jerry Desmonde, June Laverick, Hattie Jacques

The Heart of a Man
Director: Herbert Wilcox
Starring: Frankie Vaughan, Anne Heywood, Tony Britton, Anthony Newley

Kidnapped
Director: Robert Stevenson
Starring: Peter Finch, James MacArthur, Bernard Lee, John Laurie

The League of Gentlemen
Director: Basil Dearden
Starring: Jack Hawkins, Richard Attenborough, Roger Livesey, Nigel Patrick

North West Frontier
Director: J. Lee Thompson
Starring: Kenneth More, Lauren Bacall, Herbert Lom, Ursula Jeans

Peeping Tom
Director: Michael Powell
Starring: Carl Boehm, Moira Shearer, Anna Massey, Maxine Audley

Please Turn Over
Director: Gerald Thomas
Starring: Ted Ray, Jean Kent, Leslie Phillips, Joan Sims

The Savage Innocents
Director: Nicholas Ray
Starring: Anthony Quinn, Yoko Tani, Peter O'Toole, Marie Yang

Sink the Bismarck!
Director: Lewis Gilbert
Starring: Kenneth More, Dana Wynter, Laurence Naismith, Carl Mohner

SOS Pacific
Director: Guy Green
Starring: Richard Attenborough, Pier Angeli, John Gregson, Eddie Constantine

Upstairs and Downstairs
Director: Ralph Thomas
Starring: Michael Craig, Anne Heywood, Mylene Demongeot, James Robertson Justice

1960

The Bulldog Breed
Director: Robert Asher
Starring: Norman Wisdom, Edward Chapman, Ian Hunter, David Lodge

Carry On Regardless
Director: Gerald Thomas
Starring: Sidney James, Kenneth Connor, Charles Hawtrey, Kenneth Williams

Cleopatra (filming at Pinewood abandoned)
Director: Joseph L. Mankiewicz
Starring: Elizabeth Taylor, Richard Burton, Rex Harrison, Pamela Brown

Doctor in Love
Director: Ralph Thomas
Starring: Michael Craig, Leslie Phillips, James Robertson Justice, Virginia Maskell

Flame in the Streets
Director: Roy Baker
Starring: John Mills, Brenda de Banzie, Sylvia Syms, Earl Cameron

The Hellfire Club
Director: Robert S. Baker
Starring: Keith Michell, Adrienne Corri, Kai Fischer, Peter Cushing

The Impersonator
Director: Alfred Shaughnessy
Starring: John Crawford, Jane Griffith, Patricia Burke, John Salew

Make Mine Mink
Director: Robert Asher
Starring: Terry-Thomas, Athene Seyler, Hattie Jacques, Billie Whitelaw

Man in the Moon
Director: Basil Dearden
Starring: Kenneth More, Shirley Anne Field, Michael Hordern, Charles Gray

No Kidding
Director: Gerald Thomas
Starring: Leslie Phillips, Geraldine McEwan, Julia Lockwood, Noel Purcell

Piccadilly Third Stop
Director: Wolf Rilla
Starring: *John Crawford, William Hartnell,*
Tony Hawes, Charles Kay

The Professionals
Director: Don Sharp
Starring: *William Lucas, Andrew Faulds,*
Colette Wilde, Stratford Johns

The Singer Not the Song
Director: Roy Baker
Starring: *John Mills, Dirk Bogarde,*
Mylene Demongeot, John Bentley

Sons and Lovers
Director: Jack Cardiff
Starring: *Dean Stockwell, Trevor Howard,*
Wendy Hiller, Mary Ure

There Was a Crooked Man
Director: Stuart Burge
Starring: *Norman Wisdom, Alfred Marks,*
Andrew Cruickshank, Susannah York

The Treasure of Monte Cristo
Director: Monty Berman, Robert S. Baker
Starring: *Rory Calhoun, Patricia Bredin,*
John Gregson

Watch Your Stern
Director: Gerald Thomas
Starring: *Kenneth Connor, Eric Barker,*
Leslie Phillips, Joan Sims

1961

All Night Long
Director: Basil Dearden
Starring: *Patrick McGoohan, Keith Michell,*
Richard Attenborough, Betsy Blair

In Search of the Castaways
Director: Robert Stevenson
Starring: *Maurice Chevalier, Hayley Mills,*
George Sanders, Wilfrid Hyde White

In the Doghouse
Director: Darcy Conyers
Starring: *Leslie Phillips, Peggy Cummins,*
Hattie Jacques, James Booth

The Long Shadow
Director: Peter Maxwell
Starring: *John Crawford, Susan Hampshire,*
Willoughby Goddard,
Humphrey Lestocq

No Love for Johnnie
Director: Ralph Thomas
Starring: *Peter Finch, Stanley Holloway,*
Mary Peach, Billie Whitelaw

No, My Darling Daughter
Director: Ralph Thomas
Starring: *Michael Redgrave, Michael Craig,*
Roger Livesey, Juliet Mills

A Pair of Briefs
Director: Ralph Thomas
Starring: *Michael Craig, Mary Peach, James*
Robertson Justice, Brenda de Banzie

Raising the Wind
Director: Gerald Thomas
Starring: *James Robertson Justice, Leslie Phillips,*
Kenneth Williams, Paul Massey

Tiara Tahiti
Director: William T. Kotcheff
Starring: *John Mills, James Mason,*
Herbert Lom, Claude Dauphin

Twice Round the Daffodils
Director: Gerald Thomas
Starring: *Juliet Mills, Donald Houston,*
Kenneth Williams, Ronald Lewis

1962

Band of Thieves
Director: Peter Bezencenet
Starring: *Acker Bilk, Carol Deene, Peter Haigh,*
Norrie Paramor (all as themselves)

Bitter Harvest
Director Peter Graham Scott
Starring: *Janet Munro, John Stride,*
Anne Cunningham, Alan Badel

Call Me Bwana
Director: Gordon Douglas
Starring: *Bob Hope, Anita Ekberg,*
Edie Adams, Lionel Jeffries

Carry On Cruising
Director: Gerald Thomas
Starring: *Sidney James, Kenneth Williams,*
Kenneth Connor, Dilys Laye

Dr No
Director: Terence Young
Starring: *Sean Connery, Ursula Andress,*
Joseph Wiseman, Jack Lord

The Horse Without a Head
Director: Don Chaffey
Starring: *Leo McKern, Jean-Pierre Aumont,*
Herbert Lom, Pamela Franklin

The Informers
Director: Ken Annakin
Starring: *Nigel Patrick, Colin Blakely,*
Derren Nesbitt, Katherine Woodville

The Iron Maiden
Director: Gerald Thomas
Starring: *Michael Craig, Alan Hale Jnr,*
Jeff Donnell, Cecil Parker

Lancelot and Guinevere
Director: Cornel Wilde
Starring: *Cornel Wilde, Jean Wallace,*
Brian Aherne, George Baker

Life for Ruth
Director: Basil Dearden
Starring: *Michael Craig, Patrick McGoohan,*
Janet Munro, Paul Rogers

The Mindbender
Director: Basil Dearden
Starring: *Dirk Bogarde, John Clements,*
Mary Ure, Michael Bryant

The Mouse on the Moon
Director: Richard Lester
Starring: *Margaret Rutherford, Ron Moody,*
Bernard Cribbins, David Kossoff

Nurse on Wheels
Director: Gerald Thomas
Starring: *Juliet Mills, Ronald Lewis,*
Joan Sims, Raymond Huntley

On the Beat
Director: Robert Asher
Starring: *Norman Wisdom, Jennifer Jayne,*
Raymond Huntley, David Lodge

The Party's Over
Director: Guy Hamilton
Starring: *Oliver Reed, Clifford David, Ann Lynn,*
Louise Sorel

Play it Cool
Director: Michael Winner
Starring: *Billy Fury, Michael Anderson Jr,*
Helen Shapiro, Bobby Vee

The Primitives
Director: Alfred Travers
Starring: *Jan Holden, Bill Edwards,*
Rio Fanning, George Mikell

Stranglehold
Director: Lawrence Huntington
Starring: *Macdonald Carey, Barbara Shelley,*
Philip Friend, Nadja Regin

The Three Lives of Thomasina
Director: Don Chaffey
Starring: *Susan Hampshire, Patrick McGoohan,*
Karen Dotrice, Vincent Winter

The Traitors
Director: Robert Tronson
Starring: *Patrick Allen, James Maxwell,*
Ewan Roberts, Jacqueline Ellis

Victim
Director: Basil Dearden
Starring: *Dirk Bogarde, Sylvia Syms,*
Dennis Price, Norman Bird

Waltz of the Toreadors
Director: John Guillermin
Starring: *Peter Sellers, Margaret Leighton,*
Dany Robin, John Fraser

What a Whopper
Director: Gilbert Gunn
Starring: *Adam Faith, Sidney James,*
Carol Lesley, Terence Longdon

Whistle Down the Wind
Director: Bryan Forbes
Starring: *Hayley Mills, Bernard Lee,*
Alan Bates, Norman Bird

The Wild and the Willing
Director: Ralph Thomas
Starring: *Virginia Maskell, Paul Rogers,*
Ian McShane, Samantha Eggar

1963

80,000 Suspects
Director: Val Guest
Starring: *Claire Bloom, Richard Johnson, Yolande Donlan, Cyril Cusack*

The Bay of St. Michel
Director: John Ainsworth
Starring: *Keenan Wynn, Mai Zetterling, Ronald Howard, Rona Anderson*

The Beauty Jungle
Director: Val Guest
Starring: *Janette Scott, Ian Hendry, Ronald Fraser, Edmund Purdom*

Blind Corner
Director: Lance Comfort
Starring: *William Sylvester, Barbara Shelley, Elizabeth Shepherd, Mark Eden*

Bomb in the High Street
Directors: Peter Bezencenet, Terry Bishop
Starring: *Ronald Howard, Terry Palmer, Suzannah Leigh, Peter Gilmore*

Carry On Cabby
Director: Gerald Thomas
Starring: *Sidney James, Hattie Jacques, Charles Hawtrey, Kenneth Connor*

Carry On Jack
Director: Gerald Thomas
Starring: *Kenneth Williams, Bernard Cribbins, Juliet Mills, Charles Hawtrey*

Doctor in Distress
Director: Ralph Thomas
Starring: *Dirk Bogarde, James Robertson Justice, Mylene Demongeot, Samantha Eggar*

Dr Syn Alias the Scarecrow
Director: James Neilson
Starring: *Patrick McGoohan, George Cole, Tony Britton, Geoffrey Keen*

1964

Carry On Cleo
Director: Gerald Thomas
Starring: *Sidney James, Kenneth Williams, Jim Dale, Amanda Barrie*

Carry On Spying
Director: Gerald Thomas
Starring: *Kenneth Williams, Barbara Windsor, Charles Hawtrey, Bernard Cribbins*

Farewell Performance
Director: Robert Tronson
Starring: *David Kernan, Delphi Lawrence, Derek Francis, Alfred Burke*

From Russia With Love
Director: Terence Young
Starring: *Sean Connery, Pedro Armedariz, Lotte Lenya, Robert Shaw*

Hot Enough for June
Director: Ralph Thomas
Starring: *Dirk Bogarde, Sylva Koscina, Robert Morley, Leo McKern*

Live it Up
Director: Lance Comfort
Starring: *David Hemmings, Jennifer Moss, John Pike, Heinz Burt*

The Moon Spinners
Director: James Neilson
Starring: *Hayley Mills, Peter McEnery, Eli Wallach, Joan Greenwood*

Séance on a Wet Afternoon
Director: Bryan Forbes
Starring: *Kim Stanley, Richard Attenborough, Nanette Newman, Patrick Magee*

A Stitch in Time
Director: Robert Asher
Starring: *Norman Wisdom, Edward Chapman, Jerry Desmonde, Jeanette Sterke*

The Switch
Director: Peter Maxwell
Starring: *Anthony Steel, Zena Marshall, Conrad Phillips, Dermot Walsh*

This is My Street
Director: Sidney Hayers
Starring: *June Ritchie, Ian Hendry, Avice Landone, Meredith Edwards*

Woman of Straw
Director: Basil Dearden
Starring: *Gina Lollobrigida, Sean Connery, Ralph Richardson, Johnny Sekka*

City Under the Sea
Director: Jacques Tourneur
Starring: *Vincent Price, David Tomlinson, Susan Hart, Tab Hunter*

Devil of Darkness
Director: Lance Comfort
Starring: *William Sylvester, Hubert Noel, Carole Gray, Tracy Reed*

Goldfinger
Director: Guy Hamilton
Starring: *Sean Connery, Honor Blackman, Gert Frobe, Shirley Eaton*

Guns at Batasi
Director: John Guillermin
Starring: *Richard Attenborough, Jack Hawkins, Flora Robson, Mia Farrow*

The Heroes of Telemark
Director: Anthony Mann
Starring: *Kirk Douglas, Richard Harris, Ulla Jacobsson, Roy Dotrice*

The High Bright Sun
Director: Ralph Thomas
Starring: *Dirk Bogarde, Susan Strasberg, George Chakiris, Denholm Elliott*

A High Wind in Jamaica
Director: Alexander Mackendrick
Starring: *Anthony Quinn, James Coburn, Dennis Price, Nigel Davenport*

The Intelligence Men
Director: Robert Asher
Starring: *Eric Morecambe, Ernie Wise, William Franklyn, April Olrich*

The Ipcress File
Director: Sidney J. Furie
Starring: *Michael Caine, Nigel Green, Guy Doleman, Sue Lloyd*

The Legend of Young Dick Turpin
Director: James Neilson
Starring: *David Weston, Bernard Lee, George Cole, Maurice Denham*

Those Magnificent Men in Their Flying Machines, or How I Flew from London to Paris in 25 Hours and 11 Minutes
Director: Ken Annakin
Starring: *Sarah Miles, Stuart Whitman, Robert Morley, Terry-Thomas*

**The Magnificent Showman
(US title: Circus World)**
Director: Henry Hathaway
Starring: *John Wayne, Rita Hayworth, Claudia Cardinale, John Smith*

Masquerade
Director: Basil Dearden
Starring: *Cliff Robertson, Jack Hawkins, Charles Gray, Bill Fraser*

1965

Arabesque
Director: Stanley Donen
Starring: *Gregory Peck, Sophie Loren, Alan Badel, Kieron Moore*

The Big Job
Director: Gerald Thomas
Starring: *Sidney James, Sylvia Syms, Dick Emery, Joan Sims*

Carry On Cowboy
Director: Gerard Thomas
Starring: *Sidney James, Kenneth Williams, Jim Dale, Charles Hawtrey*

Doctor in Clover
Director: Ralph Thomas
Starring: *Leslie Phillips, James Robertson Justice, Shirley Anne Field, Joan Sims*

The Early Bird
Director: Robert Asher
Starring: *Norman Wisdom, Edward Chapman, Jerry Desmonde, Paddy O'Neil*

The Fighting Prince of Donegal
Director: Michael O'Herlihy
Starring: *Peter McEnery, Susan Hampshire, Tom Adams, Gordon Jackson*

Island of Terror
Director: Terence Fisher
Starring: *Peter Cushing, Edward Judd, Carole Gray, Eddie Byrne*

Khartoum
Director: Basil Dearden
Starring: *Charlton Heston, Laurence Olivier, Ralph Richardson, Richard Johnson*

Romeo and Juliet
Director: Paul Czinner
Starring: *Margot Fonteyn, Rudolph Nureyev, David Blair, Desmond Doyle*

Sky West and Crooked
Director: John Mills
Starring: *Hayley Mills, Ian McShane, Laurence Naismith, Geoffrey Bayldon*

Stop the World: I Want to Get Off
Director: Philip Saville
Starring: *Tony Tanner, Millicent Martin,*
Georgina Allen, Natasha Ashton

That Riviera Touch
Director: Cliff Owen
Starring: *Eric Morecambe, Ernie Wise,*
Alexandra Bastedo, Peter Jeffrey

Thunderball
Director: Terence Young
Starring: *Sean Connery, Claudine Auger,*
Adolfo Celi, Luciana Paluzzi

The Wrong Box
Director: Bryan Forbes
Starring: *Ralph Richardson, John Mills,*
Michael Caine, Nanette Newman

1966

Carry On Screaming
Director: Gerald Thomas
Starring: *Harry H Corbett, Kenneth Williams,*
Jim Dale, Fenella Fielding

Casino Royale (interiors filmed at Shepperton
and at Pinewood)
Directors: John Huston, Kenneth Hughes,
Val Guest, Robert Parrish,
Joseph McGrath
Starring: *Peter Sellers, Ursula Andress,*
David Niven, Orson Welles

A Countess From Hong Kong
Director: Charles Chaplin
Starring: *Marlon Brando, Sophia Loren,*
Margaret Rutherford, Charles Chaplin,

Deadlier Than the Male
Director: Ralph Thomas
Starring: *Richard Johnson, Nigel Green,*
Elke Sommer, Sylva Koscina,

Don't Lose Your Head
(re-issued as *Carry On Don't Lose Your Head*)
Director: Gerald Thomas
Starring: *Sidney James, Kenneth Williams,*
Jim Dale, Charles Hawtrey

Fahrenheit 451
Director: Francois Truffaut
Starring: *Oskar Werner, Julie Christie,*
Cyril Cusack, Anton Diffring

Finders Keepers
Director: Sidney Hayers
Starring: *Cliff Richard and The Shadows,*
Robert *Morley, Peggy Mount, Ellen Pollock*

Funeral in Berlin
Director: Guy Hamilton
Starring: *Michael Caine, Oscar Homolka,*
Eva Renzi, Paul Hubschmid

Kaleidoscope
Director: Jack Smith
Starring: *Warren Beatty, Susannah York,*
Clive Revill, Eric Porter

The Long Duel
Director: Ken Annakin
Starring: *Trevor Howard, Yul Brynner,*
Harry Andrews, Charlotte Rampling

The Magnificent Two
Director: Cliff Owen
Starring: *Eric Morecambe, Ernie Wise,*
Margit Saad, Cecil Parker

The Marat/Sade
Director: Peter Brook
Starring: *Glenda Jackson, Patrick Magee,*
Ian Richardson, Michael Williams

Maroc 7
Director: Gerry O'Hara
Starring: *Gene Barry, Elsa Martinelli,*
Leslie Phillips, Angela Douglas

The Quiller Memorandum
Director: Michael Anderson
Starring: *George Segal, Max Von Sydow,*
Alex Guinness, Senta Berger

To Sir With Love
Director: James Clavell
Starring: *Sidney Poitier, Christian Roberts,*
Judy Geeson, Suzy Kendall

The Whisperers
Director: Bryan Forbes
Starring: *Edith Evans, Eric Portman,*
Avis Bunnage, Nanette Newman

You Only Live Twice
Director: Lewis Gilbert
Starring: *Sean Connery, Akiko Wakabayashi,*
Mie Hama, Donald Pleasence

1967

Billion Dollar Brain
Director: Ken Russell
Starring: *Michael Caine, Oscar Homolka,*
Francois Dorléac, Karl Malden

Carry On Doctor
Director: Gerald Thomas
Starring: *Kenneth Williams, Sidney James,*
Hattie Jacques, Frankie Howerd

A Challenge for Robin Hood
Director: C. Pennington-Richards
Starring: *Barrie Ingham, James Hayter,*
Leon Greene, John Arnatt

Charlie Bubbles
Director: Albert Finney
Starring: *Albert Finney, Billie Whitelaw,*
Liza Minnelli, Colin Blakely

Chitty Chitty Bang Bang
Director: Ken Hughes
Starring: *Dick Van Dyke, Sally Ann Howes,*
Lionel Jeffries, Robert Helpmann

Deadfall
Director: Bryan Forbes
Starring: *Michael Caine, Eric Portman,*
Giovanna Ralli, Nanette Newman

Follow That Camel
(re-issued as *Carry On Follow That Camel*)
Director: Gerald Thomas
Starring: *Phil Silvers, Jim Dale,*
Peter Butterworth, Kenneth Williams

The Limbo Line
Director: Samuel Gallu
Starring: *Alan Barry, Joan Benham,*
Norman Bird, Jean Marsh

Night of the Big Heat
Director: Terence Fisher
Starring: *Christopher Lee, Peter Cushing,*
Patrick Allen, Sarah Lawson

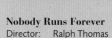

Nobody Runs Forever
Director: Ralph Thomas
Starring: *Rod Taylor, Christopher Plummer,*
Lilli Palmer, Daliah Lavi

Pretty Polly
Director: Guy Green
Starring: *Hayley Mills, Trevor Howard,*
Shashi Kapoor, Brenda de Banzie

Prudence and the Pill
Directors: Fielder Cook, Ronald Neame
Starring: *David Niven, Deborah Kerr,*
Edith Evans, Keith Michell

Work is a Four-Letter Word
Director: Peter Hall
Starring: *David Warner, Cilla Black,*
Elizabeth Spriggs, Joe Gladwin

1968

The Assassination Bureau
Director: Basil Dearden
Starring: *Oliver Reed, Diana Rigg,*
Telly Savalas, Curt Jurgens

Battle of Britain
Director: Guy Hamilton
Starring: *Laurence Olivier, Michael Caine,*
Kenneth More, Trevor Howard

Carry On Camping
Director: Gerald Thomas
Starring: *Sidney James, Kenneth Williams*
Charles Hawtrey, Barbara Windsor

Carry On ... Up the Khyber!
Director: Gerald Thomas
Starring: *Sidney James, Kenneth Williams,*
Charles Hawtrey, Joan Sims

Doppleganger
Director: Robert Parrish
Starring: *Ian Hendry, Roy Thinnes,*
Patrick Wymark, Herbert Lom

Dracula Has Risen From the Grave
Director: Freddie Francis
Starring: *Christopher Lee, Rupert Davies,
            Veronica Carlson, Barbara Ewing*

The Most Dangerous Man in the World
Director: J. Lee Thompson
Starring: *Gregory Peck, Anne Heywood,
            Arthur Hill, Conrad Yama*

The Prime of Miss Jean Brodie
Director: Ronald Neame
Starring: *Maggie Smith, Robert Stephens,
            Pamela Franklin, Celia Johnson*

Some Girls Do
Director: Ralph Thomas
Starring: *Richard Johnson, Daliah Lavi,
            Bebi Loncar, James Villiers*

1969

Carry On Again Doctor
Director: Gerald Thomas
Starring: *Sidney James, Jim Dale,
            Kenneth Williams, Hattie Jacques*

Carry On Up The Jungle
Director: Gerald Thomas
Starring: *Frankie Howerd, Sidney James,
            Charles Hawtrey, Joan Sims*

Connecting Rooms
Director: Franklin Gollings
Starring: *Bette Davis, Michael Redgrave,
            Alexis Kanner, Kay Walsh*

David Copperfield (made-for-television film
released theatrically in Europe)
Director: Delbert Mann
Starring: *Richard Attenborough, Cyril Cusack,
            Edith Evans, Ron Moody*

Destiny of a Spy (made-for-television film)
Director: Boris Sagal
Starring: *Lorne Green, Rachel Roberts,
            Anthony Quayle, Harry Andrews*

The Devil's Widow (aka *Tam-Lin*)
Director: Roddy McDowall
Starring: *Ava Gardner, Ian MacShane,
            Richard Wattis, Cyril Cusak*

The Firechasers
Director: Sidney Hayers
Starring: *Keith Barron, Anjanette Corner,
            Allan Cuthbertson, Rupert Davies*

Mister Jericho (made-for-television film)
Director: Sidney Hayers
Starring: *Patrick Macnee, Connie Stevens,
            Herbert Lom, Marty Allen*

On Her Majesty's Secret Service
Director: Peter Hunt
Starring: *George Lazenby, Diana Rigg,
            Telly Savalas, Gabriele Ferzetti*

Perfect Friday
Director: Peter Hall
Starring: *Stanley Baker, Ursula Andress,
            David Warner, T. P. McKenna*

The Private Life of Sherlock Holmes
Director: Billy Wilder
Starring: *Robert Stephens, Colin Blakely,
            Genevieve Page, Christopher Lee*

Run a Crooked Mile (made-for-television film)
Director: Gene Levitt
Starring: *Louis Jourdan, Mary Tyler Moore,
            Wilfrid Hyde-White, Stanley Holloway*

Toomorrow
Director: Val Guest
Starring: *Olivia Newton-John, Benny Thomas,
            Vic Cooper, Roy Dotrice*

When Eight Bells Toll
Director: Etienne Perier
Starring: *Anthony Hopkins, Robert Morley,
            Corin Redgrave, Jack Hawkins*

1970

Assault
Director: Sidney Hayers
Starring: *Frank Finlay, Suzy Kendall,
            James Laurenson, Freddie Jones*

The Beast in the Cellar
Director: James Kelly
Starring: *Flora Robson, Beryl Reid,
            Tessa Wyatt, T. P. McKenna*

The Blood on Satan's Claw
Director: Piers Haggard
Starring: *Patrick Wymark, Linda Hayden,
            Barry Andrews, Simon Williams*

Carry On Henry
Director: Gerald Thomas
Starring: *Sidney James, Kenneth Williams,
            Charles Hawtrey, Joan Sims*

Carry On Loving
Director: Gerald Thomas
Starring: *Sidney James, Kenneth Williams,
            Charles Hawtrey, Hattie Jacques*

Countess Dracula
Director: Peter Sasdy
Starring: *Ingrid Pitt, Nigel Green,
            Sandor Eles, Maurice Denham*

The Devils
Director: Ken Russell
Starring: *Vanessa Redgrave, Oliver Reed,
            Dudley Sutton, Max Adrian*

Doctor in Trouble
Director: Ralph Thomas
Starring: *Leslie Phillips, Harry Secombe,
            Angela Scoular, Robert Morley*

Fiddler on the Roof
Director: Norman Jewison
Starring: *Topol, Norma Crane,
            Leonard Frey, Molly Picon*

Jane Eyre
Director: Delbert Mann
Starring: *Susannah York, George C. Scott,
            Ian Bannen, Jack Hawkins*

Quest For Love
Director: Ralph Thomas
Starring: *Tom Bell, Joan Collins, Denholm Elliot,
            Laurence Naismith*

Revenge
Director: Sidney Hayers
Starring: *Joan Collins, Sinead Cusack,
            James Booth, Kenneth Griffith*

Zeppelin
Director: Etienne Perier
Starring: *Michael York, Elke Sommer,
            Marius Goring, Anton Diffring*

1971

200 Motels
Directors: Tony Palmer, Frank Zappa,
Charles Swenson
Starring: *Theodore Bikel, Mark Volman,
Howard Kaylan, Ian Underwood*

All Coppers Are ...
Director: Sidney Hayers
Starring: *Nicky Henson, Martin Potter,
Julia Foster, David Essex*

Anne and Muriel
Director: Francois Truffaut
Starring: *Jean-Pierre Léaud, Kika Markham,
Stacey Tendeter, Sylvia Marriott*

Baffled (made-for-television pilot film)
Director: Philip Leacock
Starring: *Leonard Nimoy, Susan Hampshire,
Rachel Roberts, Vera Miles*

Carry On At Your Convenience
Director: Gerald Thomas
Starring: *Sidney James, Kenneth Williams,
Charles Hawtrey, Hattie Jacques*

Carry On Matron
Director: Gerald Thomas
Starring: *Sidney James, Kenneth Williams,
Charles Hawtrey, Joan Sims*

Diamonds Are Forever
Director: Guy Hamilton
Starring: *Sean Connery, Jill St John,
Charles Gray, Lana Wood*

Doomwatch
Director: Peter Sasdy
Starring: *Ian Bannen, Judy Geeson,
John Paul, Simon Oates*

Frenzy
Director: Alfred Hitchcock
Starring: *Jon Finch, Alec McCowen,
Barry Foster, Vivien Merchant*

Hamlet (made-for-television version)
Director: David Giles
Starring: *Ian McKellen, Faith Brook,
Susan Fleetwood, John Woodvine*

Hands of the Ripper
Director: Peter Sasdy
Starring: *Eric Porter, Angharad Rees,
Jane Merrow, Keith Bell*

Kidnapped
Director: Delbert Mann
Starring: *Michael Caine, Trevor Howard,
Jack Hawkins, Gordon Jackson*

Lady Caroline Lamb
Director: Robert Bolt
Starring: *Sarah Miles, Jon Finch, Richard
Chamberlain, Margaret Leighton*

Madame Sin
Director: David Greene
Starring: *Bette Davis, Robert Wagner,
Denholm Elliot, Gordon Jackson*

The Magnificent Seven Deadly Sins
Director: Graham Stark
Starring: *Bruce Forsyth, Joan Sims,
Harry Secombe, Leslie Phillips*

Nobody Ordered Love
Director: Robert Hartford-Davis
Starring: *Ingrid Pitt, Judy Huxtable,
John Ronane, Tony Selby*

Please Sir!
Director: Mark Stuart
Starring: *John Alderton, Deryck Guyler,
Joan Sanderson, Carol Hawkins*

Twins of Evil
Director: John Hough
Starring: *Peter Cushing, Dennis Price,
Mary Collinson, Madelaine Collinson*

Vampire Circus
Director: Robert Young
Starring: *Adrienne Corri, Laurence Payne,
Thorley Walters, John Moulder Brown*

1972

The Amazing Mr Blunden
Director: Lionel Jeffries
Starring: *Laurence Naismith, Diana Dors,
James Villiers, Lynne Frederick*

Anoop and the Elephant
Director: David Eady
Starring: *Anoop Singh, Linda Robson,
Phil Daniels, Jimmy Edwards*

The Belstone Fox
Director: James Hill
Starring: *Eric Porter, Rachel Roberts,
Jeremy Kemp, Dennis Waterman*

Bless This House
Director: Gerald Thomas
Starring: *Sidney James, Diana Coupland,
Terry Scott, June Whitfield*

Carry On Abroad
Director: Gerald Thomas
Starring: *Sidney James, Kenneth Williams,
Charles Hawtrey, Joan Sims*

The Day of the Jackal
Director: Fred Zinnemann
Starring: *Edward Fox, Michel Lonsdale,
Alan Badel, Eric Porter*

Diamonds on Wheels (made-for-television film)
Director: Jerome Courtland
Starring: *Patrick Allen, George Sewell,
Dudley Sutton, Richard Wattis*

The Fourteen
Director: David Hemmings
Starring: *Jack Wild, June Brown,
John Bailey, Alun Armstrong*

Go for a Take
Director: Harry Booth
Starring: *Reg Varney, Norman Rossington,
Sue Lloyd, Dennis Price*

Innocent Bystanders
Director: Peter Collinson
Starring: *Stanley Baker, Geraldine Chaplin,
Dana Andrews, Donald Pleasance*

Live and Let Die
Director: Guy Hamilton
Starring: *Roger Moore, Yaphet Kotto,
Jane Seymour, Clifton James*

The Mackintosh Man
Director: John Huston
Starring: *Paul Newman, James Mason,
Nigel Patrick, Harry Andrews*

Miss Julie
Directors: John Glenister, Robin Phillips
Starring: *Helen Mirren, Donal McCann,
Heather Canning, Mary Allen*

Nearest and Dearest
Director: John Robins
Starring: *Hylda Baker, Jimmy Jewel,
Eddie Malin, Madge Hindle*

Nothing But the Night
Director: Peter Sasdy
Starring: *Christopher Lee, Peter Cushing,
Diana Dors, Keith Barron*

Phase IV
Director: Saul Bass
Starring: *Nigel Davenport, Lynne Frederick,
Michael Murphy, Alan Gifford*

Sleuth
Director: Joseph L. Mankiewicz
Starring: *Laurence Olivier, Michael Caine*

That's Your Funeral
Director: John Robins
Starring: *Bill Fraser, Raymond Huntley,
David Battley, Dennis Price*

A Warm December
Director: Sidney Poitier
Starring: *Sidney Poitier, Esther Anderson,
George Baker, Earl Cameron*

1973

The Abdication
Director: Anthony Harvey
Starring: *Liv Ullmann, Peter Finch,
Cyril Cusack, Graham Crowden*

Applause (filmed Broadway musical adaptation of
All About Eve)
Producer: Richard M. Rosenbloom
Starring: *Lauren Bacall, Larry Hagman,
Penny Fuller, Sarah Marshall*

Carry On Girls
Director: Gerald Thomas
Starring: *Sidney James, Barbara Windsor,
Joan Sims, Bernard Bresslaw*

The Glass Menagerie (made-for-television)
Director: Anthony Harvey
Starring: *Katharine Hepburn, Joanna Miles, Sam Waterston, Michael Moriarty*

The Great Gatsby
Director: Jack Clayton
Starring: *Robert Redford, Mia Farrow, Karen Black, Sam Waterston*

11 Harrowhouse
Director: Aram Avakian
Starring: *Charles Grodin, James Mason, Trevor Howard, John Gielgud*

Mousey
Director: Daniel Petrie
Starring: *Kirk Douglas, Jean Seberg, John Vernon, Sam Wanamaker*

No Sex Please, We're British
Director: Cliff Owen
Starring: *Ronnie Corbett, Arthur Lowe, Beryl Reid, Ian Ogilvy*

Penny Gold
Director: Jack Cardiff
Starring: *James Booth, Francesca Annis, Nicky Henson, Sue Lloyd*

QBVII (made-for-television mini-series)
Director: Tom Gries
Starring: *Ben Gazzara, Anthony Hopkins, Lee Remick, Anthony Quayle*

Terror! Il Castello Delle Donne Maledette
Director: Robert Oliver
Starring: *Rossano Brazzo, Michael Dunn, Edmund Purdom, Gordon Mitchell*

1974

Brief Encounter (made-for-television film)
Director: Alan Bridges
Starring: *Richard Burton, Sophia Loren, Jack Hedley, John Le Mesurier*

Carry On Dick
Directors: Gerald Thomas
Starring: *Sidney James, Kenneth Williams, Barbara Windsor, Hattie Jacques*

The Ghoul
Directors: Freddie Francis
Starring: *Peter Cushing, Aledandra Bastedo, John Hurt, Gwen Watford*

Gold
Director: Peter Hunt
Starring: *Roger Moore, Susannah York, Ray Milland, Bradford Dillman*

Hennessy
Director: Don Sharp
Starring: *Rod Steiger, Richard Johnson, Lee Remick, Trevor Howard*

I Don't Want To Be Born
Director: Peter Sasdy
Starring: *Joan Collins, Ralph Bates, Donald Pleasance*

Legend of the Werewolf
Director: Freddie Francis
Starring: *Peter Cushing, Ron Moody, David Rintoul, Roy Castle*

Love Among the Ruins (made-for-television)
Director: George Cukor
Starring: *Katharine Hepburn, Laurence Olivier, Richard Pearson, Colin Blakely*

The Man With the Golden Gun
Director: Guy Hamilton
Starring: *Roger Moore, Christopher Lee, Britt Ekland, Maud Adams*

Mister Quilp
Director: Michael Tuchner
Starring: *Anthony Newley, Michael Hordern, David Hemmings, David Warner*

One of Our Dinosaurs is Missing
Director: Robert Stevenson
Starring: *Helen Hayes, Peter Ustinov, Derek Nimmo, Joan Sims*

Robbery Under Arms
Director: Jack Lee
Starring: *Peter Finch, David McCallum, Ronald Lewis, Maureen Swanson*

Rollerball
Director: Norman Jewison
Starring: *James Caan, John Houseman, Ralph Richardson, Maud Adams*

That Lucky Touch
Director: Christopher Miles
Starring: *Roger Moore, Susannah York, Lee J. Cobb, Shelley Winters*

What Changed Charlie Farthing?
Directors: Sidney Hayers
Starring: *Doug McClure, Lionel Jeffries, Warren Mitchell, Hayley Mills*

The Wilby Conspiracy
Director: Ralph Nelson
Starring: *Sidney Poitier, Michael Caine, Nicol Williamson, Prunella Gee*

1975

The Bawdy Adventures of Tom Jones
Director: Cliff Owen
Starring: *Nicky Henson, Trevor Howard, Terry-Thomas, Joan Collins*

Bugsy Malone
Director: Alan Parker
Starring: *Scott Baio, Jodie Foster, Florrie Dugger, John Cassisi*

Carry On Behind
Director: Gerald Thomas
Starring: *Kenneth Williams, Elke Sommer, Bernard Bresslaw, Kenneth Connor*

Escape from the Dark
Director: Charles Jarrott
Starring: *Alastair Sim, Peter Barkworth, Maurice Colbourne, Susan Tebbs*

The Human Factor
Director: Edward Dmytryk
Starring: *George Kennedy, John Mills, Raf Vallone, Rita Tushingham*

The Incredible Sarah
Director: Richard Fleischer
Starring: *Glenda Jackson, Daniel Massey, Yvonne Mitchell, Douglas Wilmer*

The Seven Per Cent Solution
Director: Herbert Ross
Starring: *Nicol Williamson, Robert Duvall, Vanessa Redgrave, Laurence Olivier*

The Slipper and the Rose
Director: Bryan Forbes
Starring: *Richard Chamberlain, Kenneth More, Michael Hordern, Edith Evans*

1976

At the Earth's Core
Director: Kevin Connor
Starring: *Doug McClure, Peter Cushing, Caroline Munro, Cy Grant*

Candleshoe
Director: Norman Tokar
Starring: *David Niven, Helen Hayes, Jodie Foster, Leo McKern*

Carry On England
Director: Gerald Thomas
Starring: *Kenneth Connor, Windsor Davies, Patrick Mower, Jack Douglas*

Gulliver's Travels
Director: Peter R. Hunt
Starring: *Richard Harris, Catherine Schell, Norman Shelley, Meredith Edwards*

The Prince and the Pauper
Director: Richard Fleischer
Starring: *Mark Lester, Oliver Reed, George C. Scott, Rex Harrison*

The Spy Who Loved Me
Director: Lewis Gilbert
Starring: *Roger Moore, Barbara Bach, Curt Jurgens, Richard Kiel*

1977

Death on the Nile
Director: John Guillermin
Starring: *Peter Ustinov, Bette Davis, Angela Lansbury, David Niven*

International Velvet
Director: Bryan Forbes
Starring: *Nanette Newman, Anthony Hopkins, Tatum O'Neal, Christopher Plummer*

The Medusa Touch
Director: Jack Gold
Starring: *Richard Burton, Lee Remick, Harry Andrews, Alan Badel*

Meetings With Remarkable Men
Director: Peter Brook
Starring: *Gregoire Aslan, Martin Benson, Colin Blakely, Tom Fleming*

The People That Time Forgot
Director: Kevin Connor
Starring: *Patrick Wayne, Sarah Douglas, Dana Gillespie, Doug McClure*

Superman
Director: Richard Donner
Starring: *Christopher Reeve, Marlon Brandon, Margot Kidder, Jackie Cooper*

Warlords of Atlantis
Director: Kevin Connor
Starring: *Doug McClure, Peter Gilmore, Shane Rimmer, Lea Brodie*

Wombling Free
Director: Lionel Jeffries
Starring: *David Tomlinson, Frances de la Tour, Bonnie Langford, Bernard Spear*

1978

Absolution
Director: Anthony Page
Starring: *Richard Burton, Dominic Guard, David Bradley, Billy Connolly*

Arabian Adventure
Director: Kevin Connor
Starring: *Christopher Lee, Oliver Tobias, Mickey Rooney, Milo O'Shea*

Carry On Emmannuelle
Director: Gerald Thomas
Starring: *Kenneth Williams, Suzanne Danielle, Kenneth Connor, Joan Sims*

The First Great Train Robbery
Director: Michael Crichton
Starring: *Sean Connery, Donald Sutherland, Lesley-Anne Down, Alan Webb*

Ike: The War Years (made-for-television)
Directors: Boris Sagal, Melville Shavelson
Starring: *Robert Duvall, Lee Remick*

The Lady Vanishes
Director: Anthony Page
Starring: *Cybil Shepherd, Elliot Gould, Angela Lansbury, Herbert Lom*

Moonraker
Director: Lewis Gilbert
Starring: *Roger Moore, Lois Chiles, Michael Lonsdale, Richard Kiel*

The Spaceman and King Arthur
Director: Russ Mayberry
Starring: *Dennis Dugan, Jim Dale, Ron Moody, Kenneth More*

The Thirty Nine Steps
Director: Don Sharp
Starring: *Robert Powell, Karen Dotrice, John Mills, Eric Porter*

1979

Bear Island
Director: Don Sharp
Starring: *Vanessa Redgrave, Richard Widmark, Donald Sutherland, Christopher Lee*

Clash of the Titans
Director: Desmond Davis
Starring: *Laurence Olivier, Claire Bloom, Maggie Smith, Ursula Andress*

McVicar
Director: Tom Clegg
Starring: *Roger Daltrey, Adam Faith, Cheryl Campbell, Billy Murray*

North Sea Hijack
Director: Andrew V. McLaglen
Starring: *Roger Moore, Anthony Perkins, James Mason, Michael Parks*

Rough Cut
Director: Don Siegel
Starring: *Burt Reynolds, Lesley-Anne Down, David Niven, Timothy West*

Silver Dream Racer
Director: David Wickes
Starring: *David Essex, Beau Bridges, Cristina Raines, Harry H. Corbett*

Superman II
Director: Richard Lester
Starring: *Christopher Reeve, Gene Hackman, Ned Beatty, Jackie Cooper*

There Goes the Bride
Director: Terence Marcel
Starring: *Tom Smothers, Twiggy, Sylvia Syms, Martin Balsam*

The Watcher in the Woods
Directors: John Hough, Vincent McEveety (uncredited)
Starring: *Bette Davis, Carroll Baker, David McCallum, Lynn-Holly Johnson*

Why Not Stay For Breakfast?
Director: Terence Marcel
Starring: *George Chakiris, Gemma Craven, Yvonne Wilder, Ray Charleson*

The World is Full of Married Men
Director: Robert Young
Starring: *Carroll Baker, Anthony Franciosa, Sherrie Lee Cronn, Paul Nicholas*

1980

Dragonslayer
Director: Matthew Robbins
Starring: *Peter MacNichol, Caitlin Clarke, Ralph Richardson, John Hallam*

For Your Eyes Only
Director: John Glen
Starring: *Roger Moore, Carole Bouquet, Topol, Julian Glover*

Hawk the Slayer
Director: Terry Marcel
Starring: *Jack Palance, John Terry, Bernard Bresslaw, Ray Charleston*

Heaven's Gate
Director: Michael Cimino
Starring: *Kris Kristofferson, Christopher Walken, John Hurt, Sam Waterston*

Outland
Director: Peter Hyams
Starring: *Sean Connery, Peter Boyle, Francis Sternhagen, James B. Sikking*

1981

The Hunchback of Notre Dame (made-for-television)
Directors: Michael Tuchner, Alan Hume (uncredited)
Starring: *Anthony Hopkins, Lesley-Anne Down, Derek Jacobi, John Gielgud*

Ivanhoe (made-for-television)
Director: Douglas Camfield
Starring: *James Mason, Anthony Andrews, Michael Hordern, Sam Neill*

Pink Floyd The Wall
Director: Alan Parker
Starring: *Bob Geldof, Christine Hargreaves, James Laurenson, Eleanor David*

Victor/Victoria
Director: Blake Edwards
Starring: Julie Andrews, James Garner,
            Robert Preston, Lesley Anne Warren

1982

Curse of the Pink Panther
Director: Blake Edwards
Starring: Ted Wass, Joanna Lumley,
            Herbert Lom, David Niven

Krull
Director: Peter Yates
Starring: Ken Marshall, Lysette Anthony,
            Freddie Jones, Francesca Annis

Octopussy
Director: John Glen
Starring: Roger Moore, Maud Adams,
            Louis Jourdan, Steven Berkoff

Superman III
Director: Richard Lester
Starring: Christopher Reeve, Richard Pryor,
            Jackie Cooper, Marc McClure

Trail of the Pink Panther
Director: Blake Edwards
Starring: Peter Sellers (archive footage), David
            Niven, Joanna Lumley, Herbert Lom,

Who Dares Wins
Director: Ian Sharp
Starring: Lewis Collins, Richard Widmark,
            Judy Davis, Edward Woodward

1983

The Dresser
Director: Peter Yates
Starring: Albert Finney, Tom Courtenay,
            Edward Fox, Eileen Atkins

The First Olympics: Athens 1896 (made-for-television mini-series)
Director: Alvin Rakoff
Starring: David Ogden Stiers, Louis Jourdan,
            David Caruso, Honor Blackman

The Last Days of Pompeii (made-for-television mini-series)
Director: Peter R. Hunt
Starring: Ned Beatty, Lesley Anne Down,
            Brian Blessed, Ernest Borgnine

Master of the Game (made-for-television mini-series)
Director: Kevin Connor, Harvey Hart
Starring: Dyan Cannon, Donald Pleasence,
            Leslie Caron, Maryam d'Abo

The People That Time Forgot
Director: Kevin Connor
Starring: Patrick Wayne, Sarah Douglas,
            Dana Gillespie, Doug McClure

Slayground
Director: Terry Bedford
Starring: Peter Coyote, Mel Smith,
            Billie Whitelaw, Philip Sayer

Squaring the Circle (made-for-television)
Director: Mike Hodges
Starring: Bernard Hill, Alec McCowen,
            Frank Middlemass, Roy Kinnear

Supergirl
Director: Jeannot Szwarc
Starring: Helen Slater, Faye Dunaway,
            Peter O'Toole, Mia Farrow

Top Secret!
Directors: Jim Abrahams, David Zucker,
            Jerry Zucker
Starring: Val Kilmer, Lucy Gutteridge,
            Peter Cushing, Jeremy Kemp

1984

Dream Lover
Director: Alan J. Pakula
Starring: Kristy McNichol, Ben Masters,
            Paul Shenar, Gayle Hunnicutt

King David
Director: Bruce Beresford
Starring: Richard Gere, Edward Woodward,
            Denis Quilley, Cherie Lunghi

Legend
Director: Ridley Scott
Starring: Tim Curry, Mia Sara,
            Tom Cruise, David Bennent

Morons from Outer Space
Director: Michael Hodges
Starring: Mel Smith, Griff Rhys Jones,
            Paul Brown, Jimmy Nail

Santa Claus
Director: Jeannot Szwarc
Starring: David Huddleston, Dudley Moore,
            John Lithgow, Judy Cornwell

Steaming
Director: Joseph Losey
Starring: Vanessa Redgrave, Sarah Miles,
            Diana Dors, Brenda Bruce

A View To a Kill
Director: John Glen
Starring: Roger Moore, Christopher Walken,
            Tanya Roberts, Grace Jones

1985

Aliens
Director: James Cameron
Starring: Sigourney Weaver, Carrie Henn,
            Michael Biehn, Lance Henriksen

D.A.R.Y.L.
Director: Simon Wincer
Starring: Mary Beth Hurt, Michael McKean,
            Kathryn Walker, Colleen Camp

Deceptions
Directors: Robert Chenault, Melville Shavelson
Starring: Stefanie Powers, Barry Bostwick,
            Jeremy Brett, Gina Lollobrigida

Gunbus
Director: Zoran Perisic
Starring: Scott McGinnis, Jeffrey Osterhage,
            Ronald Lacey, Miles Anderson

Little Shop of Horrors
Director: Frank Oz
Starring: Rick Moranis, Ellen Greene,
            Vincent Gardenia, Steve Martin

Murder Elite
Director: Claude Whatham
Starring: Ali MacGraw, Billie Whitelaw,
            Hywel Bennett, Garfield Morgan

The Second Victory
Director: Gerald Thomas
Starring: Anthony Andrews, Helmut Griem,
            Mario Adorf, Max Von Sydow

Spies Like Us
Director: John Landis
Starring: Chevy Chase, Dan Aykroyd,
            Steve Forest, Donna Dixon

1986

Full Metal Jacket
Director: Stanley Kubrick
Starring: Matthew Modine, Adam Baldwin,
            Vincent D'Onofrio, Lee Ermey

The Living Daylights
Director: John Glen
Starring: Timothy Dalton, Maryam D'Abo,
            Jeroen Krabbé, Joe Don Baker

Max Mon Amour
Director: Nagisa Oshima
Starring: Charlotte Rampling, Anthony Higgins,
            Victoria Abril, Anne-Marie Besse

Superman IV: The Quest for Peace
Director: Sidney J. Furie
Starring: Christopher Reeve, Gene Hackman,
            Jackie Cooper, Marc McClure

1987

Consuming Passions
Director: Giles Foster
Starring: Vanessa Redgrave, Freddie Jones,
            Jonathan Pryce, Tyler Butterworth

The Dressmaker
Director: Jim O'Brien
Starring: Joan Plowright, Billie Whitelaw,
            Jane Horrocks, Peter Postlethwaite

Hazard of Hearts (made-for-television)
Director: John Hough
Starring: Diana Rigg, Oliver Reed, Edward Fox,
            Fiona Fullerton

Hawks
Director: Robert Ellis Miler
Starring: Timothy Dalton, Anthony Edwards,
            Janet McTeer, Camille Coduri

Pack of Lies
Director: Anthony Page
Starring: Alan Bates, Ellen Burstyn,
            Daniel Benzali, Terri Garr

Paperhouse
Director: Bernard Rose
Starring: Charlotte Burke, Ben Cross,
            Glenne Headly, Gemma Jones

1988

Adventures of Baron Munchausen
Director: Terry Gilliam
Starring: John Neville, Eric Idle,
Sarah Polley, Oliver Reed

Batman
Director: Tim Burton
Starring: Michael Keaton, Jack Nicholson,
Kim Basinger, Michael Gough

Dealers
Director: Colin Bucksey
Starring: Paul McGann, Rebecca De Mornay,
Derrick O'Connor, John Castle

A Dry White Season
Director: Euzhan Palcy
Starring: Donald Sutherland, Janet Suzman,
Zakes Mokae, Jurgen Prochnow

Great Expectations (made-for-television mini-
series)
Director: Kevin Connor
Starring: Anthony Hopkins, Jean Simmons,
Anthony Calf, Ray McAnally

Hellbound: Hellraiser II
Director: Tony Randel
Starring: Clare Higgins, Ashley Laurence,
Kenneth Cranham, Imogen Boorman

The Lady and the Highwayman (made-for-
television)
Director: John Hough
Starring: Hugh Grant, Lysette Anthony,
Emma Samms, Claire Bloom

Loser Takes All
Director: James Scott
Starring: Robert Lindsay, John Gielgud,
Marius Goring, Molly Ringwald

A Man for All Seasons (made-for-television)
Director: Charlton Heston
Starring: Charlton Heston, John Gielgud,
Richard Johnson, Vanessa Redgrave

Slipstream
Director: Steven M. Listberger
Starring: Mark Hamill, Bob Peck,
Bill Paxton, Kitty Aldridge

War and Remembrance (made-for-television
mini-series)
Director: Dan Curtis
Starring: Robert Mitchum, Jane Seymour,
Sharon Stone, Victoria Tennant

Without a Clue
Director: Thom Eberhardt
Starring: Michael Caine, Ben Kingsley,
Jeffrey Jones, Lysette Anthony

1989

Act of Will (made-for-television)
Director: Don Sharp
Starring: Jean Marsh, Peter Coyote,
Elizabeth Hurley, Jean Marsh

Chicago Joe and the Showgirl
Director: Bernard Rose
Starring: Kiefer Sutherland, Emily Lloyd,
Patsy Kensit, Keith Allen

The Gravy Train (made-for-television mini-
series)
Director: David Tucker
Starring: Ian Richardson, Alexei Sayle,
Judy Parfitt, Geoffrey Hutchings

Memphis Belle
Director: Michael Caton-Jones
Starring: Matthew Modine, Eric Stoltz,
Tate Donovan, D. B. Sweeney

Nightbreed
Director: Clive Barker
Starring: Craig Sheffer, Anne Bobby,
David Cronenberg, Charles Haid

The Russia House
Director: Fred Schepisi
Starring; Sean Connery, Michelle Pfeiffer,
Roy Scheider, James Fox

Treasure Island (made-for-television)
Directors: Fraser Clarke Heston
Starring: Charlton Heston, Christian Bale,
Oliver Reed, Christopher Lee

White Hunter, Black Heart
Director: Clint Eastwood
Starring: Clint Eastwood, Jeff Fahey,
Marisa Berenson, Richard Vanstone

1990

Air America
Director: Roger Spottiswoode
Starring: Mel Gibson, Robert Downey Jr,
Nancy Travis, Ken Jenkins

Buddy's Song
Director: Claude Whatham
Starring: Roger Daltrey, Chesney Hawkes,
Sharon Duce, Michael Elphick

Crucifer of Blood (made-for-television)
Director: Fraser Clarke Heston
Starring: Charlton Heston, Richard Johnson,
Susannah Harker, Edward Fox

King Ralph
Director: David S. Ward
Starring: John Goodman, Peter O'Toole,
John Hurt, Richard Griffiths

Let Him Have It
Director: Peter Medak
Starring: Christopher Ecclestone,
Paul Reynolds, Tom Bell, Eileen Atkins

Shining Through
Director: David Seltzer
Starring: Michael Douglas, Melanie Griffith,
Liam Neeson, Joely Richardson

1991

Alien 3
Director: David Fincher
Starring: Sigourney Weaver, Charles S. Dutton,
Charles Dance, Paul McGann

Bye Bye Baby (made-for-television)
Directors: Jack Rosenthal, Edward Bennett
Starring: Ben Chaplin, Jason Flemyng,
Simon Foy, James Purefoy

City of Joy
Director: Roland Joffé
Starring: Patrick Swayze, Om Puri,
Pauline Collins, Shabana Azmi

Just Like A Woman
Director: Nick Evans
Starring: Julie Walters, Adrian Pasdar,
Paul Freeman, Susan Woolridge

Kafka
Director: Steven Soderbergh
Starring: Jeremy Irons, Theresa Russell,
Joel Grey, Ian Holm

Patriot Games
Director: Phillip Noyce
Starring: Harrison Ford, Anne Archer,
Patrick Bergin, Sean Bean

1988-1991

Shadowchaser
Director: John Eyres
Starring: Martin Kove, Meg Foster,
Frank Zagarino, Joss Ackland

Year of the Comet
Director: Peter Yates
Starring: Penelope Ann Miller, Lois Jourdan,
Art Malik, Ian Richardson

1992

Being Human
Director: Bill Forsyth
Starring: Robin Williams, Maudie Johnson,
Max Johnson, Robert Carlyle

Carry On Columbus
Director: Gerald Thomas
Starring: Jim Dale, Bernard Cribbins,
Leslie Phillips, Jack Douglas

Diana: Her True Story (made-for-television)
Director: Kevin Connor
Starring: Serena Scott Thomas, David Threlfall,
Elizabeth Garvie, Donald Douglas

Great Moments in Aviation (made-for-television)
Director: Beeban Kidron
Starring: Vanessa Redgrave, John Hurt,
Jonathan Pryce, Dorothy Tutin

The Phoenix and the Magic Carpet
Director: Zoran Perisic
Starring: Peter Ustinov, Timothy Hegemann,
Laura Kamrath, Nick Klein

The Secret Garden
Director: Agnieszka Holland,
Starring: Kate Maberly, Maggie Smith,
Haydon Prowse, John Lynch

Sister, My Sister
Director: Nancy Meckler
Starring: Julie Walters, Joely Richardson,
Jodhi May, Sophie Thursfield

Son of the Pink Panther
Director: Blake Edwards
Starring: Roberto Benigni, Herbert Lom,
Claudia Cardinale, Shabana Azmi

U.F.O.
Director: Tony Dow
Starring: Roy "Chubby" Brown, Amanda
Symonds, Sara Stockbridge,
Roger Lloyd-Pack

1993

No films produced at Pinewood

1994

The Englishman Who Went Up a Hill But Came Down a Mountain
Director: Christopher Monger
Starring: Hugh Grant, Ian McNeice,
Colm Meaney, Tara Fitzgerald

First Knight
Director: Jerry Zucker
Starring: Richard Gere, Sean Connery,
Julia Ormond, Ben Cross

Hackers
Director: Iain Softley
Starring: Jonny Lee Miller, Angelina Jolie,
Jesse Bradford, Matthew Lillard

Interview with the Vampire: The Vampire Chronicles
Director: Neil Jordan
Starring: Tom Cruise, Brad Pitt,
Antonio Banderas, Stephen Rea

Jack & Sarah
Director: Tim Sullivan
Starring: Richard E. Grant, Samantha Mathis,
Judi Dench, Eileen Atkins

Loch Ness
Director: John Henderson
Starring: Ted Danson, Joely Richardson,
Iam Holm, Harris Yulin

Mary Reilly
Director: Stephen Frears
Starring: Julia Roberts, John Malkovich,
Glenn Close, Michael Gambon

Scarlett (made-for-television mini-series)
Director: John Erman
Starring: Joanne Walley-Kilmer, Timothy
Dalton, Barbara Barrie, Annabel Gish

1995

Canterville Ghost (made-for-television)
Director: Sydney Macartney
Starring: Patrick Stewart, Neve Campbell,
Joan Sims, Donald Sinden

Cold Lazarus (made-for-television mni-series)
Director: Renny Rye
Starring: Albert Finney, Ciarán Hinds,
Roy Hudd, Ganiat Kasumu

Cutthroat Island
Director: Renny Harlin
Starring: Geena Davis, Matthew Modine,
Patrick Malahide, Frank Langella

The Darkening
Director: William Mesa
Starring: Jeff Rector, George Saunders, Rebecca
Kyler Downs, Red Montogmery

Deadly Voyage (made-for-television)
Director: John Mackenzie
Starring: Omar Epps, Joss Ackland,
Sean Pertwee, David Suchet

Emma
Director: Douglas McGrath
Starring: Gwyneth Paltrow, Jeremy Northam,
Ewan McGregor, Greta Scacchi

Evita
Director: Alan Parker
Starring: Madonna, Antonio Banderas,
Jonathan Pryce, Jimmy Nail

Fierce Creatures
Directors: Fred Schepisi, Robert Young
Starring: John Cleese, Jamie Lee Curtis,
Kevin Kline, Michael Palin

Firelight
Director: William Nicholson
Starring: Sophie Marceau, Stephan Dillane,
Dominique Belcourt, Kevin Anderson

Karaoke (made-for-television mini-series)
Director: Renny Rye
Starring: Albert Finney, Richard E. Grant,
Hywell Bennett, Julie Christie

Mission: Impossible
Director: Brian De Palma
Starring: Tom Cruise, Jon Voight,
Emmanuelle Béart, Henry Czerny

Surviving Picasso
Director: James Ivory
Starring: Anthony Hopkins,
Natascha McElhone, Julianne Moore,
Joss Ackland

Turn of the Screw (made-for-television)
Director: Ben Bolt
Starring: Jodhi May, Pam Ferris, Colin Firth,
Joe Sowerbutts

1996

20,000 Leagues Under the Sea (made-for-television)
Director: Michael Anderson
Starring: Richard Crenna, Ben Cross,
Julie Cox, Michael Jayston

The Apocalypse Watch (made-for-television mini-series)
Director: Kevin Connor
Starring: Patrick Bergin, John Shea,
Virginia Madsen. Benedick Blythe

The Designated Mourner
Director: David Hare
Starring: Mike Nichols, Miranda Richardson,
David De Keyser

Fairytale: A True Story
Director: Charles Sturridge
Starring: Harvey Keitel, Peter O'Toole,
Florence Hoath, Elizabeth Earl

Hostile Waters (made-for-television)
Director: David Drury
Starring: Rutger Hauer, Martin Sheen,
Max von Sydow, Colm Feore

Incognito
Director: John Badham
Starring: *Jason Patric, Irène Jacob,*
             Thomas Lockyer, Ian Richardson

Ivanhoe (made-for-television mini-series)
Director: Stuart Orme
Starring: *Roger Ashton-Griffiths, Chris Barnes,*
             David Barrass, Niven Boyd

The Jackal
Director: Michael Caton-Jones
Starring: *Bruce Willis, Richard Gere,*
             Sidney Poitier, Leslie Phillips

The Fifth Element
Director: Luc Besson
Starring: *Bruce Willis, Gary Oldman,*
             Ian Holm, Chris Tucker

The Saint
Director: Phillip Noyce
Starring: *Val Kilmer, Elizabeth Shue,*
             Rade Serbedzija, Alun Armstrong

1997

The Avengers
Director: Jeremiah Chechik
Starring: *Ralph Fiennes, Uma Thurman,*
             Sean Connery, Jim Broadbent

Bean
Director: Mel Smith
Starring: *Rowan Atkinson, Peter MacNicol,*
             Pamela Reed, Burt Reynolds

Don't Go Breaking My Heart
Director: Will Patterson
Starring: *Anthony Edwards, Jenny Seagrove,*
             Charles Dance, Jane Leeves

Event Horizon
Director: Paul W. S. Anderson
Starring: *Laurence Fishburne, Sam Neill,*
             Kathleen Quinlan, Sean Pertwee

Eyes Wide Shut
Director: Stanley Kubrick
Starring: *Tom Cruise, Nicole Kidman,*
             Jackie Sawrie, Sydney Pollack

The Governess
Director: Sandra Goldbacher
Starring: *Minnie Driver, Tom Wilkinson,*
             Harriet Walter, Jonathan Rhys Myers

Rogue Trader
Director: James Dearden
Starring: *Ewan McGregor, Anna Friel,*
             Yves Beneyton, Betsey Brantley

Sliding Doors
Director: Peter Howitt
Starring: *Gwyneth Paltrow, John Hannah,*
             John Lynch, Jeanne Tripplehorn

Star Wars: Episode I – Phantom Menace
Director: George Lucas
Starring: *Liam Neeson, Ewan McGregor,*
             Natalie Portman, Jake Lloyd

Tomorrow Never Dies
Director: Roger Spottiswoode
Starring: *Pierce Brosnan, Jonathan Pryce,*
             Michelle Yeoh, Teri Hatcher

Tom's Midnight Garden
Director: Willard Carroll
Starring: *Anthony Way, Nigel Le Vaillant,*
             Greta Scacchi, James Wilby

1998

Entrapment
Director: Jon Amiel
Starring: *Sean Connery, Catherine Zeta-Jones,*
             Ving Rhames, Will Patton

Great Expectations (made-for-television mini-series)
Director: Julian Jarrold
Starring: *Ioan Gruffud, Laura Aikman,*
             Nicholas Blane, Justine Waddell

The Last Yellow
Director: Julian Farino
Starring: *Mark Addy, Alan Atheral, Kenneth*
             Cranham, Charlie Creed-Miles

Lighthouse
Director: Simon Hunter
Starring: *Rachel Shelley, James Purefoy, Don*
             Warrington, Christopher Adamson

Little White Lies (made-for-television)
Director: Philip Saville
Starring: *Tara Fitzgerald, Cherie Lunghi,*
             Peter Bowles, Gerald Butler

Mansfield Park
Director: Patricia Rozema
Starring: *Hannah Taylor-Gordon, Lindsay*
             Duncan, James Purefoy, Harold Pinter

Plunkett & Macleane
Director: Jake Scott
Starring: *Robert Carlyle, Jonny Lee Miller,*
             Liv Tyler, Michael Gambon

Still Crazy
Director: Brian Gibson
Starring: *Stephen Rea, Billy Connolly,*
             Jimmy Nail, Timothy Spall, Bill Nighy

With or Without You
Director: Michael Winterbottom
Starring: *Christopher Eccleston, Dervla Kirwan,*
             Yvan Attal, Julie Graham

1999

Birthday Girl
Director: Jez Butterworth
Starring: *Nicole Kidman, Ben Chaplin,*
             Vincent Cassell, Mathieu Kassovitz

The Golden Bowl
Director: James Ivory
Starring: *Kate Beckinsale, James Fox,*
             Anjelica Huston, Nick Nolte

Jesus Christ Superstar (made-for-television)
Directors: Gale Edwards, Nick Morris
Starring: *Glen Carter, Renee Castle,*
             Fred Johnason, Rik Mayall

Joseph and His Amazing Technicolor Dreamcoat (made-for-television/video)
Directors: David Mallett, Steven Pimlott
Starring: *Donny Osmond, Maria Friedman,*
             Richard Attenborough, Joan Collins

Longitude (made-for-television mini-series)
Director: Charles Sturridge
Starring: *Michael Gambon, Jeremy Irons,*
             Ian Hart, Peter Vaughan

The Man Who Cried
Director: Sally Potter
Starring: *Cate Blanchett, Johnny Depp,*
             Christina Ricci, Harry Dean Stanton

Natureboy (made-for-television mini-series)
Director: Joe Wright
Starring: *Mark Benton, Victoria Binns,*
             Lee Ingleby, Paul McGann

Return to the Secret Garden
Director: Scott Featherstone
Starring: *Mercedes Kastner, Michelle Horn,*
             Josh Zuckerman, Guy Siner

RKO 281 (made-for-television)
Director: Benjamin Ross
Starring: *Liev Schreiber, James Cromwell,*
             Melanie Griffith, John Malkovich

The 10th Kingdom (made-for-television mini-series)
Directors: David Carson, Herbert Wise
Starring: *Kimberly Williams, Dianne Wiest,*
             Rutger Hauer, Scott Cohen

Quills
Director: Philip Kauffman
Starring: *Geoffrey Rush, Kate Winslet,*
             Joaquin Phoenix, Michael Caine

The World Is Not Enough
Director: Michael Apted
Starring: *Pierce Brosnan, Sophie Marceau,*
             Robert Carlyle, Robbie Coltrane

---

2 0 0 0

2000

Dinotopia (made-for-television mini-series)
Director: Marco Brambilla
Starring: *Tyron Leitso, David Thewlis, Wentworth Miller, Katie Carr*

Enigma
Director: Michael Apted
Starring: *Dougray Scott, Kate Winslet, Saffron Burrows, Jeremy Northam*

Jack and the Beanstalk – The Real Story
(made-for-television mini-series)
Director: Brian Henson
Starring: *Matthew Modine, Vanessa Redgrave, Mia Sara, Daryl Hannah*

Lara Croft: Tomb Raider
Director: Simon West
Starring: *Angelina Jolie, Jon Voigt, Noah Taylor, Leslie Phillips*

Last Orders
Director: Fred Schepisi
Starring: *Michael Caine, Tom Courtenay, David Hemmings, Bob Hoskins*

The Merchant of Venice (made-for-television)
Director: Trevor Nunn
Starring: *David Bamber, Peter De Jersey, Andrew French, Henry Goodman*

The Mummy Returns
Director: Stephen Sommers
Starring: *Brendan Fraser, Rachel Weisz, John Hannah, Arnold Vosloo*

Ma Femme est une Actrice (My Wife is an Actress)
Director: Yvan Attal
Starring: *Charlotte Gainsbourg, Yvan Attal, Terence Stamp, Laurent Bateau*

Proof of Life
Director: Taylor Hackford
Starring: *Meg Ryan, Russell Crowe, David Morse, Pamela Reed*

Revelation
Director: Stuart Urban
Starring: *Terence Stamp, Natasha Wightman, Udo Kier, Celia Imrie*

Vertical Limit
Director: Martin Campbell
Starring: *Chris O'Donnell, Robin Tunney, Scott Glenn, Bill Paxton*

Wit (made-for-television)
Director: Mike Nichols
Starring: *Emma Thompson, Christopher Lloyd, Eileen Atkins, Harold Pinter*

2001

Below
Director: David Twohy
Starring: *Matthew Davis, Bruce Greenwood, Olivia Williams, Scott Foley*

The Car Man: An Auto-Erotic Thriller
(made-for-television)
Director: Ross MacGibbon
Starring: *Alan Vincent, Saranne Curton, Will Kemp, Etta Murfitt*

Charlotte Gray
Director: Gillian Armstrong
Starring: *Cate Blanchett, Billy Crudup, Michael Gambon, James Fleeet*

The Hours
Director: Stephen Daldry
Starring: *Nicole Kidman, Julianne Moore, Meryl Streep, Miranda Richardson*

Iris
Director: Richard Eyre
Starring: *Judi Dench, Jim Broadbent, Kate Winslet, Hugh Bonneville*

K-19: The Widowmaker
Director: Kathryn Bigelow
Starring: *Liam Neeson, Sam Spruell, Peter Stebbings, Sam Redford*

The Lost World (made-for-television)
Director: Stuart Orme
Starring: *Bob Hoskins, James Fox, Peter Falk, Elaine Cassidy*

Miranda
Director: Marc Munden
Starring: *Christina Ricci, John Simm, Kyle MacLachlan, John Hurt*

Planet of the Apes
Director: Tim Burton
Starring: *Mark Wahlberg, Tim Roth, Helena Bonham Carter, David Warner*

The Seventh Stream (made-for-television)
Director: John Gray
Starring: *Scott Glenn, Saffron Burrows, Simon Delaney, Fiona Shaw*

2002

Bright Young Things
Director: Stephen Fry
Starring: *Emily Mortimer, James McAvoy, Michael Sheen, Dan Ackroyd*

Die Another Day
Director: Lee Tamahori
Starring: *Pierce Brosnan, Halle Berry, Toby Stephens, Judi Dench*

Finding Neverland
Director: Marc Forster
Starring: *Johnny Depp, Kate Winslet, Julie Christie, Dustin Hoffman*

Jeffrey Archer: The Truth (made-for-television)
Director: Guy Jenkin
Starring: *Damian Lewis, Greta Scacchi, Polly Walker, Geoffrey Beevers*

Lara Croft Tomb Raider: The Cradle of Life
Director: Jan de Bont
Starring: *Angelina Jolie, Gerard Butler, Chris Barrie, Noah Taylor*

LD 50 Lethal Dose
Director: Simon De Selva
Starring: *Katharine Towne, Melanie Brown, Tom Hardy, Ross McCall*

Mee-Shee: The Water Giant
Director: John Henderson
Starring: *Bruce Greenwood, Daniel Magder, Joel Tobeck, Phyllida Law*

What a Girl Wants
Director: Dennie Gordon
Starring: *Amanda Bynes, Colin Firth, Kelly Preston, Eileen Atkins*

2003

Alexander
Director: Oliver Stone
Starring: *Anthony Hopkins, Angelina Jolie,*
            Val Kilmer, Fiona O'Shaughnessy

Alfie
Director: Charles Shyer
Starring: *Jude Law, Jane Krakowski,*
            Marisa Tomei, Jeff Harding

Henry VIII (made-for-television)
Director: Pete Travis
Starring: *Ray Winstone, Joss Ackland,*
            Charles Dance, Helena Bonham Carter

The Phantom of the Opera
Director: Joel Schumacher
Starring: *Gerard Butler, Emmy Rossum,*
            Patrick Wilson, Miranda Richardson

Ripley Under Ground
Director: Roger Spottiswoode
Starring: *Tom Wilkinson, Willen Dafoe,*
            Barry Pepper, Jacinda Barrett

Thunderbirds
Director: Jonathan Frakes
Starring: *Brady Corbet, Debora Weston,*
            Lou Hirsch, Soren Fulton

Tooth
Director: Edouard Nammour
Starring: *Yasmin Paige, Rory Copus,*
            Maisie Preston, Jim Broadbent

2004

Beyond the Sea
Director: Kevin Spacey
Starring: *Kevin Spacey, Kate Bosworth,*
            John Goodman, Bob Hoskins

Charlie and the Chocolate Factory
Director: Tim Burton
Starring: *Johnny Depp, Freddie Highmore,*
            David Kelly, Helena Bonham Carter

The Chronicles of Riddick
Director: David Twohy
Starring: *Vin Diesel, Colm Feore, Judi Dench,*
            Linus Roache

The Descent
Director: Neil Marshall
Starring: *Shauna Macdonald, Natalie Mendoza,*
            Alex Reid, Saskia Mulder

Harry Potter and the Goblet of Fire
Director: Mike Newell
Starring: *Daniel Radcliffe, Emma Watson,*
            Rupert Grint, Timothy Spall

King Arthur
Director: Antoine Fuqua
Starring: *Clive Owen, Ioan Gruffudd,*
            Ray Winstone, Keira Knightley

Kinky Boots
Director: Julian Jarrold
Starring: *Joel Edgerton, Chiwetel Ejiofor,*
            Leo Bill, Kellie Bright

Nanny McPhee
Director: Kirk Jones
Starring: *Colin Firth, Emma Thompson,*
            Angela Lansbury, Celia Imrie

Revolver
Director: Guy Ritchie
Starring: *Jason Statham, Ray Liotta,*
            Mark Strong, Francesca Annis

Stoned
Director: Stephen Woolley
Starring: *Will Adamsdale, Yousef Altin,*
            Paddy Considine, David Morrissey

2005

Basic Instinct 2
Director: Michael Caton-Jones
Starring: *Sharon Stone, David Morrissey,*
            Charlotte Rampling, David Thewlis

Cashback
Director: Sean Ellis
Starring: *Sean Biggerstaff, Emilia Fox,*
            Shaun Evans, Michelle Ryan

The Children of Men
Director: Alfonso Cuaron
Starring: *Clive Owen, Julianne Moore,*
            Michael Caine, Michael Klesic

The Da Vinci Code
Director: Ron Howard
Starring: *Tom Hanks, Ian McKellen,*
            Audrey Tautou, Alfred Molina

Footprints in the Snow (made-for-television)
Director: Richard Spence
Starring: *Caroline Quentin, Kevin Whately,*
            Kerry Fox, Annette Crosbie

Goal!
Director: Danny Cannon
Starring: *Kuno Becker, Anna Friel,*
            Sean Pertwee, Kieran O'Brien

I Could Never Be Your Woman
Director: Amy Heckerling
Starring: *Sarah Alexander, Brittany Benson,*
            Jed Bernard, Twink Caplan

Kenneth Williams: Fantabulosa (made-for-television)
Director: Andy DeEmmony
Starring: *Michael Sheen, Cheryl Campbell,*
            David Charles, Beatie Edney

The Line of Beauty (made-for-television mini-series)
Director: Saul Dibb
Starring: *Jake Border, Tim Elliott,*
            Elize du Toit, Joseph Morgan

Riot at the Rite (made-for-television)
Director: Andy Wilson
Starring: *Adam Garcia, Aidan McArdle,*
            Emma Pierson, Griff Rhys Jones

Sixty Six
Director: Paul Weiland
Starring: *David Bark-Jones, Helena Bonham*
            Carter, Stephen Greif, Daniel Marks

Stormbreaker
Director: Geoffrey Sax
Starring: *Alex Pettyfer, Ewan McGregor,*
            Mickey Rourke, Bill Nighy

To the Ends of the Earth (made-for-television mini-series)
Director: David Attwood
Starring: *Benedict Cumberbatch, Victoria*
            Hamilton, Daniel Evans, Brian Pettifer

United 93
Director: Paul Greengrass
Starring: *Christian Clemenson, Khalid Abdalla,*
            Opal Alladin, David Alan Basche

V for Vendetta
Director: James McTeigue
Starring: *Natalie Portman, Hugo Weaving,*
            Stephen Fry, John Hurt

2006

Bourne Ultimatum
Director: Paul Greengrass
Starring: *Matt Damon, Joan Allen,*
            Julia Stiles, Brian Cox

Casino Royale
Director: Martin Campbell
Starring: *Daniel Craig, Eva Green,*
            Mads Mikklesen, Judi Dench

Eragon
Director: Stefen Fangmeier
Starring: *Edward Speleers, Jeremy Irons,*
            Sienna Guillory, Robert Carlyle

Fred Claus
Director: David Dobkin
Starring: *Vince Vaughn, Paul Giamatti,*
            Kevin Spacey, Kathy Bates

Frequently Asked Questions About Time Travel
Director: Gareth Carrivick
Starring: *Anna Faris, Chris O'Dowd,*
            Marc Wootton, Dean Lennox Kelly

Miss Potter
Director: Chris Noonan
Starring: *Ewan McGregor, Renee Zellweger,*
            Emily Watson, Bill Paterson

Stardust
Director: Matthew Vaughn
Starring: *Charlie Cox, Claire Danes,*
            Robert De Niro, Michelle Pfeiffer

2007

The Bank Job
Director: Roger Donaldson
Starring: *Jason Statham, Saffron Burrows,*
            James Faulkner, David Suchet

The Best Time of Our Lives
Director: John Maybury
Starring: *Keira Knightley, Cillian Murphy,*
            Sienna Miller, Matthew Rhys

Incendiary
Director: Sharon Maguire
Starring: *Michelle Williams, Ewan McGregor,*
            Matthew Macfadyen, Enzo Squillino

Mamma Mia!
Director: Phyllida Lloyd
Starring: *Meryl Streep, Pierce Brosnan,*
            Amanda Seyfried, Christine Baranski

Sweeney Todd
Director: Tim Burton
Starring: *Johnny Depp, Helena Bonham Carter,*
            Alan Rickman, Timothy Spall

PINEWOOD *Television Listings*

The following television shows and series have also been made at Pinewood Studios. From 1958-2000, the most well-remembered television output is shown. Pre-2000, where a series has returned to Pinewood for further programme runs, the first year of production only is listed. After 2000, the titles of all television productions made at Pinewood are listed.

1958
Interpol Calling

1964
Court Martial

1966
The Avengers (two episodes)
Man in a Suitcase

1968
Foreign Exchange
Strange Report

1969
Destiny of a Spy
From a Bird's Eye View

1970
The Persuaders
UFO (nine episodes)

1971
Shirley's World

1972
Never Mind the Quality Feel the Width

1973
Space 1999
The Zoo Gang

1976
The New Avengers

1977
The Professionals

1986
Crazy Like a Fox
Mio My Mio

1989
Press Gang

1990
Heil Honey I'm Home

1991
The Camomile Lawn
Jeeves and Wooster

1992
The Borrowers
Moving Story
Parallel 9
Spender

1994
Chandler and Co
Poirot
Scavengers
Space Precinct
Strike It Lucky
The Vacillations of Poppy Carew

1995
Class Act
The Final Cut
Ken Russell's Treasure Island
Last of the Summer Wine

Little Orphan Annie
Poldark
Potamus Park
You Bet!
The Young Indiana Jones Chronicles

1996
Born to Run
Jonathan Creek
The Preventers

1997
Crime Traveller
Invasion Earth
Merlin
Perfect Blue
The Trial of Jasper Carrott
The Vanishing Man

1998
The Dark Room
French & Saunders
Friends
Harbour Lights
Hornblower
Midsommer Murders
Mrs Merton & Malcolm
The New Professionals
Roger Roger
Teletubbies

1999
Doctor Who – The Curse of the Fatal Death
Heartburn Hotel

2000
Hornblower
One Foot in the Grave
The Play
Queen of Swords
Thursday the 12th

2001
Dog Eat Dog
Jonathan Creek
Lenny Henry in Pieces
My Family
The Queen's Nose
Sam's Game
Shafted
Sirens
Survivor/Survivor Live
Teletubbies
Tomorrow's World Live Lab
The Weakest Link
You Don't Know Jack (Pilot)

2002
The Chair
Dog Eat Dog
Hornblower
My Family
Trial & Retribution
The Weakest Link
Wild West

2003
Auf Wiedersehen, Pet
The Catherine Tate Show
Deadringers
My Family
Rescue Robots
Spooks
The Weakest Link

2004
20th Century Roadshow
According to Bex
All About Me
Auf Wiedersehen, Pet
Brainiac
Captain Scarlet

Deadringers
Jonathan Creek
Last of the Summer Wine
My Dad's the Prime Minister
My Family
Planet Cook
Restoration (Series Two)
Spooks
Sport Relief
The Weakest Link
Xperimental

2005
A Bear's Tail
Avid Merrion's XXXmas Special
Brainiac
Deadringers
Extras
Foyle's War
Hollywood Greats
Last of the Summer Wine
Little Britain
London Floods
Marchioness
Planet Cook
The Chosen One (game show pilot)
Two Pints of Lager

2006
The Apprentice
Balderdash and Piffle
Brainiac Science Abuse
Dead Ringers
Death Wish Live
My Family
Test the Nation
Vorderman's Big Brain Game
The Weakest Link

PINEWOOD

Index

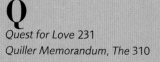

PINEWOOD *Bibliography*

The following publications and associated media have proved most useful in researching this book and ensuring accuracy of both facts and quotes:

BOOKS

American Cinematographer (January 1979)
Academy Award Winners (Admiral Books, 1986)
Ash, Russell, *The Top 10 of Film* (Dorling Kindersley, 2003)
Bright, Morris and Ross, Robert, *Mr Carry On – The Life and Work of Peter Rogers* (BBC Worldwide, 2000)
Box, Betty, *Lifting the Lid* (Book Guild, 2000)
Brewer's Cinema (Cassell, 1995)
Caine, Michael, *What's It All About* (Random House, 1992)
Cinema Year by Year 1894-2003 (DK Publishing, 2003)
Bright, Morris, *Our Thora – Celebrating The First Lady of Showbusiness* (Hodder & Stoughton, 2001)
McFarlane, Brian, *An Autobiography of British Cinema* (Methuen, 1997)
More, Kenneth, *More or Less* (Hodder & Stoughton, 1978)
Owen, Gareth & Burford, Brian, *The Pinewood Story* (Reynolds & Hearn, 2000)
Petrou, David Michael, *The Making of Superman The Movie* (W. H. Allen, 1978)
Perry, George, *Movies from the Mansion* (Pavilion Books, 1986)
Quinlan, David, *Quinlan's Film Directors* (B.T. Batsford, 1999)
Radio Times Guide to Films, 2004 Edition (BBC Worldwide, 2003)
Robertson, Patrick, *The Guinness Book of Movie Facts and Feats* (Guinness Publishing, 1991)
Sellar, Maurice, *Best of British* (Sphere Books, 1987)
Sims, Joan, *High Spirits* (Partridge, 2000)
Walker, John, *Halliwell's Film Guide 2004* (HarperCollins Entertainment, 2003)
Walker, John, *Halliwell's Who's Who in the Movies*, 14th Edition (HarperCollins Entertainment, 2001)
Warren, Patricia, *British Film Studios – An Illustrated History* (B.T. Batsford, 1995)
Wisdom, Norman, with Hall, William, *My Turn* (Arrow, 2003)
Wood, Mary and Alan, *Silver Spoon* (Hutchinson & Co, 1954)

AUDIO COMMENTARIES AND FEATURES ON DVD

Genevieve (Carlton International, 2000)
The James Bond Special Edition DVD Collection (MGM Home Entertainment, 2000)
An Evening with Sir Donald Sinden (BrightSide Productions & Marc Sinden Productions, 2002)

INTERNET SITES

www.pinewoodgroup.com
www.imdb.com
www.littlegoldenguy.com
www.bafta.org
www.bfi.org.uk
www.mi6.co.uk
www.wikipedia.org

ACKNOWLEDGEMENTS

It was late April 1996 and I was in the final throes of putting on an event at Pinewood bringing together Betty Box, Ralph Thomas and the former cast and crew of their *Doctor* films for a one-off reunion and plaque unveiling at the Studios' new "Hall of Fame". Everyone warned me that Dirk Bogarde would never come. He hadn't been back to Pinewood since making his last film, *Doctor in Distress*, in 1962, and certainly wouldn't turn up for a plaque unveiling in honour of "those" films. I had been in touch with Dirk via mail and he had indicated he might come along to see Betty. I may have emphasized that the event was in honour of his former producer, for whom I knew Dirk had great affection, rather than the *Doctor* films themselves, for which Dirk had increasingly less time. Still, everyone warned me he would back out at the last minute. Dirk Bogarde, I was told, was a temperamental man.

The day before the event *The Times* published an article in which Dirk claimed to have introduced the English-speaking world to Brigitte Bardot and that her appearance in *Doctor at Sea* (1955) was very much down to him. They'd obviously seen the press release sent out about the event and given him a call. They asked him about his feelings on coming back to Pinewood to unveil a plaque to the *Doctor* films. (I hadn't even asked him to unveil the

plaque, thinking that that request might best be left until the day itself – if he was there – when I could then perhaps drop a cord into his hand for him to pull at the appropriate moment.) He made it quite clear in the article that he found the whole idea troubling and that he would ask his driver to keep the engine running and that he would only stay for 10 minutes. Well, that was 10 minutes more than some had predicted and this was *The Times*, so maybe he would come after all.

The next day, I waited as noon approached and the other guests arrived. Betty Box and her husband Peter Rogers, Ralph Thomas and his wife Joy, Shirley Eaton, Jim Dale, Muriel Pavlow, Jeremy Lloyd – but still no sign of Dirk. Suddenly, I saw a big black car come into view and watched it drive into the car park at a snail's pace. A driver in uniform opened the passenger door and, emerging slowly and purposefully, out of the car came Sir Dirk Bogarde.

I remember seeing his feet first. I think I was bending so far forward at the "royal" guest's arrival that that was all I could see. As he stood there I searched for the words. Eventually, I spluttered: "Sir Dirk, how good to see you. How kind of you to come." He took one look at me and smiled that smile that had lit up so many cinema screens 40 years previously and gently replied: "No, no, how kind of you to invite me." And that was it. We shook hands and he smiled again – he couldn't have been nicer. I guided him slowly through the mansion house. He walked now with a stick. He looked at the images on the walls and stopped at the fireplace in the bar pointing out that that was where the Anglo-Irish agreement has been signed back in the 1921.

He saw his former director Ralph Thomas first as we emerged from the admin block to the Hall of Fame. The two elder statesmen locked walking sticks. "Dear Raif" he proclaimed without effect, "we're both fucking lame". And then Sir Dirk joined the guests and, reunited with Betty Box, Ralph Thomas and the others, unveiled the plaque to the *Doctor* films. He stayed for a drink. He undertook some interviews, signed a few books, and shared a few stories. After an hour and a quarter he had to go. He stayed for 75 minutes. He told *The Times* he'd stay for 10. Everyone said he'd never come at all. It was and remains one of my happiest memories of Pinewood Studios. Magic.

But then Pinewood is a magical place. Nothing can beat the feeling of driving through Pinewood's front gates. I have heard producers, directors, actors and crew all say the same thing – the "Sunday afternoon, can't wait to come to work on Monday" feeling. That's what you get when you enter Pinewood and there are precious few places in the world that can boast such recognition. After almost 15 years, I still get that feeling every time I come to the Studios.

To be asked then to write a book about the Studios' long and illustrious history was both a daunting and exciting task. So many hundreds of films and thousands of people have been associated with Pinewood since it opened some seven decades ago. How can one cover everyone's contribution, the part that each person played in making Pinewood what it is – a premier Studios of film and television excellence? The answer is you cannot. The best you can do is try to give a flavour of what has been and what is now and hope that those who have been to Pinewood or who have watched and continue to view output from the Studios will get that same feeling by reading and looking at this book.

To accompany the wonderful images in this book are many happy reminiscences, and my thanks go to the many contributors, including Leslie Phillips OBE, Sir Norman Wisdom, Sir Donald Sinden, Shirley Eaton, Jim Dale, Norman Hudis, Anthony Waye, Paul Hitchcock, Virginia McKenna OBE, Martin Campbell, Alan Hume, Peter Rogers, the late Betty Box OBE, the late Sir Dirk Bogarde, Gerry Anderson MBE, Graham Hartstone, Terry Ackland-Snow, Daniel Craig and Lord Attenborough.

I am indebted to Dame Judi Dench for adding a further dash of class by writing the Foreword and to Tim Burton for taking time out of his busy production schedule for *Sweeney Todd* to work on the Introduction for this book.

Enthusiasm for this publication appears to mirror enthusiasm for the Studios in general and many people have played a part in making this a fun and exciting project to work on. My thanks go to reporter Helen James at ITV Meridian for allowing me access to interview material undertaken in reports that so energetically promoted Pinewood's 70th anniversary. Louise Dixon and the team at publishers Carroll and Brown, who have been kind and responsive from the moment they took on this project. Pinewood's Vicky Joy, Rob Langridge, Bob Langston and Peter Wicks for helping to guide me through the Studios' own magical archive of images, and for their work in getting these images scanned, tidied up and into the book. Pinewood's marketing and PR team have wholeheartedly supported both the project and me, and I am indebted to group research and marketing manager, Julia Hillsdon, and her colleagues Aisling Magill and Daniel Lennox.

The Studio management has been equally as responsive and always happy to talk and inform, especially about where Pinewood is going now and in the years ahead. My thanks to Michael Brown who has overseen the building of stages at Pinewood for several decades, to group sales and marketing director Nick Smith, always busy but never too busy for this book, chief executive Ivan Dunleavy, one of the saviours of these great Studios, and to Board chairman Michael Grade, whose enthusiasm for Pinewood was, and still is, quite palpable. I wouldn't have started this project at all if it hadn't been for the confidence of Tim Forrester, now managing director of photographic agency Retna Pictures. And I wouldn't be at Pinewood at all if it wasn't for the former Studios' managing director Steve Jaggs.

To Kirsty, my new bride – we married at Pinewood on 5 November 2006 – and my two dear children, Alexander and Amber, I offer my heartfelt gratitude and continuing love for their patience and tolerance while I'm locked away in dusty vaults and archives or tapping away on the keyboard into the late hours.

Morris Bright

COPYRIGHT

Almost 1500 movies in 70 years including ... LONDON MELODY • RYAN 'S DAUG
GOLDENEYE • DOCTOR IN THE HOUSE • SIMBA • **SHAKESPEARE IN LOVE** • INTERVAL FOR ROMANCE
THE SAINT • BLACK NARCISSUS • GREAT EXPECTATIONS • GENEVIEVE • THE MUMMY • PLANTER'S WIFE
• 28 DAYS LATER • **LITTLE VOICE** • THE HELL BELOW ZERO • 28 WEEKS LATER • A TOWN LIKE ALICE • E
THE SHOWGIRL • FANNY AND ELVIS • DOCTOR AT LARGE • THE ONE THAT GOT AWAY • A TALE OF TWO
ODESSA FILE • NO ESCAPE • THE HEART OF A MAN • **CARRY ON SERGEANT** • INTERPOL CALLING • UPST
• **BRIDGET JONES 'S DIARY** • STRICTLY SINATRA • PEEPING TOM • CARRY ON CONSTABLE • THE LEAGU
II • **NOTTING HILL** • WHISTLE DOWN THE WIND • THE WALTZ OF THE TOREADORS • **DR NO** • CARRY O
THE IPCRESS FILE • THE HEROES OF TELEMARK • CASINO ROYALE • CARRY ON DOCTOR • **CHITTY CH**
ON CAMPING • THE PRIVATE LIFE OF SHERLOCK HOLMES • LEGEND • DAVID COPPERFIELD • DOCTOR IN
THE GOLDEN COMPASS • DIAMONDS ARE FOREVER • CARRY ON MATRON • SLEUTH • CARRY ON ABF
THE ROOF • NO SEX PLEASE, WE'RE BRITISH • REBECCA • CARRY ON GIRLS • BEYOND RANGOON • **THE**
MALONE • AT THE EARTH'S CORE • RIPLEY'S GAME • **THE PRINCE AND THE PAUPER** • THE SPY WHO L
OF THE TITANS • FOR YOUR EYES ONLY • LA FLOR DE MI SECRETO • **TRAIL OF THE PINK PANTHER** •
UMBRIA • LITTLE SHOP OF HORRORS • **ALIENS** • THE LIVING DAYLIGHTS • THE GATHERING • **FULL M**
CHILDREN & IT • RUNAWAY TRAIN • THE SECRET GARDEN • **CASINO ROYALE** • JACK AND SARAH • STR
KNIGHT • **MISSION IMPOSSIBLE** • EMMA • **EVITA** • HOPE AND GLORY • **THE FIFTH ELEMENT** • TO PA
NEVER DIES • **BOURNE ULTIMATUM** • THE AVENGERS • STAR WARS • THE CONSTANT HUSBAND • **ENTR**
THE BELLBOY • DR. JEKYLL AND MR.HYDE • AS YOU LIKE IT • THE LAND THAT TIME FORGOT • **ENIGMA**
DIE ANOTHER DAY • EVER AFTER • TOMB RAIDER II • BRIGHT YOUNG THINGS • CHASING LIBERTY • HI
I DREAMED OF AFRICA • THE CRIMSON CIRCLE • LONDON TOWN • AN IDEAL HUSBAND • A MAN ABOU
QUEEN • BRASSED OFF • BEAUTIFUL STRANGER • MOULIN ROUGE • AN INSPECTOR CALLS • HIGH HEEL
• THE END OF THE AFFAIR • FRED CLAUS • **CHARLOTTE GRAY** • THE GOOD DIE YOUNG • THE MAN W
FRENCH MISTRESS • **THE GUNS OF NAVARONE** • SNATCH • THE DAY OF THE TRIFFIDS • INFORMATION R
• **DR STRANGELOVE** • THE MAN WHO CRIED • THE EYES OF ANNIE JONES • THE SERVANT • NIGHT TRAIN
• THE MAN WHO WOULD BE KING • THE GREAT ST. TRINIANS TRAIN ROBBERY • WHAT A GIRL WANTS •
MONTE CRISTO • SCROOGE • WUTHERING HEIGHTS • A PASSAGE TO INDIA • THE WICKER MAN • THE
BROWNING VERSION • THE RETURN OF THE PINK PANTHER • **THE OMEN** • SWEENEY TODD • SIMPLY IRRE
TEN FROM NAVARONE • THE FOUR FEATHERS • THE REVENGE OF THE PINK PANTHER • G.I. JANE • THE EN
• BRIMSTONE AND TREACLE • CHOCOLAT • NIJINSKY • FEAR AND LOATHING IN LAS VEGAS • **ALFIE** • TH
BEGINNERS • CRY FREEDOM • SHANGHAI SURPRISE • POOR LITTLE RICH GIRL • ENDLESS GAME • LES MISE
OF THE MOON • A KISS BEFORE DYING • THE RAINBOW THIEF • **ROBIN HOOD - PRINCE OF THIEVES** • TH
• FRANKENSTEIN • GREYSTOKE • SHADOWLANDS • JUDGE DREDD • THE MADNESS OF KING GEORGE
BORROWERS • IN LOVE & WAR • PINK FLOYD:THE WALL • SHOOTING FISH • WINGS OF THE DOVE • RKO
BABY • F.I.S.T. • 102 DALMATIANS • BEDAZZLED • THE FOURTH PROTOCOL • **ABOUT A BOY** • ANITA &
OPS • **CALENDAR GIRLS** • ELLA ENCHANTED • **JOHNNY ENGLISH** • WONDROUS OBLIVION • BAND OF
WIMBLEDON • SHAUN OF THE DEAD • HARRY POTTER AND THE PHILOSOPHER'S STONE • SAHARA •
CHOCOLATE FACTORY • **THE DA VINCI CODE** • BASIC INSTINCT: RISK ADDICTION • STORMBREAKER •